MIYAMOTO MUSASHI

## Also by William de Lange

*Musashi: Fact & Fiction*

*The Real Musashi, I, II, III*

*Famous Japanese Swordsmen, I, II, III*

*A History of Japanese Journalism*

*A Dictionary of Japanese Proverbs*

*A Dictionary of Japanese Idioms*

*Pars Japonica*

*Iaido*

## Available in eBooks

*The Real Musashi, I, II, III*

*Famous Samurai: Kamiizumi Nobutsuna*

*Famous Samurai: Yagyū Munenori*

*Famous Samurai: Ono Tadaaki*

*Through the Eye of the Needle (Pars Japonica)*

## Available in Apps

*A Dictionary of Japanese Proverbs*

*A Dictionary of Japanese Idioms*

# MIYAMOTO MUSASHI

## A Life in Arms

A BIOGRAPHY OF JAPAN'S GREATEST SWORDSMAN

WILLIAM DE LANGE

FLOATING WORLD EDITIONS

For more on books by William de Lange visit:
**www.williamdelange.com**

First edition, 2014

Published by Floating World Editions
26 Jack Corner Road, Warren, CT 06777
**www.floatingworldeditions.com**



Printed in the U.S.A.

ISBN 978-1-891640-62-9

Library of Congress Cataloging-in-Publication data available upon request.

For my beautiful Letitia
the source of my joy
who allows me to be myself

# CONTENTS

I came to the realization it had not been because of my excellence in the art of *heihō* that I had been victorious.

—— Miyamoto Musashi

It is in falling short of your own goals that you will surpass those who exceed theirs.

—— Tokugawa Ieyasu

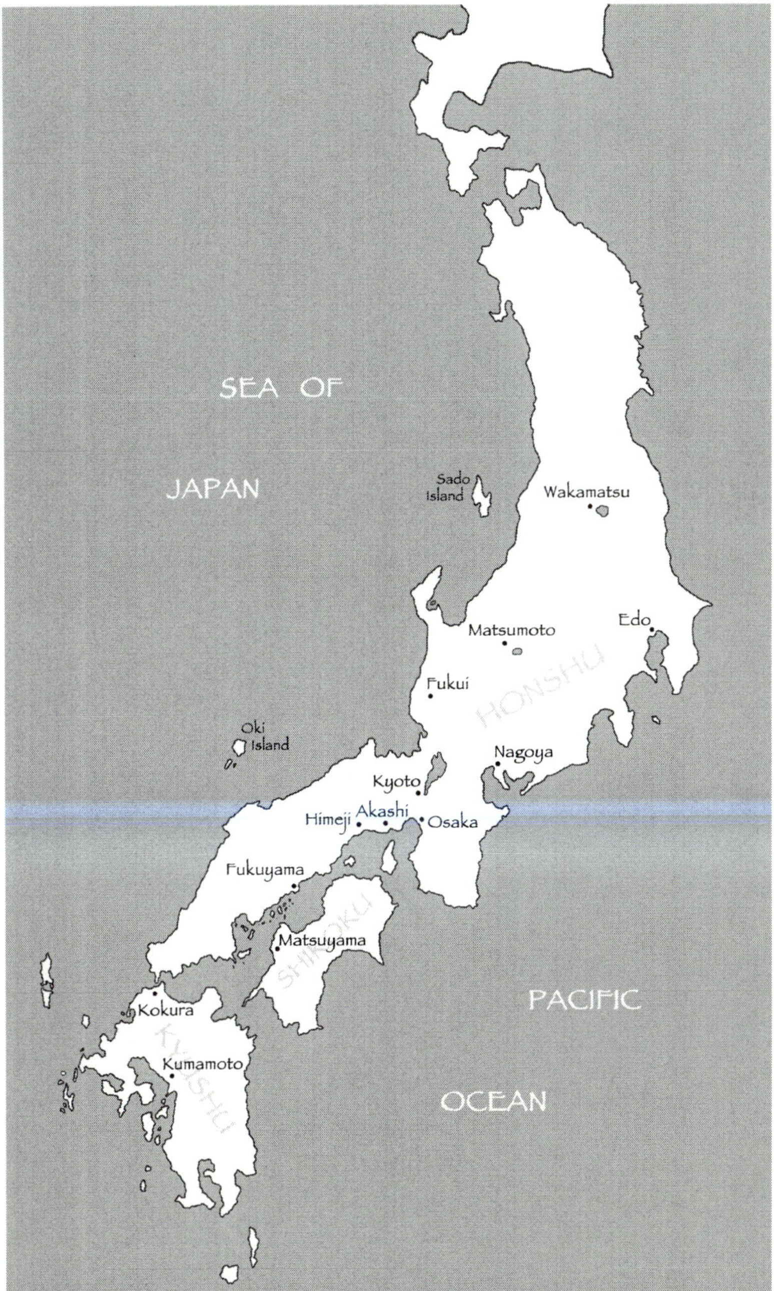
SEA OF
JAPAN
Sado Island
Wakamatsu
Matsumoto
Edo
Fukui
HONSHU
Oki Island
Nagoya
Kyoto
Himeji
Akashi
Osaka
Fukuyama
SHIKOKU
Matsuyama
Kokura
KYUSHU
Kumamoto
PACIFIC
OCEAN

# INTRODUCTION

This book is a quest for the real Miyamoto Musashi (1584–1645).

When I began to delve into Musashi's life more than a decade ago, naturally the first thing I did was to look into what original sources there were on Japan's greatest swordsman. Of course there is Musashi's own work, but sadly, Musashi seems to have had little interest in preserving for posterity his personal experience of the epoch-making events through which he lived. Instead, he concentrated—and perhaps wisely so—on what he had learned in their course. Thus, the *Gorin no sho* (*Book of Five Rings*), the only work from Musashi's own hand to shed any direct light on his life, dedicates just a few paragraphs to its most essential events, the rest taken up with his exposition on the art of combat, or *heihō*.[1]

I therefore had to look elsewhere, to accounts of Musashi written by his contemporaries, or their close descendants who recorded what was passed down to them by men who had known Musashi alive. I soon found that, contrary to widespread belief, there is a great wealth of different sources, some more, some less reliable. Both Japanese and Western authors who had delved into Musashi's life had come across these classical texts and partly quoted from them. Yet only few Japanese authors had taken the trouble to fully translate them into modern Japanese, while Western translators concentrated on the few extant works from the master's hand.

It was then that I decided to carefully translate all surviving records on Musashi before setting out to write his biography. I wanted to become intimately familiar with every scrap of ancient writing that mentioned Musashi. Over the years I compiled and translated a body of texts comprising some 150,000 words, mostly written during Japan's feudal era. They ranged from original accounts of duels, battles and sieges, local histories, and topographies, down to personal correspondence, clan records, family lineages, and roll calls. Indeed, they include a string of dedicated biographies, the two earliest and most reliable of which, the *Bushū denraiki* and the *Bukōden*, have meanwhile been published.

In the course of this fascinating exploration, it became clear to me that well before the idiosyncratic swordsman drew his last breath he had created a following that would ensure the survival of his legacy, as well as his life's story. Already within a few decades of his death Musashi began to appear in records and chronicles. While these works sometimes relate to Musashi tangentially, the swordsman invariably makes a striking impression—a man known, noted, and esteemed for his qualities. Soon more dedicated accounts appeared, describing in detail the feats and events that had brought him fame during his lifetime. It would only take a few more decades, well within Musashi's centenary, for his first biography to appear.

Sadly, with the end of Japan's feudal era and the country's rapid Westernization, many of these classical and at times inaccessible works became neglected and were gradually covered by the dust of time. This seems a sad loss, to say the least, for their authors made great efforts to record their knowledge for posterity to the best of their abilities. In this book I want to go back to these early works and in doing so paint an image as close as possible to the real Musashi.

One of the oldest records of the life of Miyamoto Musashi is the *Kokura hibun*. A lengthy epitaph celebrating the life, exploits, and character of Musashi, it is inscribed on a fifteen-foot obelisk-like stone memorial. The monument was erected in 1654 on the initiative of Musashi's adopted son, Miyamoto Iori, nine years after Musashi passed away. It stands on the crest of Temukeyama, a small hill some two hundred feet in height on the outskirts of Akazaka, situated in the northern district of the port of Kokura. At the time of its erection the monument lay within Iori's fief in the district of Kikunokōri within the Kokura fiefdom in Buzen.[2]

The *Kokura hibun* is believed to have been written at Iori's request by Akiyama Gentei Wanao (1618–73), abbot of the Taishō temple in Kumamoto, who (according to the *Bukōden*) befriended Musashi during the latter's last years in Kumamoto. Though the *Kokura hibun* was recorded by someone who knew Musashi personally and recounts the major events of his life, being carved in stone, it inevitably does so merely in outline; only occasionally (as in the case of the duels with the members of the Yoshioka clan) does it describe them in detail.

Soon the swordsman began to appear in other handwritten accounts. One such record is the *Kaijō monogatari*. Completed in 1666, it was written by a certain Echū (1628–1703), a by now largely forgotten monk of the Sōtō sect, who began his monastic life in Kumamoto's Ryūchō monastery. Later in life Echū moved to Edo (today's Tokyo), where he became an acolyte of the more well-known Suzuki Shōsan (1579–1655), the author of the *Inga monogatari* and the *Nenbutsu sōshi*, both works in the *kanazōshi* tradition.[3]

Given that Echū originally hailed from Kumamoto—the place where Musashi spent the latter part of his life—it is surprising that he does not dwell on Musashi's early and later life in Kyūshū, even though he published his work more than two decades after the swordsman's death. Instead, the *Kaijō monogatari* merely deals with the swordsman's life during his stay at Akashi castle, in particular Musashi's encounter with the rival swordsman Musō Gonnosuke Katsuyori. Moreover, that duel, though described in vivid detail, is the only such encounter mentioned in the *Kaijō monogatari*.

That Musashi appeared in such an early work itself attests to the fame he had already acquired within a decade of his death. Musashi's art, too, already had left left a deep impression, for a considerable part of the *Kaijō monogatari* is concerned with Musashi's artistic legacy. It also suggests that in between his work as a military advisor to Ogasawara Tadazane's Magistrate of Construction, Musashi managed to dedicate a considerable amount of his time to writing calligraphy and painting *sumi-e*, or ink wash paintings.

Another source to shed light on Musashi's life in Akashi is the *Seiryūwa*, the private records of the Ogasawara clan, which relate how Musashi was approached by Tadazane to design the gardens on his castle grounds. Yet while these records give an interesting glimpse of Musashi's life and activities during his stay in Akashi, only the *Kaijō monogatari* mentions Musashi's background, but in far less detail than the *Kokura hibun*.[4]

Musashi next makes a short appearance in the *Numata kaki*, the family records (*kaki*) compiled in 1672 by a descendant of Numata Nobumoto. Nobumoto was the keeper of Moji castle, situated some ten miles northwest of Kokura, and the place where Musashi stayed at the time of his duel with Sasaki Kojirō on the nearby island of Funashima.

Though the *Numata kaki* does not dwell on the events on the island itself, it does offer a fascinating insight into the conflict that erupted among the followers of both swordsmen in the wake of the duel. According to the *Numata kaki*, the disturbance took on such ugly dimensions that Nobumoto's lord, Hosokawa Tadatoshi, provided Musashi with an armed escort when the latter departed for the province of Bungo to visit his aging father in Kitsuki.[5]

The *Yoshioka-den* (also *Yoshioka kaden*) is one of the few records to give us a perspective from Musashi's adversaries, the famous Yoshioka brothers, Seijūrō and Denshichirō. It was compiled in 1684 by Fukuzumi Dōyū. Born in 1625 in the province of Awa, Dōyū studied medicine under a man named Kinoshita Kyōrin and began practicing in Osaka in his early twenties. He seems to have been a competent physician, for many of his contemporaries studied medicine under him, yet his real interest lay in the field of history. From an early age he had been gathering old records, genealogical tables as well as war records. By the time he reached his fifties he had become a well-known genealogist and biographer.

Driven by his passion for history rather than his medical expertise, Dōyū entered the service of Matsudaira Yoritsune in 1684 at the age of 59. He had been asked to manage the huge archive of the Takamatsu fiefdom. Dōyū did not serve Yoritsune for long. He died in 1689, having served the *daimyō* for only five years. Yet during his five years in Takamatsu the historian must have come into the possession of the family records of the famous Yoshioka clan.[6]

It took another four decades for more lengthy and detailed accounts of Musashi's life to appear. By now, however, their authors had to rely on accounts passed down to them at least one generation.

Completed in 1714 and published two years later, the *Honchō bugei shōden* is the first such work to shed any light on the events surrounding the duel on Funashima Island. This is not surprising since its author, Hinatsu Shigetaka (1660–1731), was a renowned practitioner of the Takeda-ryū, a school of equestrianism closely linked to the Ogasawara clan. Yet it seems that Shigetaka had only very little information at his disposal, for his account is very brief on the duel itself. Perhaps to disguise his limited knowledge of what actually took place on Funashima the author instead describes at length the melancholy and portentous dialogue between Kojirō and the humble oarsman who ferried him toward the island where he was to meet his fate.[7]

We have to wait one more decade to learn more about this pivotal duel as well as the other events in Musashi's life, when the first of four fully fledged biographies, or *denki*, of the master swordsman appeared. They are the *Bushū denraiki*, the *Heihō senshi denki*, the *Bukōden*, and the *Nitenki*. All were written during the eighteenth century, and by renowned masters of Musashi's Niten Ichi school of swordsmanship. Yet while all four works equally concern themselves with Musashi's life and exploits they represent two separate narrative strands. To understand this distinction it is necessary to take a closer look at each work and its author.[8]

The earliest and for that simple reason most reliable work is the *Bushū denraiki*. It was written in 1727 by Tachibana Minehira, alias Tanji Hōkin, an inhabitant of the province of Chikuzen and a former retainer of the house of Kuroda, a clan closely associated with Musashi's early military career. The *Heihō senshi denki* was written half a century later, in 1782.

Its author was Niwa Nobuhide, who had lost (his copy of) Hōkin's writings and sought to recapture for posterity what he remembered. The *Bukōden* was written in 1755 by Toyoda Masanaga. Masanaga hailed from the nearby province of Higo and was a senior retainer to the house of Nagaoka, vassals of the Hosokawa clan, who were closely associated with events of Musashi's later life.

Last of the four, the *Nitenki* was written in 1776 by Masanaga's son Kagehide. Given that he succeeded his father as fencing instructor to the Nagaoka and inherited his father's writings, Kagehide had no reason to recreate what he already possessed. He had, however, noticed that his father's labored and uncompromising style of writing had given rise to a number of misunderstandings. With a view to improve on his father's work and make it more accessible to his followers Kagehide rewrote the *Bukōden* and gave it the title *Nitenki*. It is a mark of Kagehide's success in achieving his objective that the *Nitenki* has become the most widely known of all *denki* on Musashi.

It is clear, then, that the *Bushū denraiki* and its spin-off, the *Heihō senshi denki*, represent one strand in the Musashi narrative. They recount the events of Musashi's life as they had been passed down by the retainers of the Kuroda clan. The *Bukōden* and its spin-off, the *Nitenki*, by contrast recount the events of Musashi's life as they had been passed down by the retainers of the Nagaoka and the Hosokawa clans.

Far from contradicting each other and thereby diminishing each other's value, all four works tend to complement each other in two important ways. One, they provide their own specific slant on those episodes they have in common. More importantly, all works recount their own unique anecdotes. Musashi's encounter with the Takenouchi-ryū practitioner Takagi Umanosuke, for instance, cannot be found in the

*Bukōden*, while his bout with the Yagyū Shinkage-ryū adept, Ujii Yashirō, does not appear in the *Bushū denraiki*. Similarly, the *Nitenki* is the only record to mention Musashi's friendly bout with Okuzōin at the Hōzō monastery, while the *Heihō senshi denki* is the only document to record the poignant scene at Musashi's deathbed. By thus complementing each other's lacuna, the four works together provide many of the scenes that make up the fascinating tapestry of Musashi's life.

Other episodes in Musashi's life are illuminated by yet other works. One of these is the *Gekken sōdan*. Written in 1790 it is a loose collection of anecdotes and descriptions of various schools of swordsmanship, their history, and their founders, including Musashi and Sasaki Kojirō. Apart from giving its own account of the duel on Funashima Island, it recounts how Musashi sought to extricate himself from his father's art of combat and develop his own style of fencing.

Author of the *Gekken sōdan*, Mikami Genryū, was born into a family of financial officers to the Ikeda clan, masters of the Okayama fiefdom in the neighboring province of Bizen. In the preface to his work, Genryū describes how, in the course of two decades of arduous work, he painstakingly gathered his material—a road undoubtedly traveled by many of the early biographers:

> During that time I collected, among others, accounts of how the various schools of combat performed in some of the most significant duels, accounting to some one hundred entries in all. Or, given that there were also those who, for reasons of a certain standing among their peers were apt to divulge the inner secrets of a certain school, I would indulge such persons in their preferred way

> and leave it to them to recall what they could so that I could record it for posterity.[9]

A particular light on Musashi's adopted son, Iori, is shed in the *Harima kagami*. Largely completed in 1762, this work, an eclectic collection of articles on the customs, places and people related to the province of Harima (today's Hyōgo prefecture), was written and compiled by Hirano Yōsai, a physician from the village of Hirazu (today a part of the city of Kakogawa). It seems only logical that Yōsai should know so much about Musashi's adopted son, for Hirazu lay only a few miles from Yoneda, the village where Iori was born. Iori spent his early childhood in Yoneda until, sometime during the second decade of the seventeenth century, he first encountered Musashi while (according to the *Bukōden*) out fishing for loaches, small eel-like fish, in a local paddy field.[10]

Musashi's activities following his return to Harima in the wake of the Osaka campaign are traced by the *Bisan hōkan*. Compiled by a certain Kosuge Ren, it is a topography not of Harima, but Owari (today's Aichi prefecture). It seems odd that knowledge of Musashi's life in Harima should be found in Owari. One reason why this might be the case is that many of Musashi's followers in Nagoya studied under Musashi during his stay in Himeji and Akashi. Nagoya, after all, was the breeding ground of Musashi's Enmei-ryū, even after Musashi developed his Niten Ichi-ryū when he moved to Kyushu.[11]

The one source to shed light on Musashi's stay in Nagoya and the spread there of his Enmei-ryū is the *Mukashibanashi*, a collection of anecdotes recorded in thirteen scrolls by Chikamatsu Shigenori (1697–1778). Shigenori came from a clan of Owari retainers. His father had served the Owari Tokugawa during their stay in Edo (under the *sankin kōtai* system, requiring a daimyo and his family's alternating attendance in the capital). At a young age Shigenori entered the service of Tokugawa Tsugutomo (1692–1731) lord of the fiefdom of Owari. Shigenori served most of his life in the *umamawarigumi*, the daimyo's elite household mounted guards. In was in that capacity that Shigenori must have gathered the many anecdotes surrounding Musashi that were passed down by those who had known him during his two-year stay stay in Nagoya.[12]

One of the later works on Musashi is the *Tōsakushi*. Published in 1851, its first draft was completed in 1815 by a man named Masaki Teruo, who served Matsudaira Yasuchika (1752–92), daimyo of the Tsuyama fiefdom in the neighboring province of Mimasaka (today's Okayama prefecture), as an instructor in the Kōshū-ryū Gungaku, a school of military strategy connected to he house of Takeda Shingen. Like the *Harima kagami* and the *Bisan hōkan*, the *Tōsakushi* is in essence a topography, in this case of the province of Mimasaka. Given the author's background, it is perhaps not surprising that he came to the conclusion Musashi hailed from Mimasaka and not from Harima as the swordsman himself claimed. As such, the *Tōsakushi* is considered to be a work in the so-called Mimasaka tradition, i.e., a work advancing the theory that Musashi hailed from Mimasaka, rather than from Harima.[13]

Another work in the Mimasaka tradition is the *Mimasaka ryakushi*. Published in 1881, it is a historical record of the old province of Mimasaka, from ancient times to the end of the Tokugawa Bakufu, or shogunate. It was recorded by Yabuki Masanori (1833–1906), a retainer of Matsudaira Naritami (1814–91), the then daimyo of the Tsuyama fiefdom in the province of Mimasaka, and the master of Tsuyama castle. A native of Mimasaka, Masanori was trained in history as well as the art of gunnery. Masanori spent much of his free time writing and editing histories on local clans. Thus we learn that, like Musashi's father, the former lord of Miyamoto, Shinmen Munetsura, also moved down to Kyushu to enter the service of the Kuroda.[14]

One of the records to shed light on Musashi's role in the suppression of the Shimabara Rebellion is he *Sōkyū sama o-degatari*. It was written by Oba Heizaemon Toshiyuki, a close retainer of Mizuno Katsunari (1564–1651). Though the record carries no date, Toshiyuki wrote his work probably sometime during the middle of the seventeenth century. Sōkyū sama, or master Sōkyū, after all, is the Buddhist name of Katsunari, who, shortly after the rebellion, passed on the reins of his estate to his son and took the tonsure.[15]

It is the reticence of all these works on Musashi's role during the winter and summer sieges of Osaka castle that gives the *Kōkō zatsuroku* its historical value in this context. Its author was Matsudaira Kunzan (1697–1783), a Confucianist scholar-warrior who was born in Nagoya. At the age of twenty (and like the author of the *Mukashibanashi*), Kunzan entered the service of Tokugawa Tsugutomo, lord of the fiefdom of Owari. In 1743 Kunzan was appointed *kakimono bugyō*, the magistrate in charge of the fiefdom's immense archive (which comprised some 3700 works), a post he was to occupy for the next thirty-eight years.

By the time Kunzan put pen to paper, the Osaka campaigns lay more than a century in the past. Yet the intimate knowledge of the Owari archive that he built up in the course of his career gives considerable credence to his claim that during the summer campaign Musashi fought among the troops of Mizuno Katsunari. Kunzan's claim is backed by other records recovered during the twentieth century. Most important among these are records from the Mizuno fiefdom of Fukuyama in which a certain Miyamoto Musashi is listed among the troops fighting under Katsunari during this decisive campaign.[16]

A few sources even give us a glimpse into Musashi's love life. The *Bushū denraiki* mentions the birth of a baby daughter, almost certainly the result of an illegitimate affair the swordsman had when he was already in his early fifties. Living in an age when many a warrior sought diversion in the pleasure quarters of Japan's major cities, Musashi also seems to have frequented one of Edo's *ageya*, the luxurious restaurants where geisha entertained their guests with song and music. This much is borne out by the *Dōbō goen*, which claims that during his stay in Edo:

> Among Kawai Kenzaemon's women in Shinmachi there was a low-class geisha who had an affair with the adept in the art of fighting with two swords, Miyamoto Musashi, causing him to regularly visit the *ageya* of Jinzaburō in the same quarter.

Written in 1720, the *Dōbō goen*'s author was Shoji Kasutomi, sixth generation descendant of Shoji Jineimon, the founder of the Yoshiwara pleasure quarters in Edo. Katsutomi's contribution is a valuable one, for it gives us a fascinating insight in the courtly, almost tender way in which the hardened swordsman related to the women of his time.

Thus equipped with ammunition, the challenge to the historian is to carefully compare and contrast these works, both against each other and against the larger canvas of history, and derive the closest approximation of the truth. By thus piecing together the scattered jigsaw of Musashi's life we are able to fill most, though not all, of the gaps in this fascinating narrative. This work does not purport to be a scholarly work.

Yet by drawing on the extensive research of Japanese historians it is possible (if only for the sake of its own narrative) to set straight some of the major misconceptions that have crept into Musashi's life story over time.

One stubborn misconception is that in 1600 Musashi fought among the western forces in the great battle of unification at Sekigahara. This is all the more curious since not one among the many sources available claims Musashi (who was only sixteen years of age at the time) did so. Indeed, the *Bushū denraiki*, which does dwell at length on Musashi's whereabouts at this time, unequivocally states that while the Battle of Sekigahara was raging at the heart of the main island of Honshū, the young Musashi was far away on the southern island of Kyūshū, taking part in the siege of Tomiku castle on behalf of his father's lord, Kuroda Yoshitaka.[17]

Not all the enigmas of Musashi's life can be dispelled on the basis of extant records. There is, for instance, still much uncertainty about the identity of the swordsman with whom Musashi dueled on the island of Funashima. The *Kokura hibun*, the lengthy epitaph found on the monument erected near Kokura in 1654 in Musashi's honor, merely mentions the man was called Ganryū. The *Numata kaki* by contrast refers to him as "a man by the name of Kojirō who used the Gan-ryū method of combat." The *Bukōden* goes a step further by identifying Musashi's opponent as Ganryū Kojirō. So does its spin-off the *Nitenki*, although, surprisingly, the latter also uses the name Sasaki Kojirō. The family name of Sasaki occurs in a number of other works that appeared during the eighteenth century, leading some to believe his real name must indeed have been Sasaki Kojirō. This still does not give us absolute certainty. The *Bushū denraiki* and the *Heihō senshi denki*, for instance, mention the family name of Tsuda. Indeed, some

Japanese scholars believe the name Sasaki Kojirō may even have been an invention of the early eighteenth-century *kabuki* playwrights, who gave their villain such varying names as Sasaki Ganryū, Ganryū Kojirō, or Sasaki Kojirō.[18]

In the end, it seems not so important by what name exactly this man went through life (he might well have done so under several pseudonyms). What is important is that somewhere during the Keichō era Musashi engaged in a duel on the island of Funashima, with a practitioner of the Gan school of swordsmanship who apparently went by the name of Kojirō and who probably was a member of the Sasaki clan. It is for that reason that this account has chosen to refer to Musashi's famous opponent by his most widely known name of Sasaki Kojirō. Similarly, unless they are waylaid by firm historical fact, it seeks to give as much credence as possible to these early accounts. This is done, not only because they are the only true sources we have, but to do justice to the great efforts of those early historians. Many of them dedicated the better part of their lives in long and painstaking quests to uncover all they could about the man they had so come to admire.[19]

What this book attempts to do, ultimately, is not to prove or disprove the many controversies surrounding Miyamoto Musashi, but to walk in the footsteps of these early explorers and sketch this solitary swordsman's path through life. If, in doing so, it gives the reader a truer, more complete portrait of the man Musashi, it will have fulfilled its objective, even if, at close scrutiny, not all of the canvas may be covered by the paint of historical evidence.

## A Note on Dates and Names

The authors of the old *denki* quoted in this book recorded events according to the Japanese, lunisolar calendar. Adapted from the Chinese system of keeping time, the calendar was based on the moon's cycle of 29.5 days in that months were given either twenty-nine or thirty days. This, however, caused a discrepancy between the calendar months and the seasons, so that every few years an additional month (*uruzuki*) was inserted to produce years with thirteen months. It is made all the more complex by the Japanese tradition of beginning a new Era (*nengō*) following the death of an emperor, a major calamity such as an earthquake, or an auspicious event.

This method of keeping time can lead to some confusion, particularly among Western readers, as the Japanese day, date, and year all fail to correspond to the Gregorian calendar. Thus, going by the lunisolar calendar, the *Bukōden* mentions how, on the twelfth day of the fifth month in the second year of Shōhō, Musashi handed the *Gorin no sho* to his star pupil, or *deshi*, Terao Magonojō Nobumasa. According to the Gregorian calendar this would have been on June 6, 1645. More importantly, the *Bushū denraiki* claims Musashi died on the nineteenth day of fifth month in the second year of Shōhō. According to the Gregorian calendar, however, he passed away on June 13, 1645. For historical interest, here the Japanese dating has been preserved in quotations, but to aid the Western reader Western dates have been added in brackets.

Another way in which the Japanese method of keeping time differed from the West is by how hours were noted. In Musashi's day, the Japanese lived by so-called temporal hours (*jūnijishin*), in which the day was divided into two sets: six daytime hours from sunrise to sunset, and six hours from sunset to sunrise.

Each hour was named according to the signs of the Japanese zodiac: Rabbit (6:00), Dragon (8:00), Snake (10:00), Horse (12:00), Goat (14:00), and Monkey (16:00); and Rooster (18:00), Dog (20:00), Pig (22:00), Rat (24:00), Ox (2:00), and Tiger (4:00). Given the seasonal changes, daylight hours are longer in summer and shorter in winter, while the opposite is true for nighttime hours. Roughly, however, a Japanese hour equalled two Western hours.

Under the influence of the Western method of keeping time the long Japanese hours were subdivided, either in two, three, or four parts. Thus, when the *Bukōden* states Musashi's duel with Sasaki Kojirō was scheduled to take place in the first third of the hour of the Dragon, we know that Musashi was expected to arrive at Funashima roughly somewhere between 7:00 and 7:40 Western time. For the sake of convenience, here only significant events are marked by their Japanese hour.

When considering time it is also important to take into account the traditional East Asian method of expressing age. Called *kazoedoshi* in Japan, this system dictates that newborns start life at the age of one. Furthermore, each passing of a Lunar New Year, rather than the passing of one's birthday, adds a year to one's age. Given this way of counting, it might happen that people are up to two years older under the *kazoedoshi* system, when compared to the Western method of counting. Thus, when the *Kokura hibun* states that Musashi was thirteen years old when he fought his first duel, he was in fact not more than twelve years old by our reckoning. Similarly, he was only eight years old when he left his father to seek out his stepmother in Hirafuku.

Names are one of the most inconstant factors in medieval Japanese texts. Birth, coming of age, succession, profession, high office, retirement, and death all had to find their expression in a person's name, and there are few, if any, persons of significance in medieval Japan who went through life under a single name. Musashi himself is a case in point. Though born as Bennosuke, by the time the swordsman fought his series of duels with the members of the Yoshioka clan, the chroniclers generally called him Musashi, or Bushū, the old way of referring to the eponymous province. Both the *Bukōden* and the *Bushū denraiki* introduce their subject as Shinmen Musashi no Kami Genshin. In doing so both *denki* closely follow Musashi's own example, for in his prologue to the *Gorin no sho* Musashi introduces himself as Shinmen Musashi no Kami Fujiwara Harunobu—Harunobu being the pronunciation (of the same two character as Genshin) by which Musashi would have been addressed during his lifetime.

It is clear why Musashi did so. Shinmen, the clan into which his father had married, was an ancient breed of warriors who had been involved in Emperor Godaigo's (1288–1339) failed attempt to restore powers to the throne. That involvement had led to exile, an exile from which his ancestors were eventually allowed to return and resume their roles under the name of Shinmen, or "newly absolved."

Less easy to explain is his claim to Fujiwara descent. The Fujiwara had ruled the realm by proxy throughout the Heian period. As such they successfully kept in check the two great military clans, the Taira and the Minamoto, and helped maintain the effeminate world of the court nobility. That world had been swept away by the ascent of the Taira (Heike), who hailed from the central province of Ise. They in turn finally lost out to the Minamoto (Genji) from the eastern Kantō region in that epic struggle of the Genpei War (1180–85). From then onward court rule had made way for a world of martial rule that would last for more than six centuries.

Probably because of the Fujiwara's great influence at court many a clan in Musashi's time claimed Fujiwara descent. Key to the Fujiwara success had been the strategic way in which they had intermarried with the imperial family as well as other powerful families—which was at least part of the reason why so many clans could rightfully claim Fujiwara descent, including the Honda of Mikawa, the Itō of Hyūga, the Arima of Hizen, and the Ikoma of Owari. Indeed, even the great Tokugawa Ieyasu, who was believed to be of Seiwa-Minamoto descent, thought it prudent to maintain an alternative line of descent suggesting Fujiwara roots.

Finally, in the face of impending death, Musashi had to address another important aspect of his life as a warrior: how to assess his life's accomplishments and find peace with his own mortality. Both the *Bushū denraiki* and the *Bukōden* mention that shortly before his death Musashi received the Buddhist name of Niten Dōraku, which may be crudely translated as the "Niten dilettante." This tells us that while Musashi wanted to be remembered for his Niten Ichi school of swordsmanship, at the same time he viewed his martial accomplishments with a healthy dose of self-effacement.

For the sake of clarity, here Musashi is referred to by his infant name of Bennosuke until he reaches adulthood. After that he is referred to as Miyamoto Musashi, as he would have been when alive. For the same reason most characters in the text are identified by their common names, and not, as so often happens, by their long titles of office or posthumous names. Similarly, Musashi's Buddhist name of Niten Dōraku is only mentioned once. One of the functions of these *dharma* names is to prevent the deceased from returning when their name is called. In our case, we warmly welcome the return of our hero, if only in spirit.

# CHAPTER 1

## Beginnings

The hills around the hamlet of Miyamoto stretched for miles and miles. They straddled the width of the island of Honshū, running all the way from Cape Kyōka, on the Sea of Japan, to the port of Akashi, on the Inland Sea. Among them one could feel safe and secure from the terrible events in the world beyond. Only the odd passing army, bound for yet another battlefield, yet another siege, would occasionally disturb the quiet and remind the rural populace, simple, hardworking people, that the country was still at war. These armies were highly disciplined. For though they would often stop for food and shelter, they strictly refrained from the rape and pillage that followed in the wake of the terrible wars that had ravaged the country over previous generations. Those who lived in Miyamoto could take comfort in the knowledge that nothing affecting their daily lives was done without the approval of their new lord and master, Toyotomi Hideyoshi, the most powerful warlord in the realm.

In this pocket of peace, in the spring of 1584, one house in Miyamoto was alive with the cries of a newly born boy.[1]

The boy was of relatively noble birth, for his mother, Omasa, was the daughter of Shinmen Munesada, once a minor local chieftain. He had been the lord of Takeyama castle, which stood on a steep and rugged hill overlooking Miyamoto village, on the eastern border of Mimasaka province.

The boy's father, Muni, was a warrior by descent, who had married Omasa during the sixties, when he entered the service of her brother, Munetsura. The latter at that time was working hard to restore his clan's fortunes. Only a decade before, in 1554, his father's domains had been overrun by the forces of Amago Haruhisa, who at that time controlled no less than eight of Honshu's western provinces. To strengthen his position Munetsura became a vassal of the powerful local warlord Ukita Naoie. It was a shrewd move. By the early eighties, when Naoie passed away and was succeeded by his even more successful son, Hideie, Munetsura had recovered much of his father's domain. He was again the master of Takeyama castle, employing close to two hundred men and women, and had a force of some sixty samurai.[2]

As one of Munetsura's most trusted retainers, Muni steadily climbed to the rank of *taishō*, or chief warrior, and had under his command some fifty *teppō ashigaru*, foot soldiers bearing rifles. Such promotion came at great personal risk. In the spring of 1578, when one of Munetsura's adversaries, Kusakari Shigetsugu, attacked Takeyama castle, Muni had as usual been in the front line, risking his life for victory. The *Shinmen kaki* describes how, at the turning point of the battle:

> When Muni advanced with his *yari* [lance], seven warriors among the enemy sought to strike Muni

> down with their *yari*, but he skillfully took hold of their *yari*, running down as many as three warriors, taking their heads and giving chase to the remainder, thereby defeating the Kusakari forces.

During his many years in Munetsura's service Muni had grown into a great warrior. He was an accomplished practitioner of the art of *jujitsu*. He was highly adept with the sword, practicing a style of swordsmanship developed by his ancestors called the Tōri-ryū. His real talent, however, lay in the art of fighting with the *jitte*, an iron rod with a fork-like extension by which one could parry an attack with a sword or lance.[3]

In his thirties, at the height of his powers, Muni had been invited to the capital by none other than shogun Ashikaga Yoshiaki. In the shogun's presence he had dueled with the great Yoshioka Matasaburō Naokata, a practitioner of the famous Yoshioka-ryū. It had been a close duel, but Muni emerged as victor by winning two of the three bouts. And while he had failed to gain an outright victory over Naokata, it had been enough to establish his name as Heihōsha Without Equal in Japan, a title sanctioned by none other than the shogun himself.

In Muni's world, the birth of a boy was an auspicious event, for his was a clan of retainers, and in a feudal society, only boys could hope to succeed their fathers and fulfill their clan's duty to their lord. His clan had a proud tradition to uphold, with its own school of swordsmanship going back many generations. All this he now hoped to impart to his newly born and only son, whom he named Bennosuke.

Tragically, the birth that should have sealed family bliss spelled its very end, for the young Omasa died in childbirth. And there were more setbacks in store for Muni, none hitting him harder than the death of one of his pupils at his own hand.

## A Cruel Twist

Being Munetsura's chief retainer, Muni was also called upon to oblige his master in matters of a more delicate nature.

On a beautiful spring day in 1586, when the cherry trees around Takeyama were erupting into color, Munetsura was entertaining some women of pleasure from one of Kyoto's high-class brothels. After a day filled with entertainment under the flowering cherry blossoms, the company spent a night under the open sky amidst yet more merriment.

The following morning, having satisfied the amorous whims of their host, the female guests were escorted back to Takeyama castle, hidden from public gaze in a long file of palanquins. The *Shinmen kaki* describes how, that very moment:

> Honiden Gekinosuke, who had been visiting Edōji Sanzuke, was just on his way back when he ran into the procession as it entered the main gate and, being taken by surprise, stood and stared as the palanquins passed by. One of the women spotted him and asked of her escort Kameemon who was the tall man glaring at them at the gate. Kameemon answered saying, "That can be no one else but our samurai Honiden Gekinosuke."

Muni, who arranged the whole visit, had at first smiled at the warrior's clumsiness in such matters. Gekinosuke was his senior deshi, who stood at least a head taller than all his lordship's other men. Yet he knew that in this towering figure dwelled a gentle, somewhat simple soul. Of course the man should have stood back and looked away discreetly, but he knew his deshi had only kept on staring in innocent surprise. Still he had felt ill at ease. Somehow it always seemed that where women of pleasure were involved, trouble was never far off.

Sure enough, not long after the incident his lordship called Muni into his presence. Munetsura had been appalled by Gekinosuke's conduct. It had brought shame on his good name, and he feared that by now he would be known in the capital as a country brute with no sense of decorum. There was only one way to restore his honor and that was for Gekinosuke to die. And since the man happened to be one of Muni's men, it fell on him to carry out the onerous duty.

The *Tōsakushi* describes how Muni was torn by conflicting emotions, realizing on the one hand his duty to his lordship, but at the same time fully aware that:

> Gekinosuke was guilty of no crime, and Muni sternly refused to do any such thing. Munetsura, however, insisted that he deal with the matter without delay, so that in the end Muni reluctantly consented. He sent a messenger to Honiden saying, "I will initiate you in the inner secrets of my school of combat. I am growing old, so be sure to come and without tarrying even a day."

Flattered by the honor his old teacher was about to bestow on him, that same day the young Gekinosuke went to Muni's house, where just then preparations were underway for an ancestral memorial service. The *Tōsakushi* goes on to describe how:

> Nakatsukasa, a monk from the Ryūdō temple (in the working-class neighborhood of Miyamoto), came to administer the rites. Muni took him aside and told him the gist of Munetsura's plot and said, "I am an

> old man, while Gekinosuke is still a man in his prime, who is intrepid and has great physical strength. If I fail, please lend me a hand."

While Muni was speaking to the monk, Gekinosuke arrived. Muni offered his unsuspecting guest tea and sake, and when they had done talking, Gekinosuke asked him about his initiation. Muni now led him into another room and took hold of his hand, tightening his grip saying:

> "This is how one grabs one's opponent's hand according to my school of combat." Muni's grip was so firm that Gekinosuke cried out in pain, but when he heard he was being arrested on Munetsura's orders he exerted the fearsome strength for which he was famed. A scuffle now ensued upon which Nakatsukasa took a *yari* and pierced Gekinosuke's chest. He thrust the weapon back and forth so that Gekinosuke quickly lost strength, at which point Muni took his head, cruel though it was.

Ironically, that day, May 31, coincided with the death of Muni's father, Buni. The ceremony marked the sixth year since he had passed away. Thus Muni spent the rest of the day in tortured piety, commemorating his beloved father, a samurai of deep integrity and impeccable behavior.[4]

From that time onward nothing was as it had been. A future that had once been so promising had been replaced with one that held only shame and disappointment. Scorned by all who were in Munetsura's service, Muni became more and more taciturn, shunning the company of his fellow retainers and choosing instead to remain indoors.

*Chapter 1*

# Rejected

Muni was already in his fifties, and to provide a home for his son, he married a second time, this time to the daughter of another deposed local lord, Bessho Shigeharu. Humbly taking on the name of Tasumi, or rice field dwellers, her clan was now eking out a living as peasants. Yoshiko had a gentle and caring nature and not surprisingly Bennosuke, who had never known his real mother, came to adore his stepmother.[5]

Different it was with father and son. Bennosuke learned fast, yet had an exceedingly stubborn nature, and from an early age the boy's relationship with his father was a troubled one.

Plagued by deep remorse over the treacherous way in which he had murdered his senior deshi, Muni became an increasingly cantankerous old man, incessantly ordering his wife about the house and scolding his son for the smallest of errors. Only a few years into their marriage, unable to bear the constant strain of an unhappy household any longer, Yoshiko asked Muni to divorce her. He refused, knowing he would have to return her substantial but spent dowry to her clan in full.[6]

With no legal recourse, Yoshiko traveled to her hometown of Hirafuku, across the border with Harima, where she found refuge with her older brother, a Buddhist monk. Before long, Muni married yet again. To his relief he had found a woman whose dowry was enough to pay off what he owed to Yoshiko's clan. But his new wife, a harsh woman, did not get on with his son and was full of complaints.

The situation was complicated by Bennosuke's affliction of eczema, which, in a superstitious society, led Muni to believe he was being punished, causing the boy in turn to feel rejected and to withdraw even further into himself. When they did meet, usually over the practice of some Tōri-ryū technique, the boy would often talk back and criticize his father instead of showing him the respect that was expected of someone his age.

The *Bushū denraiki* describes how, by the time Bennosuke was eight years old, the tension between the two came to a head when:

> One day, Muni was carving a toothpick with his knife. Bennosuke was sitting on the ground some two yards removed from his father. Suddenly, Muni took the knife and, using it as a *shuriken*, struck out at his son. Bennosuke dodged the weapon by turning away his head, causing the blade to pierce the pillar against which he had been leaning.[7]
>
> Greatly angered his father said, "Lately you have studied my art of fencing and I intended to cut the tip of your right ear lobe to remind you of the fact, but you turned your face away and sought to evade the danger. You are a thorough disgrace!" Having said this, he evicted his son from his house.

Muni's rejection and the manner in which it had come about came as a great blow to the young Bennosuke. It instilled in the boy an ever present nagging doubt about his achievements, but at the same time an insatiable desire to prove himself. It also sparked a quiet rage that would burn for the rest of his life, causing him to rebel at any authority. Instead of seeking his father's forgiveness he simply turned his back on the village of Miyamoto and set out along the Inaba Kaidō, the ancient inland route connecting the castle town of Himeji to that of Tottori, on the Sea of Japan.

Traveling southward Bennosuke crossed the Kamasake Pass, into the province of Harima, to the small village of Hirafuku, to find his loving stepmother, Yoshiko, whom he had not seen since the day she had left Miyamoto.

He soon learned she had remarried. Muni's remarriage had set her free. She was now living with a member of her own clan, a man by the name of Tasumi Masahisa. Masahisa had never come to terms with his fate. He resented the harsh life of a peasant and longed for the days when his clan commanded the respect of the very class to whom he now belonged. Nor did he take to the son of his wife's former spouse; he had heard of Muni's treachery and wanted nothing to do with the man's offspring.

At a loss what to do, Yoshiko entrusted the care of Bennosuke to her brother. Though once a warrior, the latter had long since renounced the world to dedicate himself to a life of study and meditation. He had taken on the name of Dōrin and ran a Buddhist temple called Shōrenan. At this small temple, set among a quiet bamboo grove on the edge of the village, Bennosuke spent the rest of his youth—an experience that was to have a seminal influence on his development as a swordsman, and artist, and a man of letters.

## First Duel

Dōrin was Bessho Shigeharu's third son. Not burdened by the responsibilities of his older brothers, yet endowed with a razor-sharp mind, he had spent his youth in the pursuit of learning. Given his clan's background, he was well versed in the art of *heihō*, as well as castle architecture. The monk had a sensitive side to him, for he had a gift with words and was an accomplished calligrapher and painter of sumi-e.

It was immediately clear to the monk that Bennosuke had a gift for learning. He had a natural ability to make what he had learned his own, a talent that was only reinforced by his insatiable curiosity and seemingly limitless energy.

More than anything else, however, Bennosuke was possessed by a passion for the martial arts. To take out his anger towards his father the boy spent hours in the woods, striking out with all his strength against the stern trunks of the mighty pine trees and then dashing through the undergrowth as if pursued by the old man's wrath. At times it must have felt he were both seeking and fleeing from his hated father. For making do with whatever weapon he could find he was still practicing the very skills and techniques he had learned from his father, albeit partly in play.

There was another aspect to his method of combat that troubled the budding warrior. He might be mimicking the great swordsmen of his time by wearing two white oak *bokutō* in his belt, yet like his father he was still relying on the *jitte* with many of his techniques. The *Gekken sōdan* captures the crucial line of thinking in Bennosuke's development as a warrior, as he sought to free himself from the constraints of his father's art of fighting:

> Though he practiced this art of combat, he was troubled by the thought that the *jitte* was not a weapon commonly used. He came to realize the importance of techniques by which he could defeat his enemy using the two swords that were already in his belt. And thus he invented a new style of combat and came up with a school of swordsmanship using both swords.

Bennosuke had already experimented with the use of two swords. Using both hands in combat only felt natural to him;

there were, after all, many old traditions that relied on a fine interplay between one's hands. The *Tōsakushi* describes how, even when the boy was still living with his father:

> He observed the priests of the Aramaki shrine as they pounded the shrine's great *taikō* drums, and he perceived how the sound they produced with their two drum sticks was in perfect unison. And thus, instead of using the *jitte*, he began to occasionally practice with two swords on a mallet suspended in an empty room of the house.

Bennosuke's talent with the sword was spotted by Dōrin's younger brother, Bessho Chōkurō, who had remained a warrior. He helped the boy to channel his anger and taught him the ins and outs of his own clan's style of swordsmanship.

For the next four years the young Bennosuke lived at the Shōrenan, studying and practicing under his stepuncles, until one day, visiting his mother after one of Dōrin's writing lessons, he came onto a clearing, wedged between the Inaba Kaidō and the Sayō River. He had often passed this field, but this time he immediately noticed something had changed. Staked out at the center of the field was a crude bamboo fence to create a small pen, roughly the size of a *sumō* ring.

Bennosuke knew what it was: the venue for a *shiai*, or duel. His father had often told him how, when two swordsmen met in a duel, they would stake out such a fence to mark the arena in which to test each other's strength. This was confirmed by a wooden notice, which had been placed at the pen's narrow entrance. Drawing close and reading its text, the boy saw it had been erected by a certain Arima Kihei, a warrior passing through along the Inaba Kaidō.

Bennosuke realized that Kihei was on a *musha shugyō*, or martial pilgrimage, a custom that went all the way back to the ancient practices of the *yamabushi*, the enigmatic mountain monks. Living among the inhospitable Japanese Alps, they led an austere life committed to celibacy and self-denial. In this, they very much resembled his stepuncle. In his small retreat on the edge of town, Dōrin too led a life of *shugyō*, or austere training, the aim of which was to deepen one's spiritual awareness through self-reflection and root out one's worldly weaknesses.[8]

While the true aim of *musha shugyō* was to conquer the enemy within, hardened warriors used the opportunities of a life on the road to test their prowess in duels with proponents of other schools of fencing. And so it was with Arima Kihei. On the notice, he had left his name and pedigree, challenging any swordsman in the area to come and test his mettle in a *shiai*.[9]

Without thinking twice Bennosuke took out his brush and ink stone, ground some ink with the river's water, and wrote down on the notice in bold strokes that he was Bennosuke, from the village of Hirafuku in Harima, a scion of the illustrious Shinmen, and ended his declaration with the words, "Let us engage in a *shiai* tomorrow." Having done so, he returned home to his stepuncle's retreat and prepared for the coming duel.

Dōrin, meanwhile, was utterly oblivious of Bennosuke's reckless challenge to the swordsman. But that evening a messenger arrived at their abode, announcing that his master, the great swordsman Arima Kihei, had accepted Bennosuke's challenge, and would meet him in a duel the very next day.

Aghast, the monk apologized to the messenger, explaining that the boy was far too young, and that his challenge to the swordsman was just a prank. Looking at the boy the messenger showed understanding for Dōrin's concern and, though he could not make any assurances himself, he was confident that if the monk were to reason with his master, the *shiai* would be called off. And thus Dōrin accompanied the messenger to Kihei's lodgings and begged him to call off the contest.

The *Bushū denraiki* describes how the swordsman, too, showed understanding yet noted that:

> If this was merely a prank I need not push my case. However, what good will it do to say it was only the prank of a child if it is rumored that itinerant warriors like me travel around Japan only to have their notices defiled with ink in Harima. Please accompany the child to the bamboo enclosure tomorrow. I will get ready and meet you at the place of duel. If you repeat your request there, in front of the gathered people, your request will stand and, even if at first it might reflect badly on me, it will soon be clear it was the work of an infant.

The next day Dōrin got up even earlier than usual. He was racked by nerves by the time he woke Bennosuke and said:

> "Because of you I have been put into this quandary, now follow me at a distance."
>
> Bennosuke only possessed a short *wakizashi* [auxiliary sword] and having spotted a pile of kindlewood under the veranda of his stepuncle's house, drew from it a suitable pole some two yards long, which he used as a walking staff as he followed his stepuncle, who was now in and now out of sight.

When they arrived at the enclosure they found it was thronged with people. Kihei, who had changed his attire for the *shiai*, was wearing a *karusan hakama*, and had sat down on a camp stool to await what was to come.[10]

The *Bushū denraiki* goes on to describe how the humble monk laid his hands on the fence and petitioned the swordsman saying, "Master Kihei, I repeat the words I spoke to you last night, please forgive the fledgling." But even as Dōrin spoke Bennosuke pushed open the fence and called out "Are you Kihei? Well, let's duel," upon which he ran up to Kihei and struck him with the pole. The move had the desired effect, for:

> Kihei now rose and drew his sword and struck out at the boy. Yet, as Bennosuke had run straight up to him, and Kihei had struck the moment he stood up from his camp stool, both were too close to inflict any wounds on the other and they remained locked in an embrace, their hands above each other's shoulders. Suddenly, Bennosuke dropped his pole, ducked to the floor, put his shoulders under his opponent, and toppled him head first to the floor. Then he took up the pole again, and killed Kihei with a succession of fourteen to fifteen blows.

The onlookers were utterly dumbstruck. The unthinkable had happened: a mere boy of twelve had slain the great swordsman Arima Kihei. Yet it had been the ferocity with which the boy had lashed out that disturbed the onlookers, some of whom were appalled at the merciless rage with which the boy had kept raining down blows on the swordsman's skull. Only Dōrin suspected that concentrated in that moment of rage lay the boy's deep-seated loathing of his very own father.

Kihei had been a renowned practitioner of the Shintō school of swordsmanship, and it was not long before the spectacular news of his defeat at the hands of a twelve-year-old reached the farthest corners of Harima province.

Bennosuke himself thought little of the whole event. Later, when reflecting on this early episode in his life he recalled how he had come to the simple conclusion that, "As long as I rush in and strike at the enemy ready to lay down my life I need no preparation whatsoever to conquer him."

Over the next four years the boy frequently set out from Hirafuku on his own *musha shugyō*. Traveling the length and breadth of western Honshū, he challenged anyone inclined to test his skills. In the course of those travels, Bennosuke dueled with many opponents, including a swordsman by the name of Akiyama, who hailed from the neighboring province of Tajima. But neither Akiyama nor any of the other challengers were able to beat the young swordsman.

## Reunited

Unbeaten though the young Bennosuke was, by the time he approached adulthood, he began to realize he had as yet much to learn. Able to defeat his opponents through sheer strength, he knew that with time it would steadily diminish and he would have to rely more on skill. For all his faults, Muni was a warrior of unquestionable talent, a man who had established his own school, and able to make a living by his sword. Bennosuke realized that in different ways, his father was the only person who could help him achieve his goal.

Thus, at the age of sixteen, Bennosuke left Hirafuku village and set out along the Inaba Kaidō toward Himeji. From there he took the Sanyōdō, the old highroad skirting the northern shore of the Inland Sea to the beautiful Straits of Shimonoseki.

There he hired a boat to ferry him across the water to the port of Kokura, from where he continued on foot again to Nakatsu, the castle town where his father now lived, for Muni had meanwhile left Munetsura's service.

Ever since he had been forced to kill his star deshi Muni had been pursued by guilt. For four grueling years he had carried this burden on his conscience, serving a master who had lost his respect. Then, in the same year Bennosuke had left him, Munetsura ordered him to mobilize his men. Their overlord, Ukita Hideie, was taking part in Toyotomi Hideyoshi's invasion of the Korean peninsula, and for this he needed all the men he could muster.[11]

In the course of that long campaign Muni was approached by the recruiters of Kuroda Toshitaka. Like the Ukita and many other clans, the Kuroda had embarked from Japanese shores with a huge force. To meet their military requirements at home and abroad, they were enlisting large numbers of young warriors. All of them needed to be trained and they were desperately short of skilled instructors.

Muni knew of Toshitaka. He and his older brother, Yoshitaka, had been born in Himeji. In 1567, at only twenty-one, Yoshitaka had become the castle's keeper. Over the following decade, when Oda Nobunaga launched a vast campaign to subdue the Mōri (a powerful clan from the western part of Honshu, who had their headquarters at Takamatsu castle), they had fought hard under the command of Hideyoshi, at that time still one of Nobunaga's chief generals. With Nobunaga's assassination at the Honnō temple at the hands of the treacherous Akechi Mitsuhide in 1582, and Hideyoshi's subsequent rise to power, the prestige of the Kuroda had climbed to unprecedented heights. Their reputation was further enhanced when, on the insistence of Yoshitaka, Hideyoshi sued for peace with the Mōri and chose the imposing castle of Himeji as the headquarters from which to continue Nobunaga's immense task of pacifying the country. Over the next years the Kuroda took part in numerous ensuing battles, including those at Shizugatake (1583), Komaki (1584), and Nagakute (1584).

Muni did not have to think long before he decided to take up the offer of the Kuroda recruiters. It would enable him to build a new life, to wash away his shame through new victories. He had to fight hard, especially during the Kuroda's first efforts to subdue the southern island of Kyushu. But his gamble paid off. In reward for their services the Kuroda brothers were granted vast fiefdoms in the province of Buzen.

The largest fiefdom, with a yield of more than one-hundred-and-twenty-thousand *koku* (each about eight bushels of rice, enough to feed a man for a year), had gone to Yoshitaka. He built himself a new castle in the bustling port of Nakatsu, on the Bay of Suo. Toshitaka, too, had meanwhile moved to Buzen. He now occupied Takamori castle, not far from Nakatsu. Being one of Toshitaka's retainers, Muni accompanied his lord to Takamori, where he was allotted a generous fief with a yield of two thousand *koku*.[12]

When Toshitaka died in 1596 at only forty-two, Muni entered the service of his brother, Yoshitaka, and moved to Nakatsu. He was placed under the command of Hayashi Tarōemon, a commander of a battalion of *ashigaru* (footsoldiers) since the days when the Kuroda still had their headquarters in Harima.[13]

Muni, however, was not ranked among Tarōemon's *ashigaru*. He had been appointed as one of the clan's senior fencing instructor, as well as the personal instructor to none other than Kuroda Yoshitaka and his son, Nagamasa. Given this special position, Muni was ranked as *kumihoka*, or outside the regular class of warriors.[14]

From his relatives back in Miyamoto, meanwhile, Muni had heard of his son's exploits and what he had heard had not only impressed him as a swordsman but also made him proud to be the lad's father. Stubborn old warrior that he was, he did not show it when Bennosuke, tired, disheveled, and dirty from many days on the road, one day appeared on the doorstep of his new dwelling in Nakatsu. Thus father and son once again lived under the same roof, putting up with each other to practice their fencing skills in preparation for battles to come. For both knew it would not be long before Bennosuke would get his first chance to test his mettle in combat.

First, however, Bennosuke had to go through an important ceremony, for he had not yet come of age. Called *genpuku*, the ceremony was an important event in the life of a Japanese male. Without going through the ritual, Bennosuke would not be able to marry, participate in religious ceremonies, or—most importantly to a warrior—be allowed to wear arms in public. In the olden days, a person designated by the family would cover the boy's head with an *eboshi*, the characteristic black lacquered hat worn by court nobles. By Bennosuke's time that tradition had made place for one in which his forehead was shaved and he received his adult name. It was one of the reasons why Bennosuke had felt compelled to seek out his father, for tradition required that father and son visit the family shrine and together pray to the family deity.

As had so many fathers before him, Muni proudly bestowed on his son a new name: Shinmen Musashi Harunobu. The last part of that name was his son's formal name, only to be used by Muni or those superior in rank. It might well have been an expression of Muni's own ambitions for his son, for Harunobu was a clear allusion to that great and indomitable warrior, Takeda Shingen, whose given name was also Harunobu.[15]

It was from the vast plains of Musashi, through which Muni had passed on his many travels up to Edo, that he derived his son's common name. Stretching all the way from Yotsuya to the Pacific coast, it took a man on foot several days to cross them, its ever restless and rustling pampas grasses growing tall enough to make even a man on horseback disappear. Perhaps it was the spiritual depth and breadth he sensed—and envied—in his son that inspired the aging swordsman to do so.[16]

## Into Battle

It was the fifth year of Keichō (1600), and the drive for unification, started under Oda Nobunaga and continued by Toyotomi Hideyoshi, was beginning to reach its culmination. In 1598, the great *taikō*, Hideyoshi, had passed away. His work was continued by his vassal Tokugawa Ieyasu, a Kantō warlord who had set his mind on crushing the resistance of his western rivals led by the ambitious Ishida Mitsunari. The Kuroda had wisely chosen Ieyasu's side. Yoshitaka's son, Nagamasa, who had meanwhile succeeded his father, amassed his troops near the post town of Akasaka, not far from Sekigahara, the gateway between east and west Japan. Huge armies had pitched camp, both eastern and western. All knew that the coming battle would decide the country's future.[17]

While Hayashi Tarōemon and his *ashigaru* had embarked for the main island, Muni and his son, who had only just reached adulthood, remained behind. They were both ordered to pick up their armor, go up to Nakatsu castle, and prepare for battle. They were to serve in an ad-hoc army assembled to deal with hostile warlords intent on grabbing part of the vast Kuroda possessions or those of their allies.

Exactly such a fate had befallen Hosokawa Tadaoki. Early in October that same year, his stronghold of Kitsuki castle was besieged by the forces of the Bungo warlord Ōtomo Yoshimune. Tadaoki, at that time, still had his headquarters at Miyazu castle, on the northern coast of the main island of Honshū, only a day's travel from where Musashi was born. Kitsuki had been awarded to Tadaoki after he had chosen Ieyasu's side against Mitsunari the previous year. Now, like Yoshitaka's son, Tadaoki had taken the main force of his troops to join Ieyasu at Akasaka, leaving behind one of his most trusted vassals, Nagaoka Yasuyuki, to guard Kitsuki castle and the rest of his possessions in Kyushu, worth some sixty thousand *koku*.

The Hosokawa and the Kuroda had long been on friendly terms. In 1590, Tadaoki and Yoshitaka had both taken part in the famous siege of Odawara castle, when Hideyoshi finally crushed the stubborn resistance of the mighty Hōjō. Two years later, when Hideyoshi launched his ambitious campaign against Korea, they had both embarked for the continent. Shared victories and hardships had drawn the chieftains together and when they were given adjoining domains in Kyushu their friendship deepened even further.

On the eve of his departure for Akasaka, Tadaoki had met with Yoshitaka to discuss a possible hostile landing. He told him he had instructed Nagaoka Yasuyuki to hold his castle at all cost and if need be call in Yoshitaka's help. Now the castle's keeper had done just that. His letter was short but urgent: he was outnumbered and unable to save his master's possessions from the clutches of the Ōtomo forces.

When Yoshitaka read Yasuyuki's letter he once more hoisted himself into his heavy armor. He had made up his mind to recapture Kitsuki castle and drive the Ōtomo forces back into the Bay of Beppu where they had landed.

Yoshitaka had prepared for just such a scenario. Following his meeting with Hosokawa Tadaoki, he feverishly labored to raise troops, calling on the help of befriended chieftains from as far afield as Shikoku, and even going so far as to pay his peasants to enlist. He was so successful that by the time he joined Yasuyuki near Kitsuki, the total number of his troops had reached nine thousand.

Muni and his son, Musashi, were among the forces of Kuroda Yoshitaka when, on October 19, 1600, they clashed head-on with those of Ōtomo Yoshimune on the plains of Ishigaki, only a few miles inland from the shore of the Bay of Beppu. The day ended in a decisive victory for the Kuroda forces. Ōtomo Yoshimune was captured, and only spared after he hurriedly took the tonsure. Building on his success at Ishigaki, Yoshitaka now launched a campaign to subdue the whole of Bungo. Beginning with Aki and Tomiku castle, he subdued the castles of Usuki, Saiki, Tsunomure, Hinokuma, Kawaradake, and Kokura in quick succession.

During four of these sieges, the young Musashi was in the vanguard of Yoshitaka's forces, often taking huge risks to show off his martial prowess. The *Bushū denraiki* describes how, during the siege of Tomiku castle, Musashi had reached the castle's ramparts some two hundred yards ahead of Yoshitaka's vanguard, when a *yari*, thrust through one of the castle's arrow loopholes, struck him in the waist. It goes on to describe how, instead of flinching back:

> Musashi became infuriated and called out to the soldiers lined up below "They stabbed me from this arrow loophole here, I will show you how to get rid of it." Saying this he put his upper leg against the loophole and waited.

> And sure enough, again the *yari* was thrust out through the loophole. Drawing his leg aside, Musashi took hold of the neck of the *yari*, just behind the blade, and began to pull the *yari* from the loophole with all his might. The man at the other side, realizing his weapon was being torn away, pulled hard in the other direction. Musashi now thrust his thighbone against the *yari* and, emitting a loud cry, broke it off half a yard below the blade. At this he called out "Friends, look, I broke the *yari*," not mentioning he had been wounded.
>
> Then, seeing everyone's surprise and in response to their concern on how to stem the flow of blood, he simply took some horse dung, pushed it into the wound and, without a trace of pain on his face, climbed back toward the castle and threw himself back into the melee.

Afterward, when they had returned to the camp, he went round to visit the wounded, leaning on a staff, and loitering without any signs of being in pain. Musashi's rare combination of reckless valor and gentle compassion quickly endeared him to his fellow warriors.

On October 21, 1600, three days after Yoshitaka had routed Ōtomo Yoshimune's forces on the plains of Ishigaki, Ieyasu did the same with those of Ishida Mitsunari on the plains of Sekigahara. And like Ieyasu's campaign against Mitsunari's western alliance, Yoshitaka's Bungo campaign proved a huge success. Within less than a month Yoshitaka had brought two complete provinces under his control.

It was his son's brilliant performance in the Battle of Sekigahara that earned the Kuroda the fief with which they would be connected during the Edo period (1603–1867). This was the Fukuoka fiefdom in the neighboring province of Chikuzen. With a staggering total revenue of five hundred twenty thousand *koku*, it was the seventh largest in the realm. The headquarters of the Kuroda clan from then on was the imposing stronghold of Fukuoka castle, erected between 1601 and 1607, just south of the port of Hakata. Lord of Fukuoka castle was now the great Nagamasa.

Feeling the onset of old age, Muni retired from active duty. He took the tonsure and adopted the spiritual name of Munisai. He moved yet again, this time to Kitsuki, in Bungo, where he lived in a large *yashiki*, a samurai mansion, on the edge of the small castle town, and overlooking Morie Bay. He wanted to spend his last days in perfecting his Tōri-ryū.

He did so on the invitation of Nagaoka Yasuyuki, the keeper of Kitsuki castle, who had met the aging swordsman during the battle of Ishigaki, and had come to admire his fighting skills. Munisai was appointed fencing instructor of the Nagaoka clan, and private fencing instructor to Yasuyuki's eighteen-year-old son, Okinaga. Word of his—and his son's—extraordinary skill with the sword soon spread, and Munisai was often asked to give demonstrations to other Kyushu chieftains.[18]

Musashi, meanwhile, had also made up his mind about what he wanted to do with the rest of his life. The military campaign had wetted his appetite for fighting. He wanted more. He still had to prove something to his father, as well as to himself. His aim in life was to become a warrior, a swordsman, a true master of his art. To do this he needed to make a mark, he must defeat other great swordsmen and, building on that reputation, go on to found his own school of fencing.

# CHAPTER 2

## The Yoshioka Clan

There were many famous swordsmen at the turn of the sixteenth century, and all of them had founded their own schools of fencing. There was the great Ono Jirōeon Tadaaki, alias Mikogami Tenzen, a warrior from the Bōsō Peninsula who had studied the art of fencing under the legendary Itō Ittōsai Kagehisa, the founder of the Ittō school of fencing. Tadaaki went on to become a *shihan*, a private fencing instructor to the shogun, Tokugawa Ieyasu. So had Yagyū Tajima no Kami Munenori, who hailed from Yamato province, where his father, Muneyoshi, had studied the art of fencing under the great Kamiizumi Ise no Kami Nobutsuna, founder of the Shinkage school of fencing. Muneyoshi developed Nobutsuna's style into the Yagyū Shinkage-ryū, which had just become the official fencing school of the Tokugawa Bakufu in Edo.

The Tokugawa Bakufu, however, had only just been established and all of these schools of fencing, though they drew much prestige from their association with the Bakufu, were relatively new. Musashi, of course, had heard of these men and their schools, yet at this time there was one school that was foremost in his mind. No school of fencing loomed larger in the young swordsman's mind than the Yoshioka-ryū, the fencing school of the famous Yoshioka clan.[1]

Prior to the establishment of the Tokugawa Bakufu the Ashikaga Bakufu had long ruled supreme in the Land of the Rising Sun. It went all the way back to 1336, when Ashikaga Takauji (1305–58) set up his headquarters in Kyoto's Muromachi district, for which reason it was also referred to as the Muromachi Bakufu. The Yoshioka-ryū had been the official fencing school of the Ashikaga Bakufu for close to a century. It had been founded in the early sixteenth century by Yoshioka Naomoto, a senior retainer of shogun Ashikaga Yoshiharu.

The *Yoshioka-den*, the family record of the Yoshioka clan, describes their proud tradition, explaining that:

> The Yoshioka school of swordsmanship derived from the school practiced by Genbō Hideyuki, as well as the old Satō, Suzuki, and Soga fencing traditions. The house of Yoshioka was an ancient, upright, and law-abiding clan, with a thorough sense of justice, for which reason the common people referred to its patriarch as Kenpō, or Justice.

It was Naomoto's brother, Naomitsu, who put the Yoshioka-ryū on the map when he became the personal fencing instructor to Ashikaga Yoshiteru (1536–65), known as the "master fencer shogun." Naomitsu founded the Heihōsho, a large *dōjō*, or martial training hall, situated in the Imadegawa district, not far from the headquarters of the Ashikaga Bakufu. And while the Ashikaga Bakufu had long since fallen, by now there was not a swordsman in the realm who did not know of the Yoshioka brothers and their prestigious school of fencing. The *Yoshioka-den* could boast with confidence that:

> There was such a large number of swordsmen who studied under their tutelage that it was impossible to count their number. Now among the swordsmen throughout the country there were only four of five with the skill to challenge them.

Many times the supremacy of the Yoshioka clan had been challenged, but it was never broken. Indeed, it had been only a few decades ago that Musashi's own father dueled with the famous Yoshioka Matasaburō Naokata. And while Muni won two of his three bouts with Naokata, he failed to attain an outright victory.

Naokata, on his part, could not come to terms with his defeat at Muni's hands. He grew morose and bellicose, picking fights with anyone on the slightest of pretexts, simply to vent his pent up frustrations. The *Bukōden* describes how, not long after his duel with Muni:

> Naokata had an argument during the festivities which celebrated the completion of the Great Buddha at the Hōkō temple in Kyoto. In the fighting that ensued some eight men found their end under the blade of his sword.
>
> Fearing the consequences, he tried to flee the scene by climbing over a mud wall, when the skirt of his *hakama* got caught on a nail on top of the wall. The sudden tug made him fall back on the *yari* of the assembled guards and lose his life.

> From then on down to the present day, all men are forbidden to wear swords during imperially sponsored functions.

Musashi realized that to fully defeat even one member of the Yoshioka clan in duel would be a first stepping stone toward serious recognition. If his father's relative victory had already earned him the title of Heihōsha Without Equal in Japan, how much more would an outright victory contribute to his own standing? More importantly, would it not prove that he was at least his father's equal?

## To Kyoto

Thus it came about that early one morning in the summer of 1604, well before the sun had risen over Morie Bay, Musashi silently rose from his futon in his father's *yashiki*, took his few belongings, and made his way to the port's roadstead. Having made arrangements with a skipper, he embarked in a small merchant vessel destined for the port of Sakai, at the far end of the Inland Sea. From there he would make his way to Kyoto via Osaka and Fushimi.

More than a week of traveling lay behind him when the young swordsman arrived in Kyoto and took up lodgings in a cheap and rundown hostel at Sagarimatsu, on the edge of town. The soothing journey across the beautiful Inland Sea had helped him to think clearly, and he knew exactly how he would go about achieving his objective. Early next morning he sent round a messenger to the Heihōsho, to throw down the gauntlet to Naokata's son, Yoshioka Seijūrō Naotsuna, now considered to be the best martial arts practitioner in Kyoto.[2]

That same day, a messenger from the Heihōsho arrived with a reply. Eager to avenge Naokata, the Yoshioka had taken up his challenge. Seijūrō would meet Musashi in a duel in the grounds of the Rendai temple, on the northern outskirts of Kyoto. Musashi knew this would be a decisive moment in his career. He would have only one chance to get it right, and to do so he would have to resort to a degree of ruse, for he intended to spare his opponent. The *Bushū denraiki* describes how, when the day of the duel finally dawned:

> Musashi excused himself, saying he was ill in bed. Sejūrō now sent round messengers several times, urging Musashi to come and fight with him.
>
> And so Musashi mounted a palanquin and arrived at the appointed place wrapped in a futon. Seijūrō went up to the palanquin and peered into its compartment inquiring "How is your illness?"
>
> At this Musashi thrust open the door of the palanquin, leaped out and floored Seijūrō in one blow with his *makura bokutō*, so that the latter passed out. His deshi placed him on a stretcher and took him home where they nursed him back to health.[3]

The treacherous defeat of their ace swordsman by an upstart from the south sent a shock wave through the Yoshioka clan. Most outraged was Seijūrō's brother, Denshichirō Naoshige, who, as soon as he heard the news, sent round a messenger to the hostel where Musashi was staying and challenged him to a duel on the very spot where his brother had been defeated. But when, the next day, he charged at Musashi with his five-foot *bokutō*, the latter simply "wrested the *bokutō* from him and slew him with it there and then."

This time Musashi had not spared his opponent, and the followers of the Yoshioka school were filled with bitterness. Realizing they could not defeat him by technical skill alone they decided to lay an ambush. It was decided that Seijūrō's son, Matashichirō, was to take a great number of their deshi and go to Sagarimatsu. They would pretend they had come to practice and strike as soon as Musashi left the safety of his hostel. The *Bukōden* describes how:

> There were several hundreds of them, all armed with sticks, bows, and arrows, for they wished to kill Musashi. But Musashi was aware of the ambush. He killed Matashichirō and dispersed his followers, and having displayed his supremacy in the art of swordsmanship, he returned to Kyoto.[4]

The demise of the Yoshioka clan, set in motion by the fall of the Ashikaga Bakufu, and hastened by the ignominious end of Yoshioka Naokata, was now sealed by Musashi's stunning victory. The young swordsman had set out to defeat merely one of its members, but had instead brought down a school of fencing that had ruled supreme in Kyoto for close to a century. In doing so, he had surpassed his father, for where the latter had merely won two bouts of one duel, Musashi had gained three victories, slaying two of his opponents.

## Hōzōin Kakuzenbō In'ei

Musashi was still only twenty, and while he had brought down a school of fencing singlehandedly, he was still a long way from establishing his own school, as his father had done.

Indeed, Musashi's own style of fencing still very much reflected his father's Tōri-ryū. He wanted to develop the art of fencing with two swords, yet he realized that in order to forge his own true style he must take on many more noted swordsmen—and not only swordsmen, he needed to measure himself with practitioners of all martial arts. Only then, when pitting his school against other, equally lethal schools, could he hope to find its true strengths and weaknesses, thus unlocking the hidden secrets of the art of *heihō*.

One prominent form of martial art that immediately sprang to mind was that of the lance, or *yari*, perhaps an even deadlier weapon than the sword on the field of battle and hugely popular among the *sōhei*, the notorious warrior monks. It had been the *sōhei* from Ishiyama near Osaka and Mount Hiei near Kyoto that had given Oda Nobunaga most trouble when he set out on his great task of unifying the country. They had allied themselves with followers of the intransigent Ikkō sect and the even more notorious *wakō*, the pirates who roamed the seas around Japan, and whose bloodcurdling exploits sent shivers down the spines of anyone brave enough to set foot in a boat. Supported in number by the Ikkō sectarians and where possible supplied over water by the *wakō*, they had turned their monasteries into impenetrable fortresses. These strongholds were guarded by huge garrisons of *sōhei* armed to the teeth with a large array of weapons, including the Western musket. Yet their weapon of choice remained the *yari*, the wielding of which they had developed into an art of its own.[5]

The unchallenged master of *sōjutsu*, the art of fighting with the *yari*, was Hōzōin Kakuzenbō In'ei. In'ei was a direct descendant of the Nakanomikado, a line of *sōhei* associated with Nara's Kōfuku temple. Drawing on their traditions, In'ei had founded his own school, the Hōzōin-ryū. In'ei was also known for his mastery in the art of swordsmanship, an art he had first acquired under the tutelage of Toda Yosaemon, whose Toda-ryū was based on Nenami Okuyama Jion's Nen-ryū, believed to be the oldest school of swordsmanship in Japan. It was said that In'ei had studied under as many as forty different masters of various weapons, chief among them the *yari*, the *naginata*, and the *tachi*. In'ei had long been the chief abbot of Nara's Hōzō monastery, but he had retired from his duties to dedicate his last few years to the perfection of his art.

Musashi knew that In'ei still organized regular *taryū shiai*, multi-discipline contests in which he pitted his warrior monks against practitioners of other martial arts, including the art of swordsmanship. Prior to Nobunaga's suppression of the monasteries, these gatherings had been massive events, drawing warriors from all over Japan and lasting for several days. At one of these functions In'ei introduced the great Kamiizumi no Kami Nobutsuna to Yagyū Muneyoshi, a meeting that had proved instrumental in the development of the Yagyū Shinkage-ryū. And while these meetings were now on a much more modest scale, Musashi knew that a duel with a practitioner of the Hōzōin-ryū would benefit his own development.

On the morning following the ambush Musashi packed up his few belongings, paid the innkeeper, and set off along the Nara Kaidō, the old highroad connecting the two former capitals of Kyoto and Nara. It was late in the afternoon when Musashi knocked the dust off his *hakama* and announced himself at the guest entrance of the Hōzō monastery, asking for a meeting with the retired abbot. To his great delight the warrior-monk was in and willing to see him in person.

In'ei was by now an old man. He had just turned eighty-four, and while he had laid down his arms, his mind was still as sharp as the blade of his lance. He was intrigued with

Musashi's way of using both swords, which in spite of his vast experience he had never seen before. He was too old to engage in combat with Musashi himself, but eager to pit him against one of his senior pupils, the talented Okuzōin.

The *Nitenki* describes how that same evening Musashi and Okuzōin met in the grounds of the Hōzō monastery to test each other's strength in a friendly duel:

> The monk was armed with his *yari*. Musashi had chosen two short *bokutō*. They fought two bouts, but in neither was the monk able to gain the upper hand. At length he bowed, expressed his deep admiration for Musashi's art of fencing, and asked him to stay at the Hōzō monastery, where he personally entertained him.

## To Edo

Over the next few years of his life as a *musha shugyōsha*, Musashi was to have many more such encounters, although not all of them were as amiable as his meeting with Okuzōin. The *Nitenki* describes how, during his stay at an inn along the Tōkaidō, while on his way to Edo, the new capital of Japan:

> Musashi ran into Oseto Hayato and Samanosuke Tsujikaze, two practitioners of the Yagyū Shinkage-ryū. They asked Musashi to engage with them in duel, and he accepted immediately.
>
> Hayato went first but before he was able to make a move, Musashi had already struck, and Hayato was defeated.

> Then it was Tsujikaze's turn to fight, but he was thrown backward by the blow of Musashi's *bokutō* and crashed into a stone bowl in the inn's garden, causing him to faint. He came to, but when he sat up, he suddenly collapsed and died.

As the new center of military power, Edo during the early seventeenth century was awash with swordsmen. All of these men had, over the previous decades, made their reputation in the course of numerous battles. It had been on and off the battlefield that they and their ancestors had developed their own unique fencing techniques over many generations, adding new branches to existing schools. Hundreds of these so-called *ryūha* had sprung into existence, each with its own style and distinct philosophy.

Now, in the wake of the great Battle of Sekigahara, Japan was pacified for the first time in several centuries, yet the practitioners of these *ryūha* had lost none of their zeal. If anything, they were even more determined to perfect and consolidate their particular schools of fencing, so that their heritage would be preserved for posterity, and the number of dojo that sought to do so was almost limitless. Edo, then, was the ideal place to be for a young man with Musashi's ambitions, and in his quest to widen his horizons he met with representatives of a great number of these new and exciting schools.[6]

## A New School

Musashi not only learned but also taught. He was gradually beginning to develop his own distinct style of swordsmanship—a style he tentatively called the Enmei-ryū, the School of the Circle of Light. He had also began to put his ideas into writing. Called the *Heidō kagami* (*The Mirror of the Martial Way*), his first exposition on the Enmei-ryū comprised a list of rules underpinning his developing style. Though still rough in outline, the *Heidō kagami* already encapsulated the principles he would come to expound in more detail later in life.[7]

One of the things he had taken away from his encounter with the two Yagyū Shinkage-ryū adepts was the trial of mental strength that underpinned any duel:

> When you want to engage in a duel it is crucial that you become even calmer than usual so that you are able to observe your opponent's state of mind. If he suddenly raises his voice, widens his eyes, grows red in the face, or becomes tense and grows violent he is an abominable swordsman.
>
> With such swordsmen one should grow even more quiet and, seeing that he becomes flustered, as if to put his mind at ease, draw your sword and, holding it at a low angle, almost leisurely withdraw the moment he is about to strike. Then, at the point where you can tell by his expression that he is questioning your intentions, strike.

The *Heidō kagami* also focused on the technical, purely physical aspects of swordsmanship, such as one's posture, how to look, and how to hold one's swords when fighting with two swords at the same time:

> When holding both swords, position the tip of the *kodachi* five inches away and six inches ahead of the *tachi*'s sword guard. At all times one should

> guard against bending one's elbows, although it would be foolish to keep them perfectly straight.

It also dealt with the more abstruse aspects of swordsmanship, the Daoist concepts of yin and yang, and how to discern an opponent's state of mind.

Though only in his twenties, Musashi was by no means the youngest swordsman to flock to the new capital. It was only natural then, that he was occasionally approached by other swordsmen for his advice—as for instance, by the young Hatano Jirōsaemon, a practitioner of the Asayama Ichiden-ryū. The *Nitenki* describes how, one evening, while resting from a long day's practice in an Ichiden-ryū dojo:

> Jirōsaemon asked Musashi to help him revise the principles of his techniques. Musashi helped him improve his style, which from then on was known as the Itten-ryū. After this Hatano took the tonsure and went by the name of Sōken. Sōken's was a unique style. It became widely known and practiced by a large number of followers.

## A Special Friendship

An encounter that was to have a lasting influence on Musashi's own life was that with Mizuno Katsunari. Like Musashi, Katsunari was still only in his twenties, but unlike Musashi, he was already a warrior of great standing. Born at Kariya castle in the province of Mikawa, he was a direct cousin of the great Tokugawa Ieyasu. He had made his career in the Tokugawa ranks and had fought numerous battles under

Ieyasu, including the famous battles at Komaki and Nagakute (1584), the only time Ieyasu and Hideyoshi ever confronted each other on the field of battle.[8]

There was an immediate rapport between the two young warriors. Like Musashi, Katsunari also had a rebellious streak. It had been during Hideyoshi's siege of Kanie castle that the fiery warrior landed himself in trouble when he killed one of his father's retainers in a fit of anger. Enraged, his father disowned him and expelled him from Mikawa province. Only through the intervention of his cousin, Ieyasu, relations with his father were eventually restored.

Katsunari practiced a lot with Musashi, so much so that on "an auspicious day in the first month of 1609," Musashi presented Katsunari with a copy of the *Heidō kagami*. In its postscript he concluded:

> Master Mizuno Hyūga no Kami,
>
> Having collected in great detail the secret techniques for the correct transmission of my school of swordsmanship and calling it the *Heidō kagami*, I hereby grant this document as a license to my deshi to whom I have conveyed in full the secrets of my art. I have recorded the unparalleled and unprecedented secrets of this art of *heihō* unrivaled in past and present, so that it may be preserved and perpetuated in eternity. No credence should be given to any license attributed to me if it does not include this secret scroll, even if it bears a signature that appears to be in my hand.
>
> Miyamoto Musashi

Through Katsunari's offices word of Musashi's art also reached Edo castle. The *Bushū denraiki* describes how, within months of Musashi's arrival in Edo:

> The shogunal house had taken notice of Musashi's art of *heihō* and word was sent to Musashi that they intended to send for him. Lord Yagyū Tajima no Kami Munenori, however, was already serving the Bakufu as shogunal *shihan*. Musashi bridled at the thought of being placed below a Yagyū and politely declined saying "From my youth I have held no ambitions for high office, and with my hair and nails untrimmed I would cut a strange figure, so please forgive me for declining."[9]

Musashi's self-effacing wording went only so far to disguise the true reason behind his refusal. In truth he resented the way in which the Yagyū and Ittō schools of fencing had established themselves as the official shogunal schools, even though their founders had taken part in fewer battles than he had. His true feelings were borne out by his less diplomatic response to a second shogunal invitation. The *Bushū denraiki* goes on to describe how shortly following his refusal:

> Musashi was invited to give a *heihō* demonstration, but again he declined, saying "It seems futile to me to give a demonstration of my art of *heihō* to someone who already esteems the Yagyū-ryū so highly."

Not surprisingly, none of the shogunal *shihan* ever went out of their way to recommend the eccentric swordsman as a fencing instructor to any of the shogun's sons. The shogun himself did not seem offended by the swordsman's overt criticism, but instead was conciliatory in his response. The *Bushū denraiki* describes how:

> In the end, the shogun, having seen one of Musashi's paintings, commissioned him to paint a folding screen. This time Musashi obliged and presented to the shogun a folding screen with a scene of a rising moon over the plains of Musashi.

For seven more years Musashi lived in Edo, perfecting his art and gaining a deeper understanding of the principles that underpinned it through diligent study. He also continued to travel, traversing the length and breadth of the country and fighting many more duels. Yet not one of the swordsmen he encountered managed to gain the upper hand.

In the spring of 1612, having reached the age of twenty-eight, he felt the time had come to return home. He had founded his own distinct school of swordsmanship. On his travels the former young upstart had grown into a swordsman who could hold his own against practitioners of any school of combat.

His popularity had also brought him a new name. His father had given him his common name of Musashi, but he was seldom addressed by his father's clan name of Shinmen. Most people instead knew him as Musashi, the swordsman from Miyamoto. From now on, therefore, the young and as yet unbeaten swordsman went under the name of Miyamoto Musashi. Little did he know as he went up in the bustling mass of people crossing the massive bridge at Nihonbashi to set off along the Tōkaidō, that one day his name would be known throughout the realm and even beyond.

# CHAPTER 3

## Coming Home

In the early summer of 1612 the twenty-eight-year-old Miyamoto Musashi crossed the Straits of Shimonoseki on one of the many boats carrying the great daily flow of travelers and cargo across its turbulent and treacherous waters. Breathing in the salty air threw Musashi's mind back to his days in Nakatsu. Back then he was just a boy. Now he was in the prime of his life and his father an old man. He was bound for his father's *yashiki* in Kitsuki, but that night he intended to stay in the port of Kokura to visit Nagaoka Okinaga.

Okinaga was the son of Nagaoka Yasuyuki, the keeper of Kitsuki castle who had appointed Musashi's father as Okinaga's private fencing instructor ten years before. Okinaga at that time was only eighteen years old, but after his older brother died in the second Korean campaign, he became the heir apparent. Only a year had passed since Okinaga's father had gone into retirement at the age of sixty-one. As expected, he passed on the reins of his estate to Okinaga, who continued to serve

Hosokawa Tadaoki. Wisely, Okinaga strengthened his ties with the powerful Hosokawa by marrying Tadaoki's daughter, the beautiful Koho.

Tadaoki, meanwhile, had moved down from Miyazu and taken up residence in Kokura castle. In reward for his contribution in the great Battle of Sekigahara, he had been promoted to the Kokura fiefdom. Okinaga was still the keeper of Kitsuki castle, but to fulfill his duties toward his lord, he was obliged to maintain an imposing *yashiki* with a great number of staff and retainers in the port of Kokura.

By now Musashi and Okinaga knew each other well. They differed only by two years in age and had both first seen action in the Battle of Ishigaki. Being the appointed heir, Okinaga had been kept from fighting in the vanguard like Musashi, but he had proven himself to be an able warrior with great tactical skill. He shared Musashi's passion for the martial arts, and prior to the latter's departure for Kyoto they had often practiced the art of fencing under Musashi's father at Kitsuki. Even now, whenever he resided at his headquarters of Kitsuki castle, Okinaga would seize the occasion to hone his skills under the guidance of the retired Munisai.

It was with great delight, therefore, that Okinaga welcomed the travel-weary swordsman, informed him his father was well, and invited him to stay at his *yashiki* as long as he wished.

## Sasaki Kojirō

While Musashi stayed at Nagaoka's *yashiki* the two men had long nocturnal talks over a good cup of sake. During one of these Okinaga told Musashi about another great swordsman who had settled in the region. His name was Sasaki Kojirō, and he hailed from the province of Echizen. He had given a demonstration of his art, which he branded the Gan school of fencing, at Kokura castle in front of Hosokawa Tadaoki. The latter had been so impressed with Kojirō's Gan-ryū that he hired him as his personal fencing instructor.[1]

Musashi had heard of Kojirō, for this was not the first time Kojirō had visited Kyushu. A decade earlier, while in his early forties, he had visited Kitsuki and challenged Musashi's father to a duel. Muni had declined, not because he was afraid of the rival swordsman, but because he knew they would probably be fighting at uneven odds. The Gan-ryū in itself was a sound school of fencing based on techniques that could also be found among other schools, and while Kojirō was admired by many, his reputation was not a good one.

The reason for Kojirō's notoriety was his weapon of choice, the infamous sword cane. The *shikomitsue*, as it was commonly called among Japanese warriors, was undoubtedly the most treacherous of the many weapons in their arsenal, in that it was crafted in such a way as to suggest its possessor was wielding nothing more than a wooden staff. In truth, however, the *shikomitsue* was a fully fledged sword, its hilt and scabbard made from the same innocent hardwood, so that when the sword was sheathed it was indistinguishable from an ordinary staff. Once a swordsman had been associated with this weapon, one could never be sure whether he was wielding a genuine wooden staff or a *shikomitsue*.

Musashi was undaunted by the prospect of meeting Kojirō in a duel. Indeed, he relished the idea. More than a decade before, he had come to the simple conclusion that as long as he rushed in to strike at the enemy, ready to lay down his life, he needed no preparation whatsoever, no matter how skillful or wily his opponent. Yet he knew that this time round he could not rely on boldness alone. Kojirō was in a league of his own, and to defeat the ace swordsman he would have to use all the mental and physical weapons at his disposal.

By the time he downed his last cup of sake and gently placed the wooden cup back on the lacquered table, he had decided how he would defeat the master swordsman. The *Bukōden* describes how Musashi looked at Okinaga and said:

> I hear that Sasaki Kojirō's art of swordsmanship is exceedingly rare and I would like to meet him in a duel. It is only because you have long been close to my father, Muni, that I now ask that you enable this contest to go forth.

## Arranging the Duel

It was with some relish, too, that Nagaoka Okinaga consented. He had seen Musashi fight in the siege of Tomiku castle and was keen to see the swordsman in action again. The very next morning he submitted a request to Lord Tadaoki's elders, who deliberated on the issue for the next two days. His lordship was not against a match. Kojirō might be his personal fencing instructor, but only because he was believed to be the best in his league. Within a few days Tadaoki's elders announced the place and time of the contest.

To avoid undue commotion, the duel would be held on an isolated island near the port of Kokura. The island, little more than a raised sand bank, lay on the border of Buzen and Nagato provinces, and was known variously as Funashima or Mukōjima. From Kokura to the island was just over five miles by boat, and only half that distance from Shimonoseki.

Yet Lord Tadaoki feared that even at this remote place things might spiral out of control. Because of his notoriety, Kojirō had gathered a great following, and it was to be expected that many would want to witness, if not take part in the event. Musashi had done his best to create bad blood, taunting them and their master by saying he would "crush him like the head of a frog." Only the heavens knew what would happen if Kojirō were to lose, let alone be killed. A day before the event, therefore, orders were issued throughout the castle town barring Kojirō's deshi from setting foot on the island. At the same time, sentries were posted at the port's roadstead to ensure that the orders were strictly observed.

That same day, Okinaga informed Musashi that he was to meet with Kojirō on the island in the first third of the hour of the Dragon (7:00–7:40) next morning, when the neap tide would ensure that the strong currents that hindered traffic would temporarily cease to run. Kojirō would be ferried across in one of Lord Tadaoki's boats, while Musashi would cross over to the island in one of Okinaga's boats. Musashi seemed more than satisfied with these arrangements, and expressed his gratitude to master Okinaga for his mediation.

On the eve of the event, however, Musashi suddenly went missing and could not be found. All of Kokura was searched, but it seemed as if he had vanished from the surface of the earth. In the taverns of Kokura the rumor soon spread that the young swordsman had been intimidated by Kojirō's unparalleled dexterity with the sword; that he had taken fright and fled. Even Okinaga, who knew Musashi well, was at a loss. The *Bukōden* describes how:

> At last, late at night, he summoned his men and said, "Considering things carefully, if indeed he

> has grown scared and fled, why wait until tomorrow? He must be up to something. He was already in Shimonoseki the day before he came here, and maybe he has gone there with the intention to cross over to the island from there."

Having said this, Okinaga immediately sent a messenger across the straits. Making inquiries at a local tavern the messenger soon found than Musashi was indeed at Shimonoseki. It appeared he was staying at the house of the local ship's chandler, Kobayashi Tarōsaemon, not far from where he had landed. There he encountered an exceedingly apologetic Musashi. The *Bukōden* goes on to describe how:

> Turning to the messenger, Musashi said, "I was indeed told I would be ferried across to the island in one of master Okinaga's boats, and I am deeply grateful for his kind consideration. However, Kojirō and I are now enemies, and it would be unbecoming if he were to cross over in a boat of Lord Tadaoki, and I in a boat of master Okinaga, who, after all, is one of his lordship's vassals. I am deeply grateful to master Okinaga for having made my wish come true, but he need not bother about these matters. I realize I should have told him this in person, but knowing that he would have insisted, I decided to come here without letting him know. Tomorrow morning I will cross over to Mukōjima in one of the local boats from here, and his lordship can rest assured that I will be there at the appointed hour."

*Chapter 3*

# The Die is Cast

Well before seven in the morning of the appointed day Sasaki Kojirō went down to Kokura's roadstead, where in the cool morning breeze dozens of small boats were bobbing up and down on a gentle swell. In spite of the early hour, many boats were already plying to and fro, making the most of the waning currents. The *Honchō bugei shōden* describes how, having taken in the scene, the swordsman went up to one of the oarsmen and addressed him, saying:

> "A lot of boats are crossing over today. What on earth is going on?"
>
> The oarsman replied, "Don't you know? Today the swordsman Ganryū is to duel with Miyamoto Musashi! It is to witness the event that they have been crossing over since the break of day."
>
> Then the swordsman said, "I am that Ganryū you speak of."
>
> At this the oarsman was greatly surprised. Speaking under his breath he said, "If you are the said Ganryū, let me row you over to another place, for you had better quickly make your escape to another province. Even if your technique is divine, there are a great number of Musashi's friends. Surely, you will not be able to get out alive."

Kojirō, however, had made up his mind. The same record recounts how, after a brief moment's pause:

> The swordsman said, "I do not desire to outlive today in such a way. Even if I am bound to die as

> you say, I have made a solemn oath and I would not be a brave warrior if I were to break my promise. If it is my duty to die on Funashima, I expect you to pour some water on my grave for the repose of my soul, for even though you are merely a lowly oarsman, I am touched by your compassion."

At length, having reconciled himself to what was to come, Kojirō embarked in the small boat and crossed over to the island of Funashima, taking with him one deshi.

In spite of Lord Tadaoki's painstaking precautions, his aim to keep the duel a low-key affair had miserably failed. Though he could bar Kojirō's deshi from setting foot on the island, there was little point in trying to prevent commoners, who could also reach the island from across the straits. Obviously, it was for this reason that Musashi had crossed over to Shimonoseki, so he could spread the word that he was to meet the great Ganryū protagonist on Funashima the next day.

On his way to Shimonoseki Musashi had also called at Moji castle, which was situated on the tip of Kitakyūshū. Moji castle was the stronghold of Tadaoki's son, Hosokawa Tadatoshi. Its keeper, Numata Nobumoto, was related to the Nagaoka and had long been friends with Musashi's father. In response to Musashi's request, and with Tadaoki's approval, Nobumoto crossed over to Funashima to witness the event and ensure the duel would be conducted in a fair manner.

## Kojirō's Arrival

The scene awaiting Kojirō on his arrival at the island was very much like the oarsman had predicted. The boats that passed the island had dropped their anchors and spectators were crowding around regardless of their position in life. Numata Nobumoto, too, had already arrived on the island and he had done so in force. He brought with him a large number of retainers armed with long lances, while he himself sat down nearby on a small stool to see how events would unfold. The *Bushū denraiki* describes how:

> When the island of Funashima came into sight Kojirō turned round to his deshi, and while he was talking to him, drew out his hidden weapon, made four or five bold strokes in the air, and cast it into the sea.

Musashi's plan had worked. Seeing the huge crowd and great number of Nobumoto's lancers, Kojirō realized that even if he conquered Musashi using his *shikomitsue*, he would not get away unpunished. And thus, rather than face the taunt of treachery, or perhaps even persecution by Nobumoto's men, he chose to rid himself of his most trusted weapon. Yet he was far from happy with the turn events had taken. The *Bushū denraiki* goes on to describe how:

> When the boat drew close to the beach Kojirō stepped onto the gunwale and jumped onto the beach. But he lost his footing and fell on his knees.
>
> Seeing this, the gathered crowd burst out laughing. Picking up his sword Kojirō went up to the keeper of Moji castle and reproached him, saying "Who do you think you are? And what gives you the right to be here?"
>
> The keeper scolded him, saying "I am a close friend of Musashi. I have come over to watch you

> duel, and I have no intention of interfering with you whatsoever. Are you out of your mind?"

Vexed by the loss of his most trusted weapon and unnerved by the presence of Nobumoto and his men, the master swordsman could do little else but await the arrival of his opponent. He felt robbed of his most lethal weapon, and, more importantly, his composure—a composure further undermined by Musashi's failure to arrive at the appointed hour.

## Delaying Tactics

The sun stood high in the sky when a messenger sent across by Nagaoka Okinaga arrived at the house of the ship's chandler, Kobayashi Tarōsaemon. Though brought in the politest of words the content of his message was simple: Musashi was late and he should make haste. Musashi, however, was still asleep, and to the messenger's great vexation, showed little sign of wanting to get up. Several times more the messenger came round, urgently requesting Musashi to make haste. At long last, Musashi rose from his bed, ate his breakfast of *miso* soup, pickles, and a roasted fish, and let himself be ferried across to the island by one of Tarōsaemon's men, a young man by the name of Muraya Kanpachirō.

There was something breathtakingly casual, almost reckless about the way in which Musashi behaved in the run-up to this great duel. Yet it was at the same time with great purpose of mind that, while he crossed over to Funashima Island in Kanpachirō's small boat, which now had to battle against the current, Musashi set about crafting the weapon with which he intended to outwit his opponent.

In all his duels thus far he had used his trusted *bokutō*, but this time he would be fighting with a different weapon. It would still be made of honest wood, but it would be longer, with more mass. The *Bushū denraiki* describes how:

> He took an oar from the boat and cut it to a length of four feet, reinforcing its edge with some boat nails he found and improving the grip of its handle by carving a series of grooves.
>
> To serve as a short *bokutō* he was carrying a handy-sized piece of wood still covered with bark, which had only been cut away at the hilt.

Finally, around ten o'clock in the morning, almost three hours late, Musashi arrived at Funashima. Kanpachirō beached the boat on the west side, where the island extended several hundred yards and where the shallows were only a few feet deep. The *Bukōden* describes how at this stage:

> Musashi was lying down in the boat, having taken from his belt a hand towel and tied it round his head. He was wearing a striped *kimono*, its sleeves tucked up with paper strings he had twisted during the crossing, and over it he wore a padded *yukata*.

Outraged at being upstaged by an upstart almost half his age, Kojirō by now had lost all his composure and was fuming with rage. The *Bukōden* goes on to describe how, when he saw Musashi approaching in the distance:

> Kojirō went to the water's edge and called out, "Why is it that you are late while I have already

> arrived? Is it that you have lost your nerve?" But Musashi remained silent and pretended he did not hear. Instead, he took off the padded garment, tucked the *tantō* into his belt, took his crafted *bokutō*, and waded across the shallows with bare feet, raising the trousers of his *hakama* and exposing his shins as he did so.

Like most swordsmen of his time dressed for a duel, Kojirō was wearing a *karusan hakama*. He had tied it at his waist over a bright-red, sleeveless *haori* and on his feet he wore straw sandals. He was utterly ready to make short shrift of Musashi, yet in his anger he made a move that betrayed his nerves and brought back to Kojirō the dark premonition that had haunted him following his somber exchange with the oarsman early that morning. The *Bukōden* describes how:

> Drawing his three-foot sword, Kojirō cast the sheath into the sea and stood at the water's edge, watching Musashi approach through the shallows.
>
> At that point Musashi halted and called out saying, "Kojirō, you've lost! Had you come to conquer, why on earth throw your sheath away?"

## The Duel

Unable to contain himself any longer Kojirō rushed forward and opened the attack. The *Bushū denraiki* describes how he lashed out at Musashi left and right with a *mizukuruma*.[2]

A flash of recognition electrified Musashi's brain. He knew the *mizukuruma*. An ancient technique by which the sword was brandished like a water mill, it was highly esteemed by those who wielded the longsword. The sword cane, too, could be handled in this fashion. Yet it could also be thrown from a distance with a fierce stroke, like the *shuriken*. It had been one of the reasons why Musashi decided to craft his own weapon from the boat's oar. Made of blue beech the oar was light and easy to wield, yet broad and as hard as iron—the ideal tool to deflect such a lethal projectile.

Now, he did not face Kojirō's treacherous *shikomitsue*, but his famous longsword, forged from the choicest steel by the master swordsmiths from Aoe. This was exactly what he wanted. Counting on the effect of Numata Nobumoto's presence, he had anticipated a scenario in which Kojirō would abandon his weapon of choice and resort to the lethal yet heavy longsword. The *Bushū denraiki* describes how:

> Wielding the boat's oar, he parried the attacks with a *migiwaki no kamae* and opened a fierce counter-attack. Both men clashed as Musashi raised his oar and struck down, while Kojirō, changing tack, also brought down his sword in a straight curve. But somehow Kojirō's grip on his weapon slipped, and its blade struck Musashi flat on the neck.[3]

The blow of Kojirō's weapon stunned Musashi for a moment but he was still standing. His own weapon *had* struck home. The oar had landed squarely on the forehead of his rival, who staggered backward a few paces and fell on his back:

> When Musashi moved in for the second strike Kojirō quickly rose to his knees and struck out horizontally, tearing through Musashi's *hakama*.

> Musashi's next strike, however, was devastating. He struck out twice at the same spot with all his might. The sturdy *bokutō* he had crafted from the oar crushed the skull of his opponent, who slumped forward and lay prostate.

After a pause Musashi threw away his oar and knelt down beside Kojirō, testing whether he was breathing by holding his hand over his nose and mouth. At length he rose and, undoing his *karusan hakama*, walked toward the water's edge. Picking up Kojirō's sword, he jumped aboard and told the waiting Kanpachirō to row him back across the water.

As they cast off toward the other shore, Musashi held his *hakama* aloft to show to the gathered crowd it was cut. Yet in the fierceness of the encounter no one noticed how he had been struck in the neck. And while it had only been the flat side of Kojirō's blade, due to the force of the blow, blood was oozing out of the wound, so that Musashi had to pull up the collar of his undergarment to hide it.

The *Bushū denraiki* goes on to describe how:

> When the onlookers crowded in to look at Kojirō's remains they found he was still alive, though his breathing was fading fast.
>
> Someone spoke to him, saying, "Kojirō! Musashi is leaving! Is that what it has come to?"
>
> Suddenly, his eyes flashed open and, raising himself up, he called out, "Has he got away? Give me some water!" Then he fell forward with a thud.

The great Sasaki Kojirō, known as the Demon of the Western Provinces, had been slain with no more than a boat's oar.

*Chapter 3*

# Aftermath

It was not to the port of Kokura that Musashi asked Muraya Kanpachirō to ferry him. Kokura was awash with Kojirō's deshi and though they had been largely barred from going to the island, news of their master's demise would spread like wildfire. Musashi was still intent on visiting his father in Bungo, but to travel to Kitsuki via Kokura at this time would be asking for trouble. Before he set out to the island of Funashima, therefore, he had spoken to Numata Nobumoto of his concerns about upsetting the peace in Kokura. Nobumoto, in turn had conveyed this to Lord Tadatoshi, who agreed to give Musashi refuge at Moji castle until things calmed down.

For several weeks Musashi remained at Moji castle, nursing the wound to his neck and waiting for the storm to settle. As expected, Kojirō's students had gone berserk. No sooner had they learned of the duel's outcome than they crossed over to the island to avenge Kojirō's death. Of course they came too late. All they could do was bury their teacher's remains on the island from then on known as Ganryū Island. It took several weeks for their tempers to cool and to reconcile themselves to the loss of their teacher.

At length, his wounds having healed and intent on seeing his father, Musashi felt the time had come to go home. The *Numata kaki*, the family records of the Numata clan, describe how in the summer of 1612:

> Musashi was brought to the province of Bungo. He was given an escort by Ishii Mitsunojō, who secured the way with men on horseback armed with muskets, ensuring Musashi arrived in Bungo unharmed.

> Upon his arrival in Kitsuki, Musashi was delivered to the house of a man by the name of Munisai.

For the next three years Musashi remained in Kitsuki, looking after his aging father and gathering around him a large number of deshi eager to learn the secret of fighting with two swords in the style of the Enmei-ryū. Being at the height of his powers and well known throughout the island of Kyushu, he had reached a position where he could raise the funds to build his own dojo to replace the small one run by his father. Larger, epoch-making events, however, were to upset those plans in ways the swordsman could not foresee.

# CHAPTER 4

## The Osaka Campaign

In the autumn of 1614 news reached the port of Kitsuki that huge numbers of troops were amassing around Osaka. It was the second great confrontation between coalitions of western and eastern warlords since the Battle of Sekigahara. The eastern forces were again fighting on behalf of Tokugawa Ieyasu. The western forces had rallied to the support of Toyotomi Hideyori, Hideyoshi's son and heir, who had safely ensconced himself in Osaka castle.[1]

Osaka castle was a formidable stronghold. On January 18, 1615, following a period of fierce fighting in which neither side made any headway, the parties had come to a settlement in which the Toyotomi forces agreed to fill up the castle's outer defensive moat. Yet when after a few months of waiting Ieyasu's forces sought to take things a step further by also filling up the inner moat, those of the Toyotomi felt a line had been crossed and hostilities again erupted. As in 1600, Ieyasu had to call on all his allies in order to deal with a stubborn adversary.

Musashi knew that one of Ieyasu's staunchest allies was Mizuno Katsunari, and it came as no surprise to the swordsman when in the spring of 1615 a messenger arrived at Kitsuki castle with a letter from Katsunari. In it Katsunari explained he was again going to take part in the siege. This time he would be joined by his eldest son, Katsushige, but since the latter was still only sixteen, he needed an escort. As one of his former students, Katsunari knew of Musashi's martial skills and asked the swordsman to serve as a member of the escort of ten mounted warriors for his young and inexperienced son.[2]

For Musashi the request was welcome news. In 1613, one year after the death of Nagaoka Yasuyuki, his father had passed away at age eighty-five. For more than a decade Munisai had practiced and taught his Tōri school of fencing at his modest dojo overlooking Morie Bay. He had had many students of note, among them Tomooka Danjūrō, a Hosokawa retainer to whom in 1607 he had left a *mokuroku*, a written inventory of the techniques and tenets of the Tōri-ryū.[3]

Musashi had not been saddened by his father death. It had rather been a relief. Even after their second reunion Munisai was full of reproaches and taunts, especially when it came to Musashi's approach to the art of swordsmanship. Following his father's death, Musashi reluctantly took on the responsibility of running the family dojo, but the three years at Kitsuki taught him the time had not yet come to settle down. Perhaps he still felt he had to prove himself—too many duels were unfought, too many questions unanswered.

Early in April, as the budding cedars turned the hills around Morie Bay into a verdant tapestry, the now thirty-year-old swordsman set sail from Kitsuki for the port of Sakai as he had done a decade before. Then it had been for purely selfish reasons: to establish his name as a master swordsman by defeating the Yoshioka clan. This time his mission was of a wholly different order: to see the young (and undoubtedly impulsive) son of one of Ieyasu's most trusted vassals through a battle. It was a huge responsibility. Were he to fail, it might spell the end of his martial reputation.

Katsunari, who had been put in command of a Tokugawa force of close to four thousand men, was ordered to advance on Osaka from Yamato province. Musashi was among the first troops to pitch camp when, at the hour of the Monkey (four o'clock in the afternoon) of June 1, they arrived at Kokubu. The hamlet, a few farms scattered along the southern bank of the Yamato river, marked a narrow pass between the river and a hill by the name of Komatsu. Immediately behind the hill the river was joined by the Ishi river from the south. At dawn three more contingents reached Kokubu, causing Katsunari's force to swell to well over twenty thousand men.

Convening a war council, Katsunari and his fellow commanders considered their next course of action. They were now only ten miles away from Osaka and some were in favor of taking up positions on Komatsu hill in case they were surprised by an enemy attack. Occupying higher ground they could dominate any hostile troops attempting to cross the Ishi river. Katsunari, however, was firmly opposed. The hill was not high and it would be difficult to rout the enemy in that manner. If there were an attack they should wait for the enemy to cross the river and ascend the hill, at which point they could make a pincer movement and trap them from both sides of the hill.

They had been right in their suspicions of an impending attack. Only a few miles downstream, at the village of Dōmyōji, an equally large enemy force under the overall command of Gotō Mototsugu had gathered. His plan was to surprise Katsunari's forces before they crossed the pass that night.

Breaking up camp at midnight amidst dense fog Mototsugu arrived on the opposite side of the Ishi river a few hours later, only to find that his allies had lost their way in the fog. His scouts, meanwhile, informed him Katsunari had already arrived and pitched camp at Kokubu. Intent on keeping the initiative, he ordered his three thousand men to ford the river and take up positions on Komatsu hill.

Katsunari's scouts, too, had spotted their enemy's movement. By the time Mototsugu and his men had negotiated the hill, Katsunari's warriors were ascending the hill's eastern slopes, pushing Mototsugu back towards the hill's shallow summit. The sun had risen and heavy fighting ensued as Mototsugu sought to make a valiant stand. Greatly outnumbered he managed to keep his position, hoping all the time his allies would come to his rescue. They failed to arrive, and when at ten o'clock, the hour of the Snake, Mototsugu was hit by a bullet and committed ritual suicide, his troops began to descend the hill toward the Ishi river in disarray.

By now Katsunari and his men had rounded Komatsu hill through the pass, thereby executing to perfection the very pincer movement he had proposed the day before. The *Mizuno Katsunari oboegaki*, the general's personal diary, captures the sprawl of battle as he and his men pursued their enemy through the lifting morning fog:

> As both sides of the path were deep with mud, there was a small stone bridge amid the rice paddies. I was the first to mount the bridge, followed by Nakayama Kageyu, my son Katsushige, and Murase Saba. Crossing the bridge, we drove back the forces of Honda Sakyō, and since the latter fled into the paddies flanking the bridge, we dismounted from

> our horses and taking our lances, pursued the enemy all the way back to Fujiidera.[4]

Having been assigned as a personal guard to Katsunari's son, Musashi was among the first troops to mount the bridge. The *Kōkō zatsuroku* describes how:

> Musashi carried a five-yard banner on which in bold characters was written the slogan, "Men from the realm of Shakya knew and practiced the laws of Buddha; we know and practice the laws of *heihō*."

It goes on to describe how, even in the thick of battle, the swordsman still relied on his most trusted weapon:

> At one stage he was standing on the bridge, brandishing a huge *bokutō*, and being cheered on, he cast the enemy soldiers off the bridge left and right.

The next day, Wednesday, June 3, the fighting around Osaka continued relentless and unforgiving. Trying to keep the initiative, the western forces sought to crush Ieyasu's troops at Tennōji, on the doorstep of the ancient Shitennō temple, a few miles south of Osaka castle. Executed as a hammer-and-anvil operation, the frontal attack was led by Sanada Yukimura, while the rear flank attack was led by the indomitable Akashi Takenori. For some time the odds hung in the balance, but finally, at three o'clock in the afternoon, at the cost of huge casualties, Ieyasu drove them back into the castle.

A scramble now ensued among the eastern troops to be the first to mount the walls of the painfully exposed castle. Musashi, still part of Katsushige's escort, was one of the first to enter the Sakura Mon, the main southern gate to the castle, north of which water still filled the castle's moats. And he was with Katsushige and his father when they planted the Mizuno banner over the imposing entrance.

It was Katsunari's shining example that had brought them this far. Throughout he had been in the vanguard, leading his men on whenever their spirits slackened. At one stage, troops under the command of Ieyasu's twenty-year-old grandson, Matsudaira Tadanao, had been flustered by Takenori's rear flank assault. Tadanao broke formation and sought protection among Katsunari's men. Rebuking the young warrior for his cowardice, Katsunari grabbed his *yari* to face off the assault. He did so at huge personal risk and at one stage was seen fighting with four adversaries at once. At the end of the day he had taken two enemy heads, while Musashi and the rest of his men had taken as many as ninety-seven heads.[5]

That night the castle's donjon went up in flames. Hideyori withdrew to the most northern tower, but early next morning he acknowledged defeat by committing ritual suicide. The Osaka winter and summer campaigns put a final and decisive end to western resistance against the Tokugawa Bakufu; from then on Tokugawa Ieyasu and his descendants were to rule supreme for more than two and a half centuries.

Musashi had fought hard and emerged unscathed. More importantly, so had Katsunari's son. The summer siege of Osaka castle was the largest military event in which Musashi had taken part. Thousands upon thousands of warriors had met their end in the fighting. Their lifeless, contorted bodies now lay scattered on the blood-soaked fields and piled up waist-deep in the half-filled moats of Osaka castle. Many of them had been younger than Musashi, but many more had been older, with far more experience on the field of battle.

With his father's acerbic words still ringing in his ear, it was almost with a pang of guilt that he later recalled how:

> Having passed the age of thirty, I reflected on what I had done so far and I came to the realization it had not been because of my excellence in the art of *heihō* that I had been victorious.
>
> Had it been the natural outcome of my pursuit of the path of *heihō* that kept me from straying from the principles of heaven? Or was it merely because of the deficiencies in the schools of *heihō* practiced by my adversaries?

These burning questions were to haunt Musashi over the next two decades, spurring him on to attain an even deeper understanding of the elusive laws of swordsmanship and to perfect the Enmei-ryū into an art of fencing that would allow its master to attain martial enlightenment.

## Settling Down

One of the older warriors among Katsunari's men to have lost his life was Nakagawa Shimanosuke. Musashi saw him fall when they stormed the castle's southern gate. Shimanosuke hailed from the province of Ise, where he had been lord of Nakagawabara castle. He had brought along three sons, the two eldest of whom had taken part in the siege. They were old enough to vie for themselves, but the youngest, an eleven-year-old by the name of Mikinosuke, needed a guardian.

Though he had already reached the age of thirty, Musashi had not married. In his quest to perfect his art his life thus far had been too uprooted, too wayward to settle down and start a family. By now he was seriously contemplating how he could insert some stability into his wandering life. Though he was not the type to serve anyone, let alone for life, he was very much in need of a place to live and practice his art. And in a feudal world, only lords could provide him with that kind of comfort and security.

Marriage into a feudal clan was one of the ways in which able warriors could attain such security. It had been the way in which Musashi's father, Muni, had made it to the level of senior retainer and acquired the name of Shinmen. Yet while these thoughts played through his head, Musashi realized that with his unsettled way of living, his limited means, and his poor looks he would probably never make a good match for the demanding daughter of a feudal lord.

There was, however, another way to gain a lord's patronage, if not his name: to have his adopted son enter a lordship's service. In an age when their warriors died by the thousands lords were always in need of able men. Nakagawa Shimanosuke had brought Mikinosuke along to help in the chores of camp life—preparing food, cleaning armor, and nursing wounds—and from what Musashi had seen of the boy he was sure he would make a splendid servant.

Not only these calculating motives drew the swordsman to the lad. Over the course of many weeks he had developed a great fondness for Mikinosuke. Somehow the boy, putting on a brave face yet clearly distraught and upset by the loss of his father, must have reminded the hardened warrior of a time long ago when he himself had been deprived of his father's guidance at the age of eight.

Ultimately, it was Musashi's fatherly instincts rather than any selfish designs that led him to take the boy under his care.

Early in June, 1615, he packed up his few possessions and set out with his new-found son Mikinosuke along the Sanyōdō, toward the castle town of Himeji. His own father having passed away too, Musashi felt free to go where he pleased, and having been raised in the province of Harima, where his stepmother still lived, it was there that he decided to turn his footsteps on that warm spring day.

Though still living in the village of Hirafuku, his stepmother was now on her own. Not long after Musashi rejoined his father in Nakatsu, Tasumi Masahisa also passed away. Yoshiko had not remarried, preferring instead to support herself by doing menial tasks at her brother's Shōrenan temple and growing vegetables on a nearby plot of land.

For two years Musashi remained at Hirafuku, looking after his aging stepmother and providing for Mikinosuke a childhood in which he could grow up and forget the horrors of warfare and come to terms with the loss of his father. Each day Musashi spent several hours together with Mikinosuke, priming him in the arts and skills he himself had learned as a boy.

Only now, as he was raising his adopted son, Musashi began to see how the changes that had upset his youth had been a blessing in disguise. It was true that his father had given him a thorough grounding in the martial arts. That training had been complemented by what he had learned from his stepuncle Chōkurō during his stay at the Shōrenan. Yet it had been his wide education under the erudite Dōrin that now enabled the warrior to instill in the young Mikinosuke the virtues of *bun* and *bu,* the literary and martial accomplishments that would make him a good retainer.

Though not the brightest of boys Mikinosuke was a diligent student, ready to learn more and to put into practice what he had learned. Alert to his surroundings and always eager to please, the boy was perfectly suited to serve a master. Yet at the same time Musashi began to wonder in whose service Mikinosuke could realize his potential.

## Miyake Gundayū

Then, in August 1617, unexpected news reached the village of Hirafuku. Ikeda Mitsumasa, the current lord of Himeji castle, was going to move. He was only seven when his father passed away the previous year and in spite of his guardian's best efforts he had proven far too young to manage the huge fiefdom. The Tokugawa Bakufu therefore decided to demote him to the smaller fiefdom of Tottori on the northern shore of Honshū, and divide his former domain into two new fiefs, that of Himeji and Akashi. The new lord of Himeji castle and its fiefdom was to be Honda Tadamasa, and it was in Tadamasa's appointment that Musashi saw a future for his adopted son.

During the storming of Osaka castle Lord Tadamasa had been in command of the second eastern phalanx, just behind the troops of Mizuno Katsunari. Tadamasa had heard of Musashi's antics in the battle on the bridge near Dōmyōji, but when he saw him storming the Sakura Mon with his own eyes, he was even more impressed with his bravery. He had introduced Musashi to his son, the nineteen-year-old, Tadatoki, who also took part in the siege. Musashi gave them a demonstration of his skills, and he and Tadatoki practiced the art of fencing with two swords at Tadamasa's encampment.

Following the fall of Osaka castle Tadamasa had invited Musashi to visit him at his castle in Kuwana, on the Bay of Ise. Impressed with the warrior's fencing skills, he wanted him to teach his clansmen the art of fighting with two swords.

But with the boy under his care Musashi deemed it better to go to Hirafuku, where he knew his stepmother would provide a warm home for Mikinosuke. Now, with Tadamasa's move to Himeji, the moment had come for Musashi to take him up on his offer and see what he could do for his adopted son.

To Musashi's delight Tadamasa not only vividly recalled their encounter at Osaka two years earlier, but showed a keen interest in Mikinosuke's plight. He had known the boy's father, whose castle of Nakagawabara was situated only a few miles down the coast from his former headquarters at Kuwana. He had been saddened by the death of the Nakagawa chieftain, a good neighbor and a staunch ally. On his return to Kuwana he had helped Shimanosuke's eldest son to establish himself as the new lord of Nakagawabara castle. Hearing that Musashi had adopted Shimanosuke's third son only deepened his respect for the swordsman and after some consultation with his elders it was soon decided Mikinosuke would be allowed to become a page to his eldest son, Tadatoki.

Not everyone in Himeji was as hospitable as Tadamasa. Some of his senior retainers, especially, were unhappy with Musashi's presence. They were outraged by the blatant effrontery with which Musashi was promoting his Enmei school of swordsmanship. Not long after he had met with Honda Tadamasa, he had opened a dojo in Himeji where he built up a large following of devoted students from all over the region.

Most offensive to Tadamasa's newly arrived retainers was a large signboard Musashi had erected in front of his dojo that read: "Miyamoto Musashi, Japan's Foremost Master of Swordsmanship." The majority of Tadamasa's men were practitioners of the Tōgun-ryū, a school of swordsmanship that had its origin in the Toda-ryū, which in turn went back to the ancient Chūjō-ryū. Founded by the great Kawasaki Kaginosuke, the Tōgun school of swordsmanship was considered by many to be the official fencing style of the house of Honda. Whenever they passed his dojo on some errand they returned to their quarters with more exasperated tales of the eccentric braggart with his odd style of dressing, his long hair, and his unusual style of fighting with two swords.[6]

Word of the unrest among his retainers came to Tadamasa's ears and before long he felt compelled to act. The *Bisan hōkan* describes how:

> When Honda Tadamasa heard of the unrest he said, "If Musashi really is the greatest swordsman in the realm, I would want to make him one of my retainers. If he is not, the shame of defeat in duel will surely make him leave on his own accord." At this he summoned Himeji's chief swordsman, Miyake Gundayū, and instructed him to put Musashi's martial skills to the test.
>
> Miyake sought out Musashi and presented him with his name card. Musashi let him into his guest room and made him wait for an hour. Miyake thought it below his standing as a commander of a garrison of *ashigaru* that he should be kept waiting. Moreover, since Musashi was no more than a wandering swordsman, it was rude to remain so aloof toward a man of his stature.

Another hour passed and still Musashi would not meet Miyake in person, leading the latter to suspect Musashi had grown fearful and sought to avoid a duel. Still Musashi did not show and before long an hour had elapsed. Yet when Miyake furtively looked into the room where Musashi was staying he found he was leisurely playing a game of *go* with one of his deshi. At length Miyake lost his composure and, calling the page, demanded a meeting with Musashi.

Aware that Miyake's anger had reached boiling point Musashi made a dignified appearance when he entered the guest room. He apologized for keeping his guest waiting and asked Miyake what had brought him to his house. Miyake explained that he had come to test Musashi's ability with the sword. Musashi laughed and said, "If I had known that is what you have come for I would not have kept you waiting." Instead I was killing time by playing a game of *go* with another guest. Let us go into the garden. And, come to speak of it, what weapon would you like to use, a sword, or a *bokutō*? I will leave it to you, my honored guest, to decide."

The *Bisan hōkan* goes on to describe how:

> Miyake now grew even more angry. While it had been his lordship's wish that he submit Musashi to a test, it was merely intended to ascertain his level of skill. He had certainly not come to fight a life-and-death duel. Not wanting to use a real sword, he cut himself a piece of bamboo from the garden so as to use it as a makeshift *bokutō*.
>
> Musashi wielded two *bokutō* from hardwood as they entered the garden. Miyake was no match for him and eventually dropped his head in defeat.
>
> Thus he returned to Lord Honda Tadamasa, conceding Musashi's claim that he was the greatest swordsman in the realm was only rightful.[7]

True to his word, Tadamasa now summoned Musashi and proposed that Musashi enter his service. Musashi, however, declined, saying, "I have ambitions of my own, and do not wish to become a retainer." In the end, Lord Tadamasa granted Musashi a stipend of two hundred *koku* in return for instructing his clansmen. They flocked to Musashi's dojo by the hundreds to study his art of swordsmanship. As a result, the fame of the Tōgun-ryū faded and Musashi's Enmei-ryū became the fiefdom's prominent school of swordsmanship.

## Designing a Castle Town

With Honda Tadamasa's patronage Musashi had been able to establish his school in Harima, yet he also had his adopted son to thank. Within the space of only a few years Mikinosuke had won the trust of his lord and master—so much so that he had his own retainer, while he and his father were allowed to wear Tadatoki's alternative family crest. Consisting of eight small whirlwind designs surrounding a larger one at its center, they were the symbol of Hachiman, the god of war.

Despite his fondness of the eccentric swordsman, Honda Tadamasa was still somewhat embarrassed by Musashi's presence. His elders, grave old men with conservative views, did not hide their dislike of this masterless swordsman with his unconventional life style and his odd approach to the sacred art of swordsmanship. They resented his popularity among the clan's young retainers.

At length, Tadamasa began to look for ways in which he could resolve the situation without upsetting either party. He found the answer in Ogasawara Tadazane, who had been appointed daimyo of the neighboring fief of Akashi. And again, events surrounding the siege of Osaka castle were the key to the new course Musashi's life was about to take.[8]

During the winter campaign, Tadamasa's younger brother, Tadatomo, a dissolute wastrel, had blundered into an ambush after a long night's debauch. Only with the help of Tadazane's father had he and his troops been saved from an ignoble end. Tadatomo had attempted to redeem himself during the summer campaign when, during the fierce fighting at Tennōji, he and his men sought to crush a contingent of some four thousand troops under the command of Mōri Katsunaga. Not long into the battle he was killed, albeit with his honor restored.

Only nine years old, Tadazane had been in the front line with his father. He had survived by the breadth of a hair. For weeks he lay on the brink of death, being wounded in seven places. His older brother had fallen at Tennōji. And while his father survived the battle, soon after, he too succumbed to the wounds sustained in trying to save Tadatomo. With his father and older brother dead, leadership of the Ogasawara clan had suddenly fallen on Tadazane's young shoulders.

Honda Tadamasa never had the opportunity to thank Tadazane's father for his help in restoring his brother's honor, and with a mixture of guilt and compassion he decided to help the new and inexperienced daimyo. Tadazane, after all, was only ten years old when he was promoted to the neighboring fiefdom of Akashi to face the daunting task of running an estate of a hundred thousand *koku*.

Not long after his move to Harima, therefore, Tadamasa invited his young neighbor to Himeji castle and offered him his daughter in marriage. Having consulted with his elders, Tadazane gratefully accepted the offer and that same year the young bride and her escort made their way to Funage castle, the makeshift headquarters of the Akashi fiefdom.

Built by a local member of the Akamatsu clan during the Muromachi Period, Funage castle proved to be outdated and far too small for a fief of such size. Again under Tadamasa's guidance, work was begun on creating a new seat for the Akashi daimyo and his bride. To maintain control over its territories, the Tokugawa Bakufu allowed only one castle to remain standing per domain, and thus all the smaller strongholds in the domain were demolished to create a single new one, many times larger than anything built before.

The foundations for the new castle were laid along the coast of the Inland Sea, right at the strategic narrow between the mainland and the island of Awaji. From there any hostile traffic through the Straits of Akashi could be stopped before it reached Osaka. A harbor was built for the small fleet of ships that would police the straits, while a newly laid-out castle town was erected to house all the retainers, mariners, merchants, and artisans who in one way or other served the young lord of Akashi castle.

Work was begun early in 1619 and carried out on a grand scale. Thousands of laborers were put to work on its construction, while a small army of architects, designers, and military specialists were put in charge of managing the huge undertaking. And here Tadamasa had a special role in mind for Musashi. With his keen mind and many years of experience, Musashi was the perfect man to help with the layout of the castle town and its environs. Given his fiercely independent nature, it was agreed Musashi would not directly enter the young Tadazane's service. Instead, he was appointed as an extraordinary advisor to the *zōei bugyō*, the Magistrate of Construction in charge of the project, helping with the strategic layout of the castle town, the construction of the castle walls, as well as the harbor's defenses.

Musashi was not only consulted on military matters. The *Seiryūwa*, the private writings of the Ogasawara clan, describe how, following the completion of the castle's main structures, the young lord Tadazane began work on embellishing the new home for himself and his wife:

> Facing the western side of the third ring of Akashi castle was a narrow strip of enclosed land stretching northward. On the part that was barren and uninhabited his lordship built a *yashiki* surrounded with trees and shrubs, so it could be used as an area for recreation and the performance of tea ceremonies, and in addition to this, a public bath with adjacent *tatami* rooms, and a field for playing ball.
>
> He put Miyamoto Musashi in charge of the construction of the tea house, miniature mountains, a miniature lake and a waterfall, as well as the planting of the many trees and shrubs.

Equally exacting in his approach to landscape gardening as to the martial arts, Musashi laid out the garden with a meticulous eye for detail, attending to every shrub, every stone, and no efforts were spared to satisfy his lordship's wishes. The *Seiryūwa* goes on to describe how:

> At the time of construction a huge force of laborers from within the lord's domain was mobilized. A large ship was sent over to the province of Awa and to Shodoshima in the province of Sanuki to transport the rocks for a miniature mountain.
>
> Trees and shrubs were collected from temples around Akashi and Miki, while others were bought at Osaka and Sakai, from where they were transferred and shipped to Akashi.

Work was carried out with such diligence and efficacy, that within one year, work on the castle walls, towers, and moats was completed, while a newly dug southern outer moat doubled as a protected harbor. In the first month of 1620, amid much festivities, Tadazane and his retinue moved into Akashi castle and took possession of their new abode.

Musashi's years in Akashi were undoubtedly the happiest in his life, advising the *zōei bugyō*, helping the young lord Tadazane with the layout of his gardens, and instructing his retainers in the art of fighting with two swords. They were made all the more enjoyable as he saw how, back in Himeji, his adopted son, Mikinosuke, continued to enjoy the favor of Tadamasa's heir and designated successor, Tadatoki.

## A Great Loss

Then, wholly unexpectedly, disaster struck in the spring of 1626, when Lord Tadatoki was taken ill with tuberculosis, an illness for which his physicians had no cure. After a few tense weeks it seemed the danger had passed and his spirit restored. To celebrate his recovery the shogun ordered that the Himeji fiefdom be increased to three-hundred thousand *koku* in anticipation of Tadatoki's succession.

It was to no avail. By the middle of May Tadatoki's health had again deteriorated, so much so that he was unable to walk and forced to keep to his quarters in Himeji castle. For several more weeks he clung to life, nursed by his devoted wife, Senhime, until on the last day of July he passed away. Following a grand ceremony, his remains were buried on the grounds of the Engyō temple. They were interred with those of his only son, who had died in infancy only five years earlier.

Tadatoki was only thirty when he passed away, but in a society that put such store on loyalty to one's lord and master Musashi knew the fate that lay in store for Mikinosuke. The *Bushū denraiki* describes how:

> Hearing of his lordship's death, Musashi, who was then at Osaka, thought "Mikinosuke will presently come and visit me. We will have to part in this life. I'll treat him to a feast."
>
> And surely after some time Mikinosuke came. Musashi was beside himself with joy and treated his adopted son to a banquet on a grand scale.
>
> Having toasted his adoptive father, Mikinosuke said, "I now will make my way to Himeji castle." Musashi saluted him with the words "It is becoming in you that you are thus prepared."

Following his last meeting with his father Mikinosuke traveled straight back to Himeji.

Seven days after Tadatoki's death, Mikinosuke and his retainer, Miyata Kakubei, made their way to the Engyō temple for an even more solemn occasion. It was a splendid summer morning, and the sun bounced off the young men's crisp white ceremonial robes as they silently made their way along the narrow moss-covered path toward the Honda family tomb behind the temple. There, screened off by a white curtain emblazoned with the Honda family crest, and in the presence of a small group of notables led by Honda Tadamasa, they made ready for the moment Mikinosuke would let his upper garment slip to his waist, tuck his sleeves under his knees, wrap the blade of his *tantō* in a piece of white paper, and plunge it into his lower abdomen. The intense pain would only last a moment. As soon as he had disemboweled himself, Kakubei would deliver him from further pain with his longsword and follow him in death.[9]

The *Honda kaki*, the family records of the Honda clan, captures Mikinosuke's final words of farewell before he gathered all his strength to embark on his final journey:

Though unexpected,
separated now
by distant clouds,
Our bond would have it
that we take the road together

## A Second Son

Mikinosuke's death left a deep emotional scar in the now forty-two-year-old swordsman. Eleven years of his life Musashi had dedicated to the kind youth, rescuing him from an uncertain future. Nurturing the boy's inborn talent, he had been able to secure Mikinosuke a position with Lord Tadatoki. With the tragic death of his lordship, Musashi had not only lost an able and eager pupil but also a young man he had come to consider a son of his own blood.

For months Musashi remained unapproachable to his deshi, preferring solitude as he tried to come to terms with the loss of his first and only son. Then, as time wore on, he came to, opening up again to the people around him. Yearning to fill the aching void, the lone swordsman began to look forward to an opportunity in which he could follow his fatherly instincts and help another youth onto the road to progress. As it was, that opportunity presented itself within a year of Mikinosuke's death, while Musashi was still living at Akashi.

The *Bukōden* describes how, while passing through the village of Yoneda, some ten miles north of Akashi castle, in the Miki district of Harima province, Musashi encountered a boy catching loaches in a wet paddy field beside the road:

> Going up to the boy, Musashi asked him whether he would share his catch with him. The boy said he would and, putting his catch into a small pail, handed them all to Musashi. At this Musashi said, "I am grateful for your kindheartedness, but I don't need this much, a few will suffice." And saying this, he scooped a few loaches out of the pail, wrapped them in a towel, and handed the pail back to the boy. The boy laughed and said, "It is not often that travelers ask me for loaches, so why should I be mean? Please, take the whole pail."

The text goes on to describe how, because of the late hour, Musashi spent the night at the boy's house and learned that his father, a poor farmer, had just passed away. Weakened by a life of grinding poverty, the boy, whose name was Iori, was unable to carry his father into the hills to bury him next to his previously deceased mother.[10]

The next day, having helped the boy bury his father, Musashi reflected for a while and said:

> "What good is there in you staying here by yourself? If you come with me, I might at some stage be able to help you find suitable employment." The boy said, "I see. I would indeed like to follow you, wherever it be, but I do not want to be a manservant for the rest of my life. However, if I can become a *bushi*,

> sitting astride a horse and carrying a lance, I would be content. If not, I would much prefer to go on living here, where I can spend my life in freedom." But Musashi said, "If you come with me, I will make sure you become a *bushi* with your own horse and lance you so desire." The boy's face lit up as he nodded and said, "In that case, let me join you!"

It did not take Musashi long to realize his newly found son would never be a *bushi* wielding a lance on horseback. The boy was simply too frail, too timid to do any such thing. But he was bold with the writing brush and very good with people. He discovered in Iori a fierce intelligence and an ability to solve complicated tasks. Unlike Mikinosuke, Iori was clearly destined for greater things. He had the potential to become a senior retainer to some lord. But whom?

Lord Tadatoki having passed away, it was impossible for Musashi to approach the grieving Lord Tadamasa for yet another favor. Lord Tadazane, however, had just turned twenty that year, an age at which he was fully able to make his own decisions, and with his ever increasing responsibilities, the number of servants and pages in his service was growing by the day.

The *Bushū denraiki* describes how one day, in the course of a conversation on the subject with his lordship, Musashi said, "By the way, I have a child in my care. I'll present him to you. He is no good for sword fighting, but he could serve you and may be of use for errands to the council of elders and the like." Musashi's eye for able young men was not mistaken. The *Bushū denraiki* goes on to describes how:

> Iori eventually rose to the rank of chief retainer, with a fief of five thousand *koku*.

The senior Bakufu officials were acquainted with Iori, and he was well known even among the common man. Indeed, such was his reputation that the various generations of Ogasawara retainers would not be allowed to sit in the same room with Iori. And when they accompanied him on the road they would keep a respectful distance of several yards for fear of soiling his attire with their splashing, thus forming a long line behind him.

Yet in spite of his high standing Iori did not display the slightest disrespect or pride.

## Keeping up the Practice

Whilst advising Tadazane's Magistrate of Construction and designing the castle gardens and tea house, Musashi continued to practice his Enmei style of fencing, and as in Himeji, he gathered around him a large number of deshi eager to acquire the art of fighting with two swords.

Among them was Aoki Jōemon. He was one of Musashi's earliest followers, who had joined him when he was still teaching at his father's dojo in Kitsuki. There, he had also studied under Musashi's father and had received from him a license to teach the Tōri-ryū. Immensely tall and strong, his nickname was Tetsujin, or "man of steel." And though he was not Musashi's brightest student, he was a loyal one, and immensely proud of being one. Yet time and again Musashi refused to grant Jōemon permission to teach his art, claiming he was not ready yet. Perhaps it was Musashi's knowledge of his father's treatment of the similarly strong but gullible Honiden Gekinosuke, whose tragic story he had heard years later from his tearful stepmother, that he finally relented and wrote out to Jōemon the coveted document. Yet it was with mixed emotions that he later learned Jōemon had gone up to Edo and founded a school called Nitō Tetsujin-ryū.[11]

Musashi regularly gave demonstrations of his Enmei-ryū on the grounds of Akashi castle. Among the hundreds of different schools of swordsmanship it stood out for its unique approach to the moment of combat. Musashi's novel approach, which did not rely solely on his incredible dexterity with the sword, was exemplified by *isshin ittō*, a technique he had put into practice during the very first duel in his life, more than thirty years earlier.

The *Gekken sōdan*, describes in detail the peculiar mixture of audacity and agility that characterize this technique:

> In this technique one boldly walks up to one's opponent while holding the longsword right in front as if one were about to bring it straight down on his head and then, aiming for the tip of his nose, bringing it down to the ground in an instant.
>
> No sooner has one struck than one moves in on one's opponent, stooping down, and achieving victory by lifting him up from his legs as he is about to strike from above.

He also continued to travel, visiting castles throughout the region. On one of these journeys he visited Mizuno Katsunari at his stronghold of Fukuyama castle. During his visit he stayed at the *yashiki* of Nakayama Kageyu Shigemori, commander of the escort of which Musashi had been part. It had been more than a decade since they had fought together on the bridge near Dōmyōji, and Shigemori was delighted to meet again with the famed swordsman. To celebrate the occasion, he held a banquet in honor of his guest.[12]

Eager to promote his Enmei-ryū, Musashi used such occasions to demonstrate the effectiveness of fighting with two swords, challenging practitioners of other schools of fencing to a *taryū shiai*. Musashi invariably emerged the victor of these multi-discipline duels. As a result, his reputation as one of Japan's master swordsmen steadily grew, putting him on a par with men like Yagyū Munenori and Ono Tadaaki, both of them famous *shihan*, personal fencing instructors of the shogun. In the course of his long stay as a guest of Lord Tadazane, swordsman of note came from all parts of the country to challenge his style of fencing.

## Musō Gonnosuke

One of the many swordsmen to seek Musashi out at his *yashiki* in Akashi was the renowned Musō Gonnosuke Katsuyori. Gonnosuke had entered the service of Kuroda Nagamasa following the latter's move to Fukuoka, and his fame as a martial artist had soon spread throughout the island of Kyushu. Gonnosuke was an adept of the art of fighting with the *jō*, a long, round staff made of tropical hardwood. He cut an impressive figure, standing as much as six feet tall. He was said to be as strong as an ox, and invariably traveled in the company of a large number of deshi of equal physical stature.

Musashi's deshi were somewhat intimidated therefore, when, one summer day in August, Gonnosuke and his followers made their appearance at Musashi's *yashiki* in Akashi. It was a blistering hot day. The air was filled with the incessant trill of cicadas and their master was languishing inside crafting a toy bow from riverside willow. The *Kaijō monogatari* describes how, having been led inside by Musashi's deshi, Gonnosuke spoke first, explaining the reason for his visit:

> I am on a *musha shugyō*. Needless to say I have traveled the Kantō region and beyond, as far up as the most northern provinces. Yet while I have engaged in a number of *shiai* I have not yet encountered my equal, so I made up my mind to also visit the western provinces. I have seen your father Muni wield the longsword, but hear that now his art has been passed on to you the use of the *tachi* has changed. Could you not give me a demonstration of the way in which it has changed?

Musashi replied that if Gonnosuke had indeed seen Muni's art of fencing with the longsword he would find it had not changed that much, so there would be little reason to see it demonstrated. But Gonnosuke insisted. He argued it would be for the sake of both their deshi if he and Musashi were to give a demonstration of their respective arts in the traditional role-play of *uchidachi* and *shidachi*, the offensive and passive roles in a bout of fencing between master and pupil. Musashi explained that his art of swordsmanship was not suitable to perform the offensive role of *uchidachi*, as it had been construed in such a manner that it would stop an opponent's sword in whatever way he responded. If, however, Gonnosuke would agree to take the initiative, he would be happy to take the passive role of *shidachi*. Gonnosuke, sensing an easy chance to win, leapt at the occasion.[13]

The *Kaijō monogatari* goes on to describe how, having gone out into the garden, Gonnosuke produced from a silk cover a four-foot *jō* reinforced with steel from top to bottom. It was crafted from biwa, a wood widely believed to cause inflicted wounds to fester. Meanwhile:

> Musashi, who was still holding the branch of riverside willow, stood up and said, "Well, go ahead and strike." At this, Gonnosuke immediately charged with his *jō*, but each time he struck out his *jō* was deflected away from its target by a few light parries of Musashi's piece of willow.
>
> Gonnosuke now changed the grip on his staff and struck out with a horizontal blow, touching the collar of Musashi's *haori* just below his sleeve. He cried out in a loud voice, "I struck you! I struck you!" But Musashi said, "No, one cannot call that a strike. What good would such a strike do?"

It goes on to describe how Gonnosuke, growing ever more red in the face as he concentrated on an opening in Musashi's defense, failed to find one. Instead, he found himself veering backward. Musashi had driven him into a corner of the garden and had landed a fierce blow on his forehead, which immediately swelled red. Regretting his folly Gonnosuke acknowledged defeat and for a time became Musashi's deshi.[14]

# CHAPTER 5

## Leaving Akashi

Musashi had finally reached a stage in life where he could look forward to growing old in comfort while his school of swordsmanship was thriving. Though not in the direct service of Tadazane, he was now a respected man in Akashi. He had played an important role in the castle town's construction and his Enmei-ryū attracted challengers and deshi from all over the country. Yet, again, events taking place on a higher plane were to alter the course of Musashi's life in unexpected ways.

In the summer of 1632 news began to spread among the dwellers of the castle town of Akashi that their lord and master was to be promoted to a larger fief. This could only mean some other lord had either passed away or had also changed fiefs, for in a feudal system in which the Tokugawa Bakufu had no newly conquered territories to distribute, the only way to allot a daimyo a different fiefdom was through promotion or demotion—musical chairs with fiefs. It was not long before Musashi learned Tadazane was to be promoted to the fiefdom of Kokura. Its most recent daimyo was none other than Hosokawa Tadatoshi, master of Moji castle at the time of Musashi's duel with Sasaki Kojirō on the island of Funashima.

A lot had happened in Kokura since Musashi took refuge at Moji castle in the wake of the now famous duel. In 1620 Tadatoshi's father, lord of the Kokura fiefdom, had gone into retirement. He passed on the reins of power to Tadatoshi, who had moved to Kokura castle. Tadatoshi did not belong to the privileged elite of *fūdai*, or vassal daimyo, but with great skill and tact, as well as a good degree of patience, he managed to enhance his standing with the Tokugawa regime over the next decade. This was achieved mainly by uniting the interests of his headstrong wife, who was of Tokugawa descent, with those of his stubborn father, who as in most other clans continued to exert his influence from behind the scenes.[1]

Tadatoshi's diplomatic qualities must have impressed the Bakufu a great deal, for in the spring of 1632 it announced he was to be promoted to the Kumamoto fiefdom in the province of Higō, on the west side of Kyushu. It was a huge honor. With an annual yield of more than five hundred thousand *koku*, the Kumamoto fiefdom was one of the largest in the country.[2]

Tadatoshi's move to Higo, then, left the Kokura fiefdom to be bestowed on someone else, and the daimyo the Bakufu officials appointed was Ogasawara Tadazane. They had done so with good reason. Tadazane, who had reached the age of thirty-six, had made Akashi into one of the most vibrant fiefdoms in Harima. By now fully completed, its castle was a paragon of modern military architecture, and though partly destroyed by fire the previous year, the castle town was still a beautiful example of efficient town planning.

One of the reasons for Akashi's economic success was its position. The port was situated along both the Sanyōdō and the

Akashi Straits, two of Japan's busiest transport arteries. Much of the merchandise carried by ship and cart was, of course, destined for Japan's metropolises of Osaka, Kyoto, and Edo. But like the many other towns and ports that had sprung up along these thoroughfares, Akashi thrived on the great volume of traffic that passed through it.

Though the Kokura fiefdom was far removed from the centers of power, it resembled that of Akashi in several important ways. It, too, was situated along a major traffic artery, the Straits of Shimonoseki, the linchpin between the Inland Sea and the coast facing the Sea of Japan. Like Akashi, the port of Kokura thrived on the constant coming and going of merchant ships, both Japanese and Chinese.

Perhaps even more important than the commercial traffic through the straits was the potential threat of military upheaval. It had been only a few decades since the Battle of Sekigahara, and even fewer years since the Osaka campaigns, and the Bakufu was always on guard for a hostile move by one of the former warlords who had been banished to Japan's outer regions. As such Kokura castle served exactly the same purpose as that of Akashi: to control the traffic, both through and across the straits along which it was built.

Tadazane had been raised to govern such a port and was by now intimately at home with all the ins and outs of policing and levying taxes. With the help of his patron and mentor, Honda Tadamasa, he had also grown into a competent administrator, whose benevolence shone on all who lived under his rule. Moreover, as the great-grandchild of Tokugawa Ieyasu (his mother was the daughter of Ieyasu's eldest son), he belonged to the inner circle of confidants of the Tokugawa regime, men who were bound to put the interests of the Bakufu before anything else. It did not take the Bakufu ministers long, therefore, to decide that Ogasawara Tadazane was the perfect man to become the new lord of Kokura castle.

Musashi was by now forty-eight years old, and though he was still in good health he no longer felt the need to set out on the long travels of his youth. Nor was there much to make him stay on in Akashi. His stepmother in nearby Hirafuku, whom he had visited often, had passed away, while his son Iori had already left for Kokura to prepare the way for his lordship. Tadazane had proven a good lord to Iori. And while Musashi had maintained his independence, he too had greatly benefited from Tadazane's patronage. With his help Musashi had built a large dojo, which had become the place of practice for many of Tadazane's retainers.

It was with mixed emotions, then, that on a windswept evening in the fall of 1632, as the leaves on the maple trees around Akashi were turning a thousand shades from red to yellow, Musashi closed the shutters of his dojo for the last time after taking leave of his many deshi. It was not a sad parting, for many of them he would see again. He had decided to follow his son and build a new life in Kokura, the place where two decades before his reputation had been established on the small nearby island that now bore the name of Ganryū.

First, however, he wanted to visit Nagoya, the breeding ground of the Owari line of the famous Yagyū Shinkage school of swordsmanship. He had been invited by Terao Naomasa. Naomasa was a retainer of the daimyo of Owari, Lord Tokugawa Yoshinao. Naomasa had a large fief of some three thousand *koku* near the village of Seto, situated only a few miles east of Nagoya. Like Musashi, he had taken part in the siege of Osaka castle as a young man and had come to admire the swordsman's valor. Since then he had climbed to the position of *karō*, a top-ranking samurai in Yoshinao's retinue.

Born in 1601 Lord Yoshinao had also taken part in the siege of Osaka castle and distinguished himself in the heavy fighting at Tennōji. He had been rewarded with Owari, an important fiefdom. Its headquarters of Nagoya castle guarded the crucial traffic artery of the Tōkaidō as it approached Sekigahara, the pass through the Ibuki and Yōrō mountains, and the gateway to the old capital and the western provinces.

From a young age Yoshinao had taken a profound interest in the martial arts. Like his father, Ieyasu, he patronized the Yagyū Shinkage school of swordsmanship. His chief fencing instructor was Yagyū Toshiyoshi, the nephew of the famed Yagyū Munenori. In his youth Yoshinao had submitted himself to five years of intensive practice under Toshiyoshi's guidance and had grown into a highly accomplished swordsman.

## To Nagoya

Musashi knew he was entering the dragon's den, when, in the summer of 1632, he arrived in Nagoya. Yet he was warmly welcomed when he passed through the front gate of Naomasa's imposing mansion in Seto and announced himself. Naomasa was a man of influence in Nagoya. Through his offices Musashi was offered a room at the Tōkōin, one of the twelve lodgings for priests of the Ryūfukuji, a temple in the town's southern quarters dating back to the eighth century.[3]

Knowing of Lord Yoshinao's passion for the martial arts Musashi was not surprised when within days of his arrival he was invited to demonstrate his art of fencing in a duel in his lordship's presence. Nor was he insulted when he was pitted against no more than one of Yagyū Toshiyoshi's star deshi. To risk defeat at the hands of a wandering swordsman would spell the end of Toshiyoshi's career as the daimyo's fencing instructor. Nor would he insult the daimyo by killing one of his retainers. He had been invited for a friendly bout, and that it would be. But he did intend to drive home an important point. The *Mukashibanashi* describes how:

> When his opponent suddenly opened the attack, Musashi crossed his two swords, training the tip of his longsword on the tip of his adversary's nose, thus steadily forcing the latter backward until they had traced the circumference of the whole dojo.

Having thus stunned his audience, Musashi broke the tense silence and said, "This is the way I fight duels." The same record relates how another Yagyū Shinkage-ryū adept took his place opposite Musashi, but that he was subdued in the same way without ever finding an opening in the master's defense.

Musashi thoroughly enjoyed his stay in Nagoya, especially his lodgings in the ancient Ryūfukuji, a temple steeped in history. Long ago his distant ancestor, Fujiwara Kanehira, a Heian court official and a renowned player of the *biwa*, had also visited the temple. He had come to pay homage to an image of the Jūichimen Kannon, the bodhisattva with eleven faces, carved from a piece of driftwood from the nearby river by the temple's founder. The rainy season had started and it was pelting down when to his dismay he found the roof of the building in which the relic was housed had long since collapsed. Only when he entered the dilapidated structure did he spot a young woman holding up an umbrella to protect the treasured Kannon from the raging elements. Touched to his romantic core, he took her to the capital and married her. From then on the temple was popularly known as the Kasadera, the Umbrella Temple.

During his stay at the Kasadera, Musashi presented its abbot with a work of calligraphy reading *Namu Tenman Daijizai Tenjin* ("I place my trust in Tenjin of the Tenma shrine, deity of absolute freedom"), expressing reverence to another great Heian court official, Sugawara no Michizane (Tenman Daijizai Tenjin). Musashi had become a great admirer of the famed poet-scholar, whose life took a tragic turn when he was unjustly exiled to Kyushu. While still living with his father in Kitsuki, Musashi had been on a pilgrimage to visit the famous Anraku temple, situated some forty miles south of Kokura and closely associated with the poet's life in Kyushu.[4]

To display his mastery with the brush, Musashi wrote the characters for *Tenman Daijizai* with his left hand, while the whole text was imposed on a delicate painting of a plum branch bearing blossom, a clear reference to the *Tenjin sutra*. A prayer invoking Tenjin's name, he had read the *sutra* daily before classes at the temple school of his stepuncle, Dōrin, when still a boy:

Wherever plums
are found
know that is where I am,
No need to search
here and there

In Nagoya, too, Musashi gathered around him a group of devoted followers, among them Hayashi Ichirōemon Suketatsu, also an Owari retainer and an old friend of Naomasa. Suketatsu was known for his fierce temper. Once, when visiting Nagoya castle, a guard who held a grudge against him pierced his sleeve with a *yari* as he was about to dismount. He seized the *yari*, pulled it toward him, drew his longsword halfway and cut off the man's hands by hauling them over the exposed blade. After that all guards kept a reverent distance whenever Suketatsu entered the gate. Though a practitioner of the Shintō school of swordsmanship, he was soon won over by Musashi's style of fencing.[5]

For almost a year Musashi enjoyed Naomasa's hospitality, demonstrating his art and instructing a steadily increasing number of followers who were keen to master his unique style of swordsmanship. Meanwhile, a lot of work had been done at the Kokura fiefdom, including extensive alterations to Kokura castle, and by now Lord Tadazane and his followers were firmly installed in their new domain. Yet when in the spring of 1633 Musashi packed up his few belongings in the Tōkōin and left Nagoya, he did not travel straight down to the Straits of Shimonoseki. He had one more important appointment to keep, for he had been invited to stay at the residence of Matsudaira Katsutaka, an important official in the Tokugawa Bakufu.

## To Matsuyama

Born in 1589, Matsudaira Katsutaka was only five years younger than Musashi and known for his great love of swordsmanship. He was the son of one of Ieyasu's most senior vassals and had held a string of important positions within the Bakufu. That same spring of 1634, he had moved down to the province of Iyo, on the island of Shikoku, to take up temporary residence on the grounds of Matsuyama castle. The former lord of Matsuyama castle had passed away and the Bakufu decided that henceforth the Matsuyama domain was to be governed by a member of the Matsudaira, the clan from which the Tokugawa themselves descended. It was Katsutaka's duty to prepare the *hikiwatashi*, the castle's smooth transfer from one clan to another.

It so happened that Katsutaka was distantly related to the Ogasawara. Several times he and Musashi had met at Akashi castle, and on each occasion the Bakufu official had pressed the swordsman to pay him a visit. At that time Katsutaka still resided in Edo, while Musashi was tied down by his various tasks in Akashi. Now things had changed. On his way to Kokura he would pass Matsuyama, and thus Musashi seized the opportunity to visit the Bakufu official at Matsuyama castle.

Musashi was warmly received by Katsutaka, who had long looked forward to this opportunity to see the swordsman in action again. He had assembled a number of warriors from Iyo, men with great ability and all eager to match themselves against Musashi in combat.[6]

Katsutaka arranged the contest to be held in the library garden of his residence on the spacious castle grounds, where one of his men was already awaiting Musashi with an eight-foot pole. At Katsutaka's cue Musashi descended the stairs, which ran parallel to the library, armed with his inseparable two *bokutō*. Expecting Musashi to face him squarely by the time he had descended the stairs, the warrior turned sideways, facing the library. But when Musashi had descended to the second step he suddenly raised his two swords to the height of the man's head. Then, while the startled warrior changed his stance, Musashi struck out hard at the man's left and right-hand wrists, and as he faltered, struck him down and claimed victory.

Katsutaka was intrigued and demanded a *shiai* with Musashi himself. When Musashi agreed Katsutaka's councilors implored him to desist and go inside, but Katsutaka paid no attention. The *Bushū denraiki* describes how:

> Musashi drove Katsutaka back three times, the third time right into the library. But still Katsutaka did

> not falter, and when he sought to drive his weapon home, Musashi intercepted the *bokutō* with his own using a *nebari o kakuru*, and then struck out at Katsutaka's *bokutō* by means of a *sekka no atari* with all his might. The force broke Katsutaka's *bokutō* in two, causing one piece to hit the ceiling.[7]

Katsutaka had seen enough. Indeed, stunned by the force of Musashi's blow, he had instinctively flinched and thrown himself on the floor out of fear of being struck. Like so many friendly duelists had done before him, he immediately became one of Musashi's deshi. He persuaded Musashi to stay for a while, and over the next few months he spent much of his free time practicing Musashi's art of fencing.

## Life in Kokura

Late in the autumn of 1634 Musashi finally crossed the Straits of Shimonoseki. His livelihood as a fencing instructor was not endangered by his move to Kokura. Establishing a large dojo with the help of his son, his following grew even larger than at Akashi. Although far removed from the capital and its many diversions, countless martial artists of various schools and their *ryūha* visited his dojo to experience the art of fighting with two swords.

Following his arrival in Kokura, Musashi had renamed his school of swordsmanship. Formerly called the Enmei-ryū, the "School of the Circle of Light," he now called it the Niten Ichi-ryū, the "School of the Two Heavens United," the two united heavens signifying the superlative strength of the long and short sword when used together in combat.

One of the many warriors to visit Musashi at his dojo in Kokura was Takagi Umanosuke Shigesada, a retainer of the house of Mōri. A practitioner of the ancient art of *jūjutsu*, Umanosuke was known for his immense strength, although many questioned his mental abilities. The rumor went that sometime during the thirties he had been summoned by the emperor to demonstrate his strength in the Forbidden Gardens of the Imperial Palace. There, under the emperor's watchful eyes, he lifted a weight of well over a thousand pounds without much effort. Then he took a number of huge bamboo poles and split them from top to bottom. The emperor had been impressed with Umanosuke's physical prowess but, suspicious of his mental powers, he presented the warrior with a thin bamboo stick with the order to subject it to the same treatment but using only one hand, a feat the brute was unable to accomplish.[8]

Musashi had heard of Umanosuke's visit to the palace, and told the giant with a smile that had he been challenged by the emperor he would have been able to prize the bamboo stick apart with just one finger by using the art of *heihō*. Vexed at having been reminded of the embarrassing episode, Umanosuke rose and angrily challenged Musashi to a duel. The *Bushū denraiki* describes how the giant immediately charged, and how, holding his *bokutō* in a backhand grip:

> Musashi stooped as Umanosuke lunged toward him and hit him hard in the face. Umanosuke was thrown back by the impact. Before he knew it Musashi was upon him, thrusting his thumb in Umanosuke's solar plexus and causing him to fall over backward. Umanosuke was terrified and those who had come to look were dumfounded.

The same record describes how, on another occasion, and this time in the presence of Lord Ogasawara Tadazane, Musashi engaged in a *shiai* with Takada Matabei, a third-generation practitioner of the Hōzōin school of spear fighting.[9]

> Musashi was armed with his inseparable two *bokutō*, while Matabei faced him with a cross-shaped *yari* made of bamboo. Three times Musashi charged, his *bokutō* held in a *chūdan* position. The third time round he said, "This time I touched you, but the tip of your *yari* deflected, striking my leg." It seems this had even escaped those who had been looking on.[10]
>
> Afterward, Matabei turned toward them and said, "Musashi's attainment of the art of *heihō* is on an altogether different plane than mine, but no matter what I say, nobody seems to understand this. Musashi claims I struck him the third time round, but I have no recollection of doing so. It must have been his good manners that caused him to say I did. His genius is beyond words indeed."

It seemed, then, that even after his move to Kokura, Musashi could look forward to a life of comfort and reward. He was a man at the height of his fame, respected by his patron, admired by his peers, and loved by his adopted son. Yet, as everyone's life, so was the life of the now middle-aged swordsman subject to the slings and arrows of fortune.

## A Personal Tragedy

Thus far Musashi had never held any official position. It was not that he was never offered an official post; he simply did not want to enter a lord's service. He had been only two years old at the time of his father's treacherous slaying of his senior deshi, the innocent Honiden Gekinosuke, at the behest of his lord, Munetsura. Yet like no other he had felt the devastating effect the people's approbation had on his father's self-esteem. For years Musashi and his stepmother, Yoshiko, had suffered under Muni's increasing melancholy, his terrible fits of anger, until both of them could stand it no longer and left the very man they had loved and admired.

The moment he left his father's house, Musashi had resolved never to enter anyone's service. Never would he allow his martial talents to be misused and abused the way his father's had been. The *Bushū denraiki* relates how, when asked why he would not contemplate becoming a lord's retainer, he brusquely replied that "One mere pail of hot water suffices to wash away the dirt of my body. I do not have the time to wash away from my soul the impurities such service would incur." It was very much by choice, then, that he remained an outsider, in spite of the love and respect with which he was treated by his superiors and peers.

Musashi's image as an outsider was compounded by his personal appearance. A lifelong sufferer of eczema, he never bathed, choosing instead to clean himself with a moistened cloth. Nor did he wear the usual attire of the swordsmen of his day, but outlandish items, such as long damask wide-sleeved undergarments reaching down to his feet, or the kind of padded *yukata* he had worn during his duel with Sasaki Kojirō. By this time he had also abandoned the customary two swords. Instead he usually carried with him a five-foot wooden staff, very much in the way of the itinerant monk. He never bothered to cut his nails or hair, so that in his prime his hair grew all the way down to his belt. These idiosyncrasies surely added to his charisma as a martial sage, but they did little to ingratiate him with the women of his day.

In spite of his outlandish appearance Musashi did have intimate liaisons with members of the opposite sex. During one of his visits to Edo he had begun an affair with a low-ranking geisha by the name of Kumoi. There was much affection between the two, for the *Dōbō goen* describes how:

> Musashi asked Kumoi to sew him a silk bag and a battle *haori* in black satin lined with the red fabric of her *kimono*, as well as a banner carrying an insignia in the shape of two crossed spatulas.

It is not certain whether it was Kumoi, but shortly afterward a woman bore him a baby girl. Having never had a child of his own, the swordsman was besotted with his daughter, but at the age of three she suddenly fell ill and died. The loss of this child was a devastating blow to the hardened swordsman. The *Bushū denraiki* describes how:

> Musashi was inconsolable with grief and wept from dawn till dusk while he cradled the body of the infant in his lap. People spoke to him and tried to console him, but he did not hear them. At length, even his followers began to murmur that this was unbecoming in their master.

Never again was Musashi to father a child, nor did any of his pupils ever discover where he buried the remains of his baby daughter, for throughout the remainder of his life Musashi never again talked about this personal tragedy.[11]

In an age in which many a child died in infancy Musashi's fate was one suffered by many a parent. To some it seemed odd that such a tough warrior could be so utterly distraught by the loss of a child, especially since it had not been a boy. These people failed to perceive the real tragedy at the core of Musashi's life—a tragedy this episode had brought home to him with devastating clarity.

Musashi was a warrior who had spent his life in the pursuit of an art the ultimate aim of which was to kill one's opponent. Death and destruction, not the giving of life, were at the core of his trade. The birth of a little girl—a girl destined one day to give birth to her own children—was a symbol of renewal and regeneration, and as such stood for everything that Musashi was not. Not only fatherly love made the blow so hard to bear for the battle-hardened warrior; the girl was living proof of the bond of love between a man and a woman, and to Musashi, she had presented a bridge, however fragile, between a world of warfare and another, more peaceful world. The tragic death of the infant, her life snuffed out long before her promise was realized, must have brought home to Musashi once and for all that he was destined not to partake of that better world.

The child's death, then, was far more than just the loss of a loved one. It was the dreadful and undeniable proof of the incompatibility between a way of life that was unique but solitary and one that was commonplace but happy—a life blessed with children. The divide that had momentarily been bridged had opened up once more, never to close again. Only later, through the creative process of his art, was Musashi able to rediscover that live-giving force and recapture the innocence of the infant child. It was this heartrending experience that gave his later works of art such power of emotion and imbued his writing with a sensitivity it had not known before.

*Chapter 5*

# The Shimabara Rebellion

It was by way of escape from the emotional turmoil of his personal life that, early in January 1638, Musashi accepted an official post of sorts. He was to serve as an escort to Tadazane's twenty-three-year-old nephew and successor, Nagatsugu, who, having been raised in a time of peace, had no experience on the field of battle. It was the same role Musashi performed during the Osaka campaigns, when he had been an escort to Mizuno Katsunari's son. This time, too, he could expect to see action, for the Bakufu had ordered Lord Tadazane and his son to raise troops and prepare for battle.[12]

An armed revolt had broken out in the province of Hizen. The rebellion was led by a the seventeen-year-old Amakusa Shiro, the son of a retainer of the Christian daimyo, Konishi Yukinaga. Shiro was also a Christian, and so were most of the rebels, who at the peak of the rebellion numbered more than twenty thousand. Among them were a considerable number of *rōnin*, masterless samurai, but most of them were simple peasants, who had been joined by their womenfolk and children. They had ensconced themselves in Hara castle, an old stronghold on the Shimabara Peninsula that had stood empty for several decades.[13]

The revolt had erupted in December of the previous year. Immediately, the governor of Nagasaki led four thousand troops down the peninsula, but the rebels fought with such tenacity that he had to retreat to Nagasaki. Determined to quell the revolt the Bakufu ordered Kyushu's daimyo to raise a force of at least a hundred thousand men.

Musashi at the time was again visiting Edo. As soon as he accepted Tadazane's request, he made his way to the latticed quarters of the Yoshiwara to take his leave of Kumoi. He was well over fifty now and, going into battle, he realized he might never see her again. The *Dōbō goen* describes the scene as Musashi departs for Shimabara wearing the black battle *haori* he had asked Kumoi to make for him on his previous visit:

> A crowd gathered at the center of Shinmachi to see Musashi take his leave. It was an age of ostentation, and it is said that Musashi said his farewell without faltering, confidently mounted his horse outside the great gate, and took off in high spirits.

It was well into March before Tadazane, his son, Nagatsugu, and his escort including Musashi arrived on the Shimabara Peninsula at the head of more than eight thousand men.

After more than two decades of peace, it took several more weeks for the Bakufu troops to reach their full strength. One daimyo taking part in the siege was Mizuno Katsunari, under whom Musashi had fought during the summer siege of Osaka castle. One of the few daimyo not from Kyushu, Katsunari arrived on the eighth of April in command of some six thousand troops. The *Sōkyū sama o-degatari* describes how:

> They arrived at nightfall, and it was still pouring down with rain when Lord Katsunari took control and ordered his troops in formation.
>
> When the troops of the house of Ogasawara, who were in the vanguard, heard the inordinate clamor from the camp, they could tell that there might well be a method to this way of arriving and that it spoke of just how good a general Lord Katsunari was at that time.

> Yet some began to talk among themselves. They wondered how it could be that if there were, for instance, a sudden night attack such numbers would be of any use.
>
> Hearing this, a man by the name of Miyamoto Musashi said he had rode into battle under Lord Katsunari some years earlier and that he was well acquainted with his manner of deploying the troops, that he was a commander whose thinking was beyond that of commoners, and that his style of leadership was above reproach.

By the end of March the number of Bakufu troops besieging Hara castle exceeded one hundred and twenty-five thousand, more than four times the number of defenders. Yet in spite of their overwhelming strength, and in spite of help from the Dutch at Nagasaki, who fired more than four hundred rounds into the stronghold from two of their ships, it took the Bakufu troops until April 15 before the stronghold finally fell. The *Bushū denraiki* describes how:

> From start to finish Musashi was at Lord Nagatsugu's side, never putting on a harness but simply wearing a silk damask wide-sleeved undergarment, and tucking into his belt two *wakizashi*, while leaning on his five-foot wooden staff. During the castle's siege the rebels threw down stones, but Musashi leapt in front of his lordship's horse and fended them off with his staff shouting, "Beware of the stones!"

Again Musashi had managed to safeguard his ward from injury or worse. His son, Iori, had also rode out with his lordship, though he did not fight in the siege. He was to play an important role in its aftermath, for shortly afterward he was asked to analyze the way in which the rebellion had been tackled.

This important appointment had come about partly through the generous mediation of Arima Naozumi. Now the lord of Nobeoka castle in the province of Hyūga, Naozumi originally hailed from Hizen, and Hara castle stood on his former domains. Due to his intimate knowledge of the terrain he had played a leading role in the castle's siege, in the course of which he had come to know Iori intimately. Writing to Naozumi in the wake of the battle, Musashi expressed his gratitude:

> that my son Iori was entrusted with the role of evaluating our military actions following the battle. I also believe I conducted your men to the positions you had in mind, and everyone was full of praise about the swiftness with which you and your father managed to press on to the castle's inner circle.
>
> As for myself, I was struck on the shins twice by rocks, making it impossible for me to put any weight on my legs at present, so I beg your pardon for not coming down to thank you in person. Please, therefore, allow me to express my respect in this manner.[14]

The siege of Hara castle was the last time the Tokugawa hegemony was disturbed and the last time Musashi saw action. He was now fifty-four years old and had taken part in as many as six battles, all of them on Kyushu soil except, of course, the Osaka campaign. More than forty years earlier, on the island's northern shore, during the fierce battle on the plains of Ishigaki, he first saw action under Kuroda Yoshitaka. In the subsequent siege of Tomiku castle he had brazenly climbed its defenses, wrestling with a lance of one of its occupants. Now he had done his utmost to keep Lord Nagatsugu from indulging in similar antics, incurring serous wounds himself as a result—he was beginning to feel old and weary of the battlefield.

Musashi's health was also in decline. Ever since he arrived in Kokura he had trouble with swallowing. At times his throat was so sore that he was unable to speak for days on end.[15]

## Visiting Kumamoto

Arima Naozumi was not the only daimyo in Kyushu with whom Musashi entertained good relations. All had come to admire his superlative martial skills and over the next few years, his wounds having healed, the swordsman visited many of them. It was partly the haunting memory of his lost child that caused Musashi to take to the road so often, hoping to find solace in the solitude of an itinerant life and the soothing comfort of nature.

Another goal that drove Musashi on was the promotion and spread of his school of swordsmanship. By now his Niten Ichiryū had many followers and to safeguard its reputation he felt it his duty to take up the challenge to measure his skills with practitioners from other schools of swordsmanship. Such *taryū shiai* were often organized by daimyo. Apart from their own enthusiasm for the martial arts, they had an obvious interest in maintaining the martial traditions of their clans and test them against others.

Not all such *taryū shiai* were the result of an open invitation. Many who knew of Musashi's reputation felt intimidated and balked at the idea of inviting the renowned swordsman to their castles. Especially the daimyo of surrounding provinces were keen to avoid an open duel between Musashi and one of their men, concerned as they were that the ignominious defeat of one of their retainers might lead to cross-border reprisals, thus damaging the fragile peace put in place in the wake of the Shimabara rebellion.

Most keenly aware of Musashi's incendiary qualities was Hosokawa Tadatoshi, once the master of Moji castle, but now the proud lord of the Kumamoto fiefdom in the province of Higo. Almost three decades had passed since Musashi defeated Sasaki Kojirō on Funashima Island and sought refuge at Moji castle, but Tadatoshi remembered the episode as if it had happened only yesterday.

Twenty-six years old at the time, he vividly recalled how impressed he had been by Musashi's inescapable presence, his physical prowess and his piercing mental sharpness. He had seen him practice with Numata Nobumoto and his men in the castle's forecourt and he could still hear the deafening crush as Musashi's red oak *bokutō* landed on his opponent's armor. Even more unsettling was his recollection of the hatred Musashi's victory over Kojirō had engendered among the latter's followers. Tadatoshi could still hear his late father complain, albeit with a humorous tinge of admiration, of the long time it had taken before calm returned to the castle town of Kokura.

Tadatoshi could not even be sure whether Musashi would behave with the same circumspection he had during his stay at Moji castle in the wake of the duel. Then Musashi had been a refugee, whose conduct had been tempered by his gratitude for a safe retreat. Now he would be an honored guest who might feel obliged to live up to his reputation.

At the same time Tadatoshi was very keen to meet Musashi again. He was a devoted practitioner of the martial arts. In his youth, when still living in Edo, he had studied under none other than Yagyū Munenori, the great master of the Yagyū Shinkage school of swordsmanship and the shogun's chief fencing instructor. Yet nothing he had seen impressed him as much as Musashi's almost supernatural ability with both swords. He was dying to test the skills of his own swordsmen against this fighting machine, yet at the same time wary of the demoralizing effect their defeat might have on his retainers in general.

When in the fall of 1639 word reached Kumamoto that Musashi was staying at the house of Shiota Hamanosuke, its lord therefore chose not to invite Musashi to Kumamoto castle. Tadatoshi knew Hamanosuke well, for the latter had long served his late father. Like Musashi in his fifties, Hamanosuke lived in a *yashiki* on the outskirts of Kumamoto on a stipend of twenty-five *koku*. In a small dojo next to his house, he still taught his special school of *jūjutsu* which included the ancient arts of *shimono* and *torikago*.[16]

No sooner did Tadatoshi learn that the famous swordsman had entered his fiefdom than he summoned his three best swordsmen, all expert in fighting with the lethal *tachi*. The *Bushū denraiki* describes how:

> Speaking to them Lord Tadatoshi said, "I hear that Musashi, the Heihōsha Without Equal Under the Heavens, is currently staying at the house of Shiota Hamanosuke. Did you know this?"
>
> His retainers spoke as if with one voice when they answered, "We were just going to raise the point when you mentioned it. As you say, Musashi is presently staying at the house of Hamanosuke. We intend to go there and test his skills in the art of *heihō*."

> Hearing this Lord Tadatoshi said, "This is a good thing. Go there immediately so that you can compare your martial skills."

It was on a cold and blustery morning that Tadatoshi's three swordsmen made their way to Hamanosuke's *yashiki* and announced themselves. Hamanosuke was very much taken aback by their visit, as he was merely a retainer of low rank and they were at the top of their class. When asked about the purpose of their visit they replied they had heard Musashi was staying at his house and that they would like to meet him. Hamanosuke led the three men into the parlor of his house and told them to wait and warm themselves as he withdrew to relay their message to his old friend.

Before long Musashi appeared and sat down with them. Ignorant of the real purpose of their visit he received them cordially and arranged with them a day on which he would give them a demonstration of his style of swordsmanship. Too timid to state the purpose of their visit, the three swordsmen thanked Musashi and took their leave, their mission unaccomplished.

The *Bushū denraiki* describes how, having reached the gate of Hamanosuke's *yashiki*:

> The three men eyed each other up and down and said, "What on earth can we do? We cannot now return and report to our lord that we were so awed and overcome with fear that we could not bring ourselves to challenge him."
>
> At this one of them said, "There is no use arguing like this. Let us go back and say that we want to test his skill in the art of *heihō*."
>
> And thus the three men turned back from the

> gate and, having called Hamanosuke, said, "As it was the first time we met we forgot to mention it, but could you convey to Musashi that we would like to test his martial skills?"

Hearing this Musashi came out into the forecourt with his usual two *bokutō*. He told them they need not stand on ceremony and suggested they have a session right there and then. By now they could do little else than agree. As they prepared themselves, he thrust the tip of his long *bokutō* into a gap in the veranda's boards, rattling their nerves by turning and twisting the weapon in the creaking floor boards.

The most talented of the three retainers, a man by the name of Jinnosuke, went and stood in the garden. The *Bushū denraiki* goes on to describe how:

> Musashi, too, went and stood in the garden and approached the man quietly, raising the long *bokutō* above his head in a *jōdan no kamae*. Jinnosuke drew near, holding his *bokutō* in front of him. Then Musashi brought down the sword on his opponent's head in a straight curve. It seemed as if the weapon had struck, but Jinnosuke had stopped it in its track, a hair's breadth above his head. Repelled by the impact, Jinnosuke was thrown to the ground.
>
> Next Musashi raised his sword high and wide and struck out at Jinnosuke's legs with a *ryūsui no uchi*. But Jinnosuke leapt in the air and let the *bokutō* pass under him. Musashi now retreated several steps, when Jinnosuke suddenly opened the attack and came straight toward him. Musashi ducked and struck Jinnosuke full in the chest, causing him to

> be propelled through the air and land on his back a few yards away and pass out, although, at length, he regained consciousness.[17]

The other two retainers refused to duel with Musashi on the grounds that Jinnosuke was the most senior swordsman among them. Musashi insisted, stressing that there was no need whatsoever to be shy. But both men firmly declined and, having taken their leave, all three went home. Back in Kumamoto, they quickly made their way to the castle and reported to their lordship what had taken place.

## Revanche

Lord Hosokawa Tadatoshi found it hard to come to terms with the lackluster way in which his ace swordsmen had ceded defeat, especially when one considered that the fencing traditions of his clan were founded on those of the famous Yagyū. It seemed that his swordsmen had failed to master Munenori's superior fencing techniques. Or could it be that the Yagyū Shinkage-ryū was inferior to Musashi's Niten Ichi-ryū?

Whatever the reason for Musashi's easy victory, Tadatoshi needed to find out, and the only way to do so was to have a duel between accomplished practitioners of both schools of swordsmanship. It was clear that he could not invite the leader of the Yagyū clan. Unlike Musashi, Munenori was now in his sixties. Moreover, in 1636 the chieftain of the Yagyū clan had been taken up in the ranks of daimyo, and Tadatoshi could hardly invite Munenori, or even his son, to a duel with somebody of Musashi's uncertain status. The best he could do was to invite Ujii Yashirō, one of Lord Munenori's star pupils, to come down to Kumamoto for a conclusive duel with this seemingly invincible Miyamoto Musashi.[18]

Thus it was that in the early spring of 1640 the exponents of the Niten Ichi and Yagyū Shinkage schools of fencing arrived at Kumamoto castle to engage in a *taryū shiai*.

Given that Yashirō was a deshi of the Yagyū, a clan whose domains were hundreds of miles removed from Kumamoto, there was less risk of endangering his clan's relations with the Ogasawara. Nevertheless, Tadatoshi took every precaution to avoid any negative fallout from the duel. Both duelists were made to sign a solemn pledge in which they would desist from criticizing each other's school of fencing, and no one else would be present at the event. Only a young page by the name of Urabe Tafu, who carried Tadatoshi's sword, was allowed to attend, and he too was made to sign a solemn pledge to speak to no one of what he was about to see.

The air was filled with excitement as the two swordsmen stepped onto the polished floor of the dojo on the grounds of Kumamoto castle, their every move and gesture followed by a tense yet elated Lord Tadatoshi. The *Bukōden* describes how:

> Up to three times Musashi dueled with Yashirō, brandishing his *tachi*, but not once was Yashirō able to break through his defense. Given that they were fighting in his lordship's presence, Musashi, on his side, was content with merely countering Yashirō's attacks, without ever striking out forcefully.
>
> Lord Tadatoshi was astonished. At length he, too, took his place opposite Musashi but equally failed to win even once. From then on Lord Tadatoshi gave up on the Yagyū-ryū and started practicing Musashi's Niten Ichi school of fencing.

# CHAPTER 6

## To Kumamoto

Lord Hosokawa Tadatoshi was relieved that the duel between Musashi and Yashirō had been conducted in utmost secrecy. At the same time he was deeply frustrated that the martial traditions of his clan had proven inferior to those of the Ogasawara, masters of a far lesser domain. Something had to be done. There just had to be a way to persuade Musashi to come and teach his retainers the art of fighting with two swords without upsetting his relations with the Ogasawara clan. Surely, the only safe and sure way to go about this was to approach Musashi through someone who enjoyed the trust of the Ogasawara.

Brooding over these matters Tadatoshi realized the key to Musashi lay through his own wife, Chiyohime, who was of Ogasawara descent. When they married, she had, as was the custom, brought along a number of pages—all former retainers of the Ogasawara clan. And thus, early in April, not long after Musashi's secret visit to Kumamoto castle, its lord summoned his Head of Pages, Sakazaki Naizen, for a secret consultation.[1]

It did not take Naizen long to come up with an even better candidate for the task at hand, and that was Iwama Rokubei Masanari, the keeper of Kumamoto castle. He, too, was a former retainer of the Ogasawara who had entered Tadatoshi's service when he escorted Chiyohime as a guard upon her marriage into the Hosokawa clan.[2]

Like Musashi, Masanari was a warrior in the old mold, who bore the scars to prove he had fought in the dying days of the Warring States period. He was a distant descendant of the great Takeda Shingen and had served the Ogasawara for most of his life. What better man to approach Musashi and offer him a position as fencing master to the Hosokawa clan than a warrior who thought and acted like Musashi and who enjoyed the trust of the Ogasawara?

Rokubei Masanari managed to persuade his fellow swordsman, as well as pull the right strings with the Ogasawara, for soon after he had departed for Kokura a messenger arrived at Kumamoto castle with a letter from Musashi dated April 1640, and addressed directly to:

> Master Sakazaki Naizen,
>
> Through Iwama Rokubei you inquired after my situation. I found it hard to reply verbally, so I have taken the liberty of responding by letter.
>
> Thus far, I have never once held an official position, no matter what house I stayed with. By now I am advanced in age and on top of that I have of late become a patient so that, as far as my social position is concerned, I have no ambitions whatsoever.

> Were I to come and stay with you, I would be content with a suit of armor and a spare horse in case, at some stage, I would have to go into battle. I have no wife or children, and since I am an old man I would be content with whatever house and furniture you would provide.
>
> From a young age I have gone into battle some six times in all, four times of which I was in the absolute vanguard. This is widely known, and of course there is also proof of it, although it is not with a view to advance myself that I mention this.
>
> I could be of help in matters concerning the use of weapons and the battlefield, and in the event, on how to subdue a province.
>
> I have dedicated myself to these pursuits from my early youth, disciplining myself over many years, so that, if required, I could be of use.
>
> Yours Sincerely,
> Miyamoto Musashi[3]

It was early in September when Musashi finally arrived in Kumamoto. Honoring Musashi's lifelong commitment to a status of independence, Lord Tadatoshi had agreed to hire the swordsman as an independent advisor. He was given a comfortable *yashiki* within the walls of Kumamoto castle, inside one of the curves of the Hirai river, on the northwestern side of the castle grounds.

The location of his *yashiki* pleased the historically conscious swordsman for it stood in the old location of Chiba castle. It had once been the residence of the Ideta, an old Kyushu clan known for their bravery on the field of battle. Erected in the second half of the fifteenth century, it was later replaced by Kumamoto castle, albeit at a slightly different location.[4]

The upkeep of a *yashiki* required considerable financial means. The man who concerned himself over these matters was Musashi's old friend, Nagaoka Okinaga, the staunch Hosokawa retainer whom Musashi had befriended during his stays in Kitsuki and Kokura. Okinaga had remained in the service of the Hosokawa ever since. In 1616, due to the Bakufu's one-castle-per-fiefdom edict, he had lost Kitsuki castle. But when Tadatoshi moved to Higo, he granted Okinaga possession of a fief with an impressive yield of thirty thousand *koku* in the Tamana and Gōshi districts, just north of Kumamoto.

Shortly after Musashi's arrival in Kumamoto, Okinaga approached Abe Tonomo to deal with the matter of Musashi's upkeep. Tonomo was Tadatoshi's *kanjō bugyō*, the Magistrate of Payments, and it was not much later, on September 28, that Tadatoshi issued an edict stating that:

> Miyamoto Musashi is to receive seven aides and a stipend of eighteen *koku*. This is to take effect on the sixth day of the eighth month in the seventeenth year of Kanei [September 21, 1640] and to be continued in perpetuity.[5]

Keen not to hurt the old swordsman's fragile sense of pride, the magistrate added a note cautioning his men that "the edict is not to be shown to Musashi himself and his aides are made to understand how to handle Musashi's stipend without causing any offense."

To meet the swordsman's needs, Tadatoshi's edict was followed by a string of additional edicts, specifying horsemen for the few occasions Musashi would be traveling, down to *miso*, salt, ink, and firewood for his *yashiki*. It seems that in spite of his age, the swordsman's presence in Kumamoto was highly valued, for within half a year of his arrival his stipend was raised from eighteen to three hundred *koku*.

## Daily Life at Kumamoto

Because Musashi stayed in Tadatoshi's domain as a guest he was not taken up in his retinue of retainers and so maintained his peculiar social status, not fully part of yet not wholly outside of the clearly defined strata of medieval society. He had come to cherish his independence, yet it was with a tinge of sadness that at times the old swordsman observed the self-important daily hustle and bustle on the castle grounds from the veranda of his *yashiki*. At such times he felt compelled to leave the protective yet strangely oppressive walls of Kumamoto castle to seek peace and quiet among nature. The *Bushū denraiki* describes how:

> Every now and then, Musashi would go into the fields, a falcon perched on his hand. Even in rainy weather he would do so, without sitting down, preferring to wander about, not caring whether his clothes were drenched.

A lover of poetry, Musashi would often attend one of the many *renga* meetings organized by Nagaoka Okinaga's adopted son, Yoriyuki. Yoriyuki's *yashiki* was situated in the second ring of Kumamoto castle, only a stone's throw away from Musashi's. And like him, Yoriyuki was known for his love of the arts, be it poetry, calligraphy, or the tea ceremony.[6]

It was on one of Musashi's visits to Yoriyuki's *yashiki* that one of his disciples, a young Hosokawa retainer by the name of Gengosaemon, noticed Musashi's increasing frailty. The *Bukōden* describes how:

> One day, as he entered the house, Musashi uttered a cry and had to hold on to the wooden paneling to lift himself onto the raised floor at the entrance. Gengosaemon went up to him and asked him if he needed a hand, but Musashi put him at ease and said he was fine.

Musashi's apparent old age could also prove deceptive. The *Bukōden* describes how, on one of their meetings, Yoriyuki approached Musashi about how one could select the right bamboo for some *hatasashi*, the poles of banners carrying the clan's crest (*kamon*). He had brought along several lengths of fresh bamboo his men had harvested in his father's domains in Tamana and thought he did the old warrior a favor with a request that would not tax his failing strength:[7]

> Musashi asked him to hand him a bunch and, holding them at their lower end with one hand, brandished them as one would a sword, causing several lengths to break under the strain. Sorting the broken from the unbroken, he took the undamaged lengths of bamboo and, giving them to master Yoriyuki, said, "These will do."
>
> Master Yoriyuki laughed heartily and said, "Truly, that is a good way of selecting the right bamboo, but who on earth is able to brandish a bunch of bamboo with one hand like you?"

Despite the onset of old age Musashi could still astound his peers with his agility when required for. The same record describes how:

> One day there was a fire in Kumamoto's Shinchō district, when a man was seen crossing a ladder he had laid across the roofs of the houses standing shoulder to shoulder in the district's cramped quarters. Seeing this the people were taken aback and inquired who it was, but no one knew and all they could do was look on in awe.[8]
>
> Only afterward it transpired that the man in question had been Musashi. Now on normal days Musashi's demeanor would be far from lively but rather serene, so that he looked exceedingly old, indeed, so old that Gengosaemon had felt obliged to help him enter master Yoriyuki's *yashiki*.

The *Bukōden* describes how, on yet another occasion:

> Musashi held a gorgeous banquet under the blossoming cherry trees in the company of master Sawamura Usaemon and half of his deshi.
>
> All were sitting down, with Musashi at the head and his pupils in two rows. The party was getting lively when master Usaemon offered a cup of sake to make a toast, while one of his attendants served appetizers.
>
> Then, as Musashi was about to take a piece of *narezushi* with his right hand, a kite descended from the sky with the speed of lightning and sought to fly off with the delicacy. Instantly Musashi drew his

> *tantō* with his left hand and impaled the bird on the dagger. All who heard of the feat were astounded that such should be the speed of his technique.

On summer days, when not attending one of the many official functions, Musashi could often be found sitting on the veranda of his *yashiki*, patiently working away at one of his artfully crafted *bokutō*, sword sheaths, or bows and arrows.

Most of his time, however, Musashi spent in and around the great dojo on the grounds of Kumamoto castle. It was here, among his many students that he felt most in his element. The *Bukōden* describes that among the many students who practiced under Musashi in Higo were Lord Hosokawa Tadatoshi, Nagaoka Yoriyuki, and "a host of Hosokawa retainers, both favored and not favored, as well as foot soldiers and administrators, some thousand men in all."

All of them were equally keen to learn and practice the art of fighting with two swords. Among his many followers, according to the *Bukōden*:

> The brothers Terao Magonojō Nobumasa and Terao Motomenosuke Nobuyuki were on intimate terms with Musashi, and would often work with him on tactics, without joining the other deshi in practice. At length, the two brothers became the sole progenitors of the Niten Ichi school of swordsmanship.

Little had changed in the essence of Musashi's art of fencing since his arrival in Higo, although he had adapted some techniques from other martial arts. One of these was the art of *hoshu jutsu*, a compendium of seizing, holding, and binding techniques employed to arrest culprits or deal with those who were captured alive during siege warfare. His good friend Shiota Hamanosuke was an adept in this art of fighting, and it was through him that Musashi had been inspired to do so.

Musashi by now was an old man and his execution of the many Niten Ichi-ryū techniques was exceedingly quiet, as if one were watching a Noh performance. Often he would not even resort to a specific technique, but rather illustrate its essence with a simple movement or a short anecdote. His old age only seemed to emphasize the concentrated force distilled over decades of relentless training. The *Bushū denraiki* describes how:

> One day Musashi and Magonojō were sparring, the master with a *tachi* and the pupil with a *kodachi*, driving each other back in turns, when Magonojō's *kodachi* broke in two in the middle.
>
> It seemed as if Musashi's *bokutō* had struck Magonojō full on the head, but in fact it had stopped short just above his forehead, and he had no wounds to his head whatsoever. It is said that Musashi always had this level of control over his hands.

## Musashi and His Deshi

While revered for his unsurpassed skill and depth of knowledge, Musashi was loved by his deshi as a father figure. This unconditional devotion was the natural result of Musashi's Confucian belief in the deep and inextricable bond between master and disciple, father and son. Musashi's paternalistic qualities were not only expressed in moral guidance, but when necessary also in material support. The *Bushū denraiki* describes how:

> Illustrious *rōnin* had attached themselves to Musashi in great numbers, and whenever they took their leave to go elsewhere he would give them money, reminding them that without money one was unable to go anywhere and feel at ease.
>
> At such moments he would fondly point out by number one of the many small hemp pouches he had filled with gold and silver coins and suspended from the cornice along the edge of the ceiling of the room in which he usually dwelt. Lifting a pouch off its hook with a bamboo stick, he would bestow it on the departing *rōnin*.

At the same time, however, Musashi could be utterly ruthless when he thought his honor was at stake. The same record describes how, one day, a foot soldier Musashi had summoned talked back to him. Musashi rebuked him, saying:

> "You'd better not use such language when you are talking to me." But the foot soldier did not learn from his mistake and again was insolent to Musashi, uttering the rudest of insults.
>
> At that point Musashi took a firmer hold of his wooden staff and crushed the foot soldier's skull in a single blow. Uttering a groan, the man fell flat on his back and lay there sprawled out, his arms and legs in the directions of the four winds, as his last breath escaped from his mouth.[9]

Even toward his deshi Musashi could be exceedingly stern, to the point of alienating those who had long been close to him. At such times it seemed as if he had never really shaken off the ghost of his father, as if Muni's long shadow still darkened his mood. The *Bushū denraiki* describes how, one day, when visiting his adopted son at Kokura:

> A banquet was held in Musashi's honor at the house of Shimamura Tōsaemon, a retainer of the Ogasawara. Several people had gathered and all were engaged in animated conversation while food was being served, when a gate guard came in saying, "A man by the name of Aoki Jōemon has called and requests to see you."
>
> Hearing this Musashi said, "I do not mind, please let him in." Then he greeted his old pupil, saying, "Well, well, it has been a long time, I'm glad to see you in good health." He asked Jōemon whether he was still practicing the art of *heihō*, to which the latter replied he did so constantly. "In that case," Musashi said, "let us see."
>
> He looked on with good grace as Jōemon went through the basic techniques, and praised him, saying "You have much improved, feel free to go and teach anywhere you desire." Jōemon was delighted to hear this and expressed his gratitude in no uncertain terms. Then he went into the adjacent room to put away his *bokutō*.

At that moment Musashi spotted a red cord attached to one of Jōemon's *bokutō* and queried him about its meaning. Jōemon was somewhat embarrassed, but when pressed he explained how, when traveling round the country, there were always people who wanted to have a *shiai*. Of course, he assured his old master, he intended to decline, but just in case they would insist he had marked the *bokutō* as the one he would use in a duel. Saying this he took out the large, octagonally carved *bokutō* with a red cord. The record goes on to describe how:

> Musashi now grew extremely angry and said, "My goodness, what a fool you are. The mere idea of engaging in a *shiai* with your level of *heihō* is ridiculous. When I praised you just now it was because I thought your skill was suitable to teach young men. If there be anyone who would want to have a *shiai* you had better run. The idea is preposterous. How do you think you can conquer someone if you have not even grasped the deeper essence of the art of *heihō*. You might stand a chance of beating one in ten thousand men if you only had the technical expertise, but with your level of skill you're unlikely to outlive the day."

Yet even now the old master was not done with the hapless Tōsaemon:

> Scolding him severely in this manner he called Jōemon's page, saying "Put some rice in a bowl and bring it over here." He placed a grain of rice on the boy's topknot and said, "Go and stand over there." Next he rose from his seat and took his sword from the alcove. In an instant he had drawn the sword and raised it high above his head. Then, from behind, he brought the sword down in a straight curve on the boy's head. He had cut the grain of rice in two. Holding the tip of his sword

> up to Jōemon's nose, he said, "Watch this!" And he repeated the feat up to three times. Jōemon marveled at this and all those present, from Tōsaemon down, were lost for words.

When the hush among the gathered men had finally lifted Musashi spoke and said:

> This is the level of skill I have reached, but even I cannot defeat an enemy with skill alone. How much more unattainable is it for you, unskilled and ignorant of the true meaning of *heihō*, to do so? What a dunce you are. Get out at once![10]

Others again were treated with special kindness. The *Bushū denraiki* describes how on another occasion a warrior of low rank brought along his son, a stout youth in his late teens, and asked Musashi to take him on as a deshi. Musashi accepted, and not long after the lad's arrival he took him aside and began to prime him by repeatedly demonstrating the technique of *katsu-totsu*, used to pin down an enemy.[11]

The *Bushū denraiki* goes on to describe how that evening, as the youth passed through his village on his way home:

> A thug who had slain a villager came rushing toward him brandishing his sword, still dripping with blood. Behind him, in hot pursuit, the villagers called out, "Stop him!"
>
> The youth, who had just been practicing, immediately drew his sword and challenged the man with Musashi's *katsu-totsu* technique. The ruffian was forced to draw back, having struck out only once

> with his *tachi*. Then the youth raised his sword so as to stab from below and struck out with his return strike. Yet the ruffian kept retreating and the sword failed to strike home.
>
> Again the youth struck out. As before he raised his sword so as to stab from below, striking out on the return strike. Five, six, seven, eight times the youth repeated this technique, and all the while the ruffian continued to withdraw.

While all this was going on the villagers quickly closed the village gate and drew across the gate bar. The youth now drove the ruffian against the gate with another *katsu-totsu* technique, just as the latter was about to strike out at him. His retreat blocked by the gate bar, the ruffian could no longer draw back and the youth finished him off with a slanted cut across his chest.

The youth's father, who had witnessed scene:

> took along his son to Musashi and thanked him saying "It was through you that my son was able to accomplish this feat; I am deeply grateful."
>
> Musashi praised the young man saying, "We are all practitioners of the art of *heihō* and it is not rare that we win by day what we practice by day. During his exchanges with the ruffian your son has adhered to what he was taught. That he finally won is due to his strong resolve and this is a good thing."

One deshi in particular had won the favor of the old swordsman, a young but talented retainer by the name of Takemura Yōemon Yorizumi. Yōemon hailed from the province of Sanuki on the northeastern tip of Shikoku. He had become one of

Musashi's deshi when he was still living and teaching in Akashi, but followed him to Kokura and from there to Kumamoto. Over the two decades Yōemon studied under Musashi he had become one of the few who was intimately familiar with the old swordsman and his style of fencing.

Musashi was now too old to visit Iori in Kokura, while Iori, occupying an important post, only occasionally found the time to visit his father in Kumamoto. Instead, Musashi relied increasingly on Yōemon. And while Yōemon was not one of Musashi's star deshi, the old warrior had by now come to regard him almost as his third son.

## A Prank

Musashi's quick temperament and great sense of pride did at times make him vulnerable to gentle ridicule, especially by those above him. The *Bukōden* describes how:

> Every now and then Musashi would be summoned before his lordship for a talk. It was prior to such a meeting that his lordship told his attendants that he wanted to pull a prank on Musashi and that they should think of one. They said this would be difficult but that they would try to think of a ruse.

Possessed of a mischievous sense of fun, it was not long before Lord Tadatoshi himself thought of a way to play a trick on the stern old warrior. Musashi frequently visited his lordship, sometimes to report on the progress of his deshi, but more often to converse with him on the art of *heihō* or to talk about the past. It was customary for retainers who were summoned to wait in the anteroom until their turn had come to join his lordship in the main room. Tadatoshi knew that, when called for, Musashi would formally sit down at the lintel in which the sliding doors ran that separated the two rooms. Then, as was the custom, he would take his fan, place it in front of him and lean forward, making a deft bow as his hands touched the lintel. At that point his head would just protrude into the room.

On the appointed day, Lord Tadatoshi waited for Musashi to arrive, his attendants in ambush, hoping to catch him out in an unguarded moment by trapping his head between the two sliding doors. the *Bukōden* goes on to describe how, precisely as anticipated:

> Musashi arrived and placed his hands on the lintel as was his wont. No sooner had he begun to greet his lordship than the sliding doors were shut with a slam. Musashi, however, remained totally unperturbed and continued to talk as if nothing had happened. His lordship was intrigued, but when he took a closer look he noticed that Musashi had placed his folding fan on top of the lintel, stopping the sliding doors and leaving a space of well over a foot and his head untouched. His lordship praised Musashi greatly, for it was clear to him now that at no instant did Musashi ever let down his guard.

## Recollections

During his years at Kumamoto, Musashi's mind would often wander back to a distant past, to the days when he had basked in the glory of martial feats. Sitting at the center of the dojo he would recount to his gathered deshi, as they listened in rapture, his duels with the great swordsmen of his youth—his first duel with Arima Kihei, his encounters with the various members of the Yoshioka clan, and, of course, the showdown with Sasaki Kojirō on Funashima Island.

Yet even this, his most celebrated of duels, was no source of pride to the old swordsman. The *Kōkai fūhansō* describes how:

> In old age, Musashi would say that it had been no more than the heat of youth that had enabled him to claim victory, and that it was not something he had expected to accomplish in his heart of hearts.

All of these duels had given him a deeper understanding of his art and the immutable laws of heaven. Yet not only the duels themselves had given him the insights for which he was now revered. The *Bukōden* describes that, while relating the run-up to his duel with Yoshioka Matashichirō to one of his deshi, Musashi recalled how:

> On my way there I passed in front of the Hachiman shrine, and I thought to myself, "What good fortune that I should come in the presence of the gods by accident at this moment. I should take this opportunity and pray for victory."
>
> However, when I went up to the shrine's altar and took the crimson cord to sound the temple gong it suddenly occurred to me: "up till now I have never put any faith in gods and Buddhas. Yet, now, in the face of danger, I am suddenly eager to pay my respects. Ah, I must be flinching from danger." At that moment I let loose the temple gong's cord

> and stepped down from the altar. I was so deeply ashamed that I felt the sweat running down by back.

While he took pleasure in recounting such episodes, even with a note of self-criticism, Musashi would be embarrassed if his past exploits were raised by others, and quickly vexed when his reputation was called into question.

At one occasion, Musashi was attending an evening ceremony to celebrate the New Year. The *Bukōden* describes how all the elders, senior retainers, and *bushi* were seated according to their rank. The ceremony had not yet started, and those in attendance were talking among themselves, when Shimizu Hōki, an ace Hosokawa swordsman, leaned over to Musashi and said, "It is rumored that when you fought Yoshioka Seijūrō long ago, it was he who dealt the first blow. Is it true?"

Without replying, Musashi suddenly stood up and sat down next to Hōki with a candle-holder, saying:

> "When I dueled with Seijūrō, he was fighting with a real sword, while I was fighting with a wooden oar. Now wouldn't you say that when you are struck by a real sword there should be a scar? So please take a close look."
>
> And saying this, he parted his hair with his right hand and held the candle up to his head with his left hand in front of master Hōki's face.
>
> Backing away, Hōki replied, "No, I cannot see any scars."
>
> But Musashi insisted, saying, "Please take a really close look."
>
> Again Hōki confirmed what he had seen, saying, "You are right, I have looked closely."

> At this Musashi immediately stood up again and, putting the candle-holder back, returned to his seat, where he stroked down his hair and sat down with utter composure.
>
> During the exchange, the gathered samurai had held their breaths, clenching their fists, their palms wet with perspiration.[12]

Had Musashi allowed Hōki to inspect his neck, the latter would have found a scar, still marking the moment Musashi had almost met his end on Funashima Island.

## A Spiritual Friendship

In the twilight of his life Musashi became increasingly contemplative, reflecting on his past life and seeking solace in the tenets of the Buddhist faith. In this new quest Musashi was guided by Akiyama Gentei Wanao, junior abbot of the Taishō temple, the family temple of the Hosokawa clan, which stood less than a mile upstream on the western bank of the Shirakawa, the river skirting the eastern walls of Kumamoto castle. Born in 1618, Wanao was thirty-four years Musashi's junior. Yet soon a deep spiritual friendship developed between these two so disparate men, a friendship forged in their shared awareness of the fleeting nature of human existence.[13]

Musashi would often visit Wanao at the Taishō temple to study Buddhist scriptures. And it was on Wanao's prompting that he finally took the tonsure under the Buddhist name of Niten Dōraku, the "Niten dilettante."

Under Wanao's influence Musashi also developed further his artistic talents, especially calligraphy and poetry. Expressing his thoughts and emotions on paper had a soothing, almost healing effect on the swordsman and helped him to find a place for the traumatic experiences in his life, in particular the deaths of his only child and his first adopted son, Mikinosuke.

Musashi found little solace in love. Aware of his appearance, he shunned the company of women of his own class. Instead, most of his liaisons with women had been of a mercenary nature, even his affair with Kumoi. The resulting outlook on love was expressed in a poem he wrote during these years:

When in love,
do not write letters
do not write poems
But watch your money
every single penny[14]

While at a superficial level this forlorn, almost cynical poem expresses Musashi's obvious disappointment in the opposite sex, at a deeper level it unmistakably reveals Musashi's human side, his simple need for love and affection.

In spite of Musashi's talent in the arts, inspiration did not always come easily to the swordsman. Less confident of his artistic than his martial talents, he found it especially hard to paint commissioned works. At such moments it was again his belief in the power of *heihō* that saved the day, as it had done so often throughout his life. The *Kaijō monogatari* describes how, when he was still living in the castle town of Akashi as the guest of Ogasawara Tadazane:

> Musashi was ordered by his lordship to do a painting of Daruma. Musashi applied himself to the painting, but somehow his brush refused to do its

> work and Musashi felt unusually inadequate. In the end, he was unable to complete the painting that day and he turned in for the night.
>
> That night, however, he unexpectedly woke up and realized that he had been unable to complete the painting because it had not been done in the true spirit of *heihō*. And, indeed, when he lit a candle and returned to the painting, he found that he was able to do it well.
>
> When asked by one of his deshi about the incident, Musashi replied, "Forgetting the art of *heihō* I grew fearful of his lordship, so that I was unable to paint. I speak of *heihō* with good reason, for when I seize my sword, neither I nor my opponent exists; heaven and earth collapse, and there is no longer any distinction whatsoever between men of high rank and lowly commoners. Thus, when I painted with this principle in mind, I found I was able to complete the painting for his lordship."

Musashi's belief in the universality of the art of *heihō*, a notion that had come to him very early in life and that had sustained him throughout his military career, only grew stronger in old age. It was this awareness, this sense that the principles on which he had founded his fencing career transcended the martial realm and had their bearing on all walks of life, that led Musashi to find a new purpose in old age. For it was during the last years of his life, as his ailments were beginning to take their toll, that Musashi embarked on an endeavor that would prove to be of greater consequence to the future tradition of Japanese swordsmanship than all of his martial successes of the past.

# CHAPTER 7

## Working on His Legacy

Though his glory years lay far behind him, Musashi was not content simply to dwell on the victories he had achieved in his past. Time and time again, while drilling his students in a specific technique or aspect of his school of swordsmanship, he would return to their basic principles and the laws of *heihō* that governed them until his voice grew hoarse and brittle with the strain. These were not the deeply esoteric teachings found among some of the other schools of swordsmanship at the time. Instead they were succinct and sound pieces of practical advice, forged in the course of numerous battles and countless duels—they were based, in short, on a life of success through perseverance in the face of great hardship.

Early in 1641 Lord Tadatoshi summoned Musashi to his residential quarters at Kumamoto castle. In a time when few lived beyond the age of sixty, the now fifty-five-year-old Tadatoshi was also beginning to feel the onset of old age and keen to preserve for posterity the traditions and values that had made his clan so successful. It was normal for feudal chieftains to write on the eve of their deaths so-called *kakun*, family instructions by which they expected their descendants to conduct the affairs of the clan. He had already done this for his eldest son, Mitsunao, but he was eager that his retainers, too, should have a set of injunctions by which they could conduct themselves, especially those who practiced Musashi's art of *heihō*, which had become the chief fencing tradition of the Hosokawa clan.

Tadatoshi recognized the universal value of Musashi's teachings and the positive influence they had on his men's frame of mind. He wanted to ensure that the benefit of the swordsman's teachings would last beyond his immediate disciples and their offspring. This time there was no play with sliding doors as Tadatoshi lifted his arm from his lacquered armrest, leaned forward, and solemnly asked Musashi to commit his thoughts about the Niten Ichi art of *heihō* to paper.

Musashi readily responded to Lord Tadatoshi's request. Already in his early twenties, while developing his thoughts on the art of swordsmanship during his stay in Edo, he had written the *Heidō kagami*, exploring the main principles that underpinned his style of swordsmanship.

In essence, however, the *Heidō kagami* was a catalogue of the various techniques comprising his Enmei-ryū: how to attack an opponent's hands or legs, how to avoid his sword, and how to use the *shuriken* and *jitte*. The inclusion of these two weapons revealed the extent to which his style of fencing had been under the influence of his father's Tōri-ryū. Now he set out to expand on his original work and distill the essence of his Niten Ichi-ryū, a style that was truly his own.

The result of these efforts was the *Heihō sanjū-kyū kajō*, the *Thirty-nine Articles on the Art of Heihō*. Clearly, the work was a catalogue, an enumeration of important aspects of the art of *heihō*, rather than a lengthy treatise. Yet it was Musashi's first serious attempt at organizing his thoughts on the Niten Ichi school of fencing. And while it covered only a few pages, like his earlier work, it dealt with many of the essential principles on which his school of swordsmanship was founded.[1]

The *Heihō sanjū-kyū kajō* dealt with the physical aspects of the art of swordsmanship, such as body stance, grip, foot placement, rhythm, and the ideal trajectory of a sword in motion. It also dwelt on the less tangible yet equally important aspects of the art of *heihō*. And here, in Musashi's penetrative look at the mental aspects of his art, we already find distilled some of the insights on which he was to expand in the work that would make him immortal.

Thus Musashi dedicated a whole article to a swordsman's state of mind. In the Niten Ichi school of swordsmanship:

> One's state of mind should not be dejected, flustered, willful, or fearful, but straight and wide. It should be light in thought, heavy in essence, like water, adjusting itself to one's enemy, able to respond to any event, however sudden, however unexpected. For water is ever changeable, from a single drop to a vast ocean.[2]

Lord Tadatoshi was more than pleased with Musahi's contribution to the continuation of his clan's martial traditions. All the fiefdom's retainers were invited to a grand ceremony at which Musashi's work was presented as the standard textbook of the retainers of the Hosokawa clan. As Lord Tadatoshi had foreseen, Musashi's writings would go on to shape not only the frame of mind of his own warriors, but of Japanese warriors in general.

## The Reigan Cave

As it turned out Lord Tadatoshi had been right in anticipating his own death, for it was soon after he had read Musashi's work that, on April 26, 1641, he passed away. Only a few weeks earlier he had handed the reigns of his estate to his twenty-two-year-old son, Mitsunao.

While Lord Tadatoshi had been pleased with Musashi's work, the swordsman himself, always eager to perfect what he had begun, was far from happy with the *Heihō sanjū-kyū kajō*. Though satisfied with the essence of its content, he felt that many of the points he had touched on needed elaboration and clarification, especially where it concerned the mental and spiritual aspects of the art of swordsmanship.

He raised his concerns with the new Lord of the Kumamoto domain. Mitsunao had fought with his father in the suppression of the Shimabara Rebellion and was a fervent practitioner of the Niten Ichi school of swordsmanship. He had carefully read the *Heihō sanjū-kyū kajō* and showed an understanding of Musashi's thoughts beyond his youth. Widely read, and with a long training in the Chinese classics, even Mitsunao struggled with the esoteric nature of some of the existing writings on swordsmanship. He therefore urged Musashi to work out his ideas in greater detail and do so in a style accessible to all before he too would have to join his father in the hereafter.

Thus it came about that on November 19, 1643, at the age of fifty-nine, Musashi sat down at his writing table in his *yashiki* and drafted a short letter to Lord Mitsunao:

> I have of late been climbing Mount Iwato to comply with your lordship's wish to broadly put into writing my ideas on the school of swordsmanship

> that I have spent my whole life practicing and perfecting. Hence, if there are men, besides those who enjoy the martial arts, who want to apply themselves to the principles of other crafts or arts, or again, if there are those who have queries on my art of *heihō*, even concerning its Confucian or Buddhist aspects, it is my fervent wish that they come and visit me here. However, they need not visit me solely to pay their respects.[3]

Many times before Musashi had climbed Mount Iwato. From its top, casting his gaze toward the west, he could clearly see the Ariake Sea, shimmering in the glow of the afternoon sun before its red disc would descend behind the dark silhouette of the Unzen mountains on the Shimabara Peninsula. Then it had been to spend time in meditation and contemplation. Now it was with another purpose—to write—for here, amid the stillness of a cave in the mountain's eastern slope, he found the peace and clarity of mind to put even his most ephemeral thoughts to paper.[4]

The cave was called the Reigan Cave, and inside its hushed silence stood a statue of Kannon. There, at the foot of the statue, Musashi sat down and wrote the preface to the work that would come to define his philosophy of the art of *heihō*:

> I wish to record in writing for the first time an art of *heihō* I have practiced for many years and to which I have given the name of Niten Ichi-ryū. It is early in the tenth month of the twentieth year of Kanei [November 1643] that I have climbed Mount Iwato in the province of Higo in Kyushu and that I look up to heaven, pray to Kannon, and turn to Buddha.

Over the next eighteen months Musashi kept up his daily visits to the Reigan Cave to work on his book. And every time he entered the cave, before he sat down to grind ink and spread out the scroll on which he was working, he would kneel before the statue of Kannon, the bodhisattva of compassion, to pray for wisdom and inspiration in the task at hand.

## The Enmei-ryū

One other thought preoccupied Musashi. During the first half of his life, he had devoted himself to the development and spread of his Enmei school of swordsmanship. With old age had come new insights into concepts which he had taken almost for granted when still young. Yet already during his time with his stepuncle Dōrin, he had come to the realization that a samurai's two swords were an inseparable unity. Not only should both weapons be worn together; they should be used in combat together, too.

Musashi had already made good headway on his life's work. Committing his thoughts to paper had enabled him to bring into sharp focus the principles that had induced him to rename his art the Niten Ichi-ryū, or the school of swordsmanship of the Two Heavens United. He wrote that it was:

> so-called because it is the role of a *bushi*, whether a military commander or a rank-and-file foot soldier, to wear two swords. In ancient times they were called the *tachi* and the *katana*. Nowadays they are called the *katana* and the *wakizashi*. I need not write in detail about why it is that those who call themselves *bushi* wear two swords. In our country it is the

> way of all *bushi* to tuck two swords into their *obi*, whether or not they know the reason. It is to make them understand the advantages of this custom that I have called my art of fencing the Niten Ichi-ryū.

It was to mark a turning point in his life that Musashi renamed his style Niten Ichi-ryū when he took up teaching his old students in Kokura, where most of his deshi from Akashi had moved with their lord and master, Ogasawara Tadazne.

Not only the move had made Musashi change the name of his school of swordsmanship; its content had also changed. By now he placed great emphasis not only on stance and bearing, but also on the mental aspects of combat. Thus he had dedicated a special passage in his *Heihō sanjū-kyū kajō* to the difficult concepts of *zanshin* and *hōshin*: to remain alert and leave one's mind on the fallen opponent (*zanshin*) and to empty one's mind and allow it to respond to new challenges (*hōshin*).

Other formerly important aspects of his style of fencing had become less prominent. Techniques using the *jitte* and the *shuriken*, which had played such a prominent role in his father's Tōri-ryū—and that were still being practiced by adepts of his Enmei-ryū—had been silently dropped. And while he still occasionally used Daoist terms such as *yin* and *yang*, he did not dwell at length on the metaphysical aspects of his art, preferring instead to explain its principles using concrete examples from persons his students could relate to and situations they could expect to encounter in real life.

Now, as he began to feel the onset of various afflictions and knowing he was rapidly nearing the end, he realized that in order to create some consistency in the way his school of swordsmanship was taught throughout the country, he needed to relate these changes to his followers outside Higo.

Especially, the practitioners of the Owari line of his Enmei-ryū were unaware of all these changes. The style of fencing practiced by these men reflected his art as he had perceived and practiced it more than a decade earlier, and he wanted his followers in Nagoya to share in his new insights. He realized he could not expect to bring across the full content of his teachings in Nagoya without being present. For that he was too frail. What he could do was to send one of his most trusted students in the hope of instilling the basic principles of his teachings among his many followers in Owari.

On September 27, 1644, he for once refrained from visiting the Reigan Cave. Instead, he sat down at his writing table in his *yashiki* to write a letter to his old friend Terao Naomasa in Nagoya. Not sure whether Naomasa was still alive he addressed the letter to:

> The honorable Terao Naomasa and those close to him,
>
> I would be grateful if you could be so kind as to take care of my man [Takemura] Yōemon who will be visiting your fiefdom.
>
> You must feel offended, as I have not written to you since my departure. I have by now moved to Higo, through whose master's kind benevolence I am allowed to stay.
>
> Thus it is that through such kind offices I am grateful to have found a new lease on life. For I am by now an old man and I no longer mingle among people as much as I should.
>
> Likewise, it seems I am no longer capable of practicing the art of *heihō* myself. If it were only

> possible it would be my fervent wish to meet you once again. However, I have instructed the Yōemon of whom I speak in the art of *heihō* for many years. As you will see, he has become a full-fledged practitioner of my school of swordsmanship, and I would be grateful if you could be so kind as to look after him henceforth.
>
> Yours most respectfully,
> Miyamoto Musashi[5]

Not yet having completed his life's work, Musashi sent Yōemon on his way with a copy of the *Heihō sanjū-kyū kajō*, so that it might serve as a reference for his followers in Owari. Soon he himself would depart on a journey from which he would not return. It made it easier for the old swordsman to part from his trusted Yōemon, a man he had come to regard almost as his third adopted son.

## The *Gorin no sho*

In the early spring of 1645, Musashi finally completed the first draft of his life's work. It had taken him five seasons to write, two of them winter. Each season had seen the completion of one long scroll of continuous text in his accomplished hand. He named them the scrolls of Earth, Water, Fire, Wind, and Heaven. Collectively, he called them the *Gorin no sho*, the *Book of Five Rings*, after the *gorintō*, the five-storied stupa.[6]

It was with good reason that Musashi named the five scrolls of his *Gorin no sho* after the five elements. Just as the ancient Chinese sages had distinguished five basic elements constituting all existence, Musashi perceived five different elements in the realm of the art of *heihō*.

Thus the Scroll of Earth, while serving as an introduction to the rest of the work, deals with the fundaments of martial arts, the importance of training as the foundation for anyone who calls himself a warrior, as well as the requirements for a military leader. Leading men into battle, Musashi explains, is like the task of a master carpenter:

> When a master carpenter employs other carpenters, he must know the degree of ability of each and assign them to their tasks accordingly, some to the building of the alcove, some to the doorway and paper windows, some to the threshold, lintels and ceiling, those who are less skilled to joist making, and those who are least skilled to the shaving of wedges, thus bringing the best out of those at one's disposal.

Having set out his views on the fundamentals of the art of *heihō*, Musashi goes on to describe in the Scroll of Water (*Sui no maki*) "the essence" of the sword techniques of his school of swordsmanship. Using plain language he describes the core concepts underpinning his style of swordsmanship, concepts such as one's state of mind and posture in combat and, very importantly, how to hold the longsword:

> Hold the sword lightly with the thumb and the index fingers, the grip of the middle fingers being neither tight nor loose, yet tightly with the ring and little fingers. There should be no slackness in the hand(s) with which you hold the sword.

The same attention to detail is given to footwork. When one walks on the field of battle:

> One should slightly raise the tip of one's toes and step down firmly with one's heels. Depending on the situation one may widen, shorten, slow, or hasten one's step, yet one should always tread as if one were walking.

More advanced technical aspects of the Niten Ichi-ryū, too, are dealt with in detail in the Scroll of Water, such as the all-important guard positions, or *kamae*, which he divides into five categories, that of *jōdan* (upper), *chūdan* (middle), *gedan* (lower), *migi no waki* (right side) and *hidari no waki* (left side). It was by one of these, after all, the subtle and effective *migiwaki no kamae*, that Musashi had parried the opening blows of Sasaki Kojirō's lethal *mizukuruma* technique, enabling him to escape from Funashima Island with only a wound to the back of his neck.

Where the Scroll of Water is concerned with the essentials of swordsmanship, the attainment of the art of *heihō* through diligent practice of the correct techniques, the Scroll of Fire (*Hi no maki*) dwells at length on the more advanced aspects of Musashi's art—what it is that makes it truly superior. For though important, mere devotion to technical aspects will never enable a swordsman to attain full mastery of his art:

> People have too limited a view of the principles of the art of *heihō*. Some know of the advantage of using the ends of their fingers or subtle wrist movements. They believe that victory can be decided by the speed with which one moves one's

> forearms as if one were waving a fan, or they think that if they are just a bit faster than their opponent with the *shinai* they will have the advantage. They devote themselves solely to the improvement of arm and leg techniques and put swiftness of action before anything else.

In the Scroll of Fire, therefore, Musashi seeks to elucidate the less obvious aspects of the art of *heihō*. The great importance, for instance, of "considering the site" at which one intends to engage the enemy, be they few or many. Whether engaging a large host on the field of battle or fighting man to man at close quarters in a building, one should always choose the highest position and seek to keep the sun behind one, for:

> In all situations one should force the enemy into a position where he has a difficult footing, where he has obstacles on his side. For no matter the circumstances, it is of utmost importance always to make the most of the advantages of a place. It is something that should be well studied and practiced.

The same applies to other strategic aspects of combat: how to open the attack, how to negotiate critical passages, and, more importantly, knowing the morale of one's enemy—when they are about to give in. In order to do this one should always seek to place oneself in the mind of the enemy, for only then can one perceive his real or imagined vulnerabilities.

Part of this insight into an enemy's true strengths and weaknesses, he stresses, comes from carefully observing the specific school of swordsmanship they practice. There were some fifty major schools of swordsmanship in Musashi's day, yet in the introduction of the Scroll of Wind (*Fū no maki*) Musashi states that none of them were practicing the true path:

> The other schools look on the field of martial arts as a means to raise one's status. They have strayed from the path of truth in that they put up appearances, seek to win fame, and turn their art into a commodity that can be bought and sold.
>
> Similarly, the existing arts of *heihō* merely concentrate on sword techniques. They teach how to wield the longsword on the basis of petty judgments and understand victory only in terms of how the body is used and how the hands are put to use. None of these, however, is the correct way.

To make his reader better understand what it is that makes the Niten Ichi-ryū superior to the other schools, he dedicates the rest of the Scroll of Wind to their specific demerits, such as the use of too long or too short a sword, the use of brute force, the overemphasis on guard positions, or fixing one's gaze according to set rules—all of these aspects are criticized at length, for in Musashi's view they tend to distract from the essence of true swordsmanship. For instance:

> It is erroneous to put the guard position before anything else, for such stances are only assumed when the enemy is out of sight. The reason for this is that one cannot set up rules simply because of an ancient custom or a modern law, for there is no room for such rules on the road of combat, which is only concerned with putting one's opponent at a disadvantage.

It speaks volumes about Musashi's down to earth and practical mind that the Scroll of Heaven (*Kū no maki*), the scroll concerned with the metaphysical aspects of the art of swordsmanship, is also the shortest of the five scrolls. At the same time, the Scroll of Heaven, or *kū* (space, emptiness, air) is arguably the most important of the five scrolls, for it is in this scroll that Musashi penetrates to the very core of what it is to practice the true path of *heihō*:

> For a *bushi* to understand the path of *heihō*, learning the other martial arts, observing the path of the warrior without neglect, honing one's spirit and mind every hour of every day without letting the heart go astray, and sharpening one's intuition and insight until all the clouds of delusion have lifted without a trace—this is the true meaning of *kū*.

## Last Moments

Not long after the completion of the *Gorin no sho*, before he had found the time to write a fair copy, Musashi's health, which had hitherto been relatively robust, suddenly took a turn for the worse. During the previous years he often had problems with swallowing but now he even had trouble breathing. His daily diet chiefly consisted of rice gruel and some *miso* soup, but oftentimes his food would go down the wrong way, causing severe outbursts of coughing, which only exacerbated his condition.

Sustained by his meager diet Musashi could still occasionally muster the energy and interest to receive visitors. The *Bushū denraiki* describes how, on April 10, an old friend:

> Sawamura Daigaku, a Hosokawa retainer, visited Musashi's sickbed to express his sympathy.[7]
>
> Musashi propped up his pillow and said, "I am glad you have come to see me, for this is where we will have to part in this life."
>
> Daigaku cheerily responded by saying "Come, come, your illness does not appear to be that serious. If you take care of yourself you will soon recover," upon which he went home again.

Musashi, however, was not consoled by Daigaku's words. The same record goes on to describe how:

> Afterward, when speaking to his deshi, Musashi said, "Daigaku is held in high esteem by this house, whether it be for his character or his military exploits. But to say that I would recover if I took care of myself, even though I had bade him goodbye in the sound knowledge that I would die, does not become him."

By the end of April Musashi's health had deteriorated to such an extent that he was no longer able to teach. His life's work completed and feeling that his end was near, he withdrew to his house at the former site of Chiba castle in Kumamoto. The *Bukōden* describes how:

> Not long before his death, feeling he was about to die, he expressed to master Nagaoka Yoriyuki his wish that he might be attended by someone who had shown merit during the siege of Hara castle. And thus Nakanishi Magonojō Munemasa

> was chosen to be among the men to remain by Musashi's side during his last days.

Musashi wasted no time in seeing his life's work completed. Lacking the strength to write out a clean final draft of his lengthy work, he turned to his best friend to help him achieve his goal. The *Bukōden* describes how, soon after he had fallen ill:

> Musashi asked Akiyama Wanao, the second-generation abbot of the Taishō temple, to correct his preface.
>
> Fearful that the text might lose its true meaning through any elaborations, Akiyama refrained from changing the structure of the text in any way, limiting himself to the correction of wrongly written characters and citing classical proverbs that immediately pertained to the text.

On the eighth of May, even while his friend was going through the texts of his five scrolls Musashi sat down to write a last letter to master Nagaoka Yoriyuki in which he confessed that:

> I have been sick these last years. Especially since the beginning of this year my condition has deteriorated, and I find it difficult to stand up. It is because of this that I have not been able to fulfill my functions in the fiefdom in the way I wished.
>
> The late lord [Tadatoshi] displayed a profound interest in the art of *heihō*, and I was able to teach him the general outline of my school, which caused me the greatest of joy. With his death, however,

> I have lost the desire to live … Given that I am a swordsman … I should transmit the teachings of my school myself, but I can no longer move my limbs and believe my end is drawing near.
>
> It is for these reasons that I prefer to spend my last few days among the mountains, hiding my dying body from the sight of others. Please be so kind as to convey this to the others.[8]

The *Bukōden* describes how, not long afterward:

> Musashi went up to Mount Iwato, so that he might quietly await his end in the Reigan Cave.
>
> Soon, however, strange but groundless rumors were beginning to circulate among the populace. Feigning that he had gone out to hunt with falcons, master Nagaoka Yoriyuki visited Musashi and prevailed on him to return to his old residence on the former grounds of Chiba castle.

Then, on the sixth of June, feeling his strength rapidly ebbing away, Musashi called his chief deshi to his side and ceremonially bestowed on them the possessions he had held onto in old age. Among these few but cherished items was a beautiful sword forged by the great master Ōhara Sanemori and which he gave to his old friend Sawamura Daigaku.

It was on the same oddly festive occasion that Musashi had one of his deshi grind some ink and jotted down a short tract called the *Dokkōdō* (*The Way to be Followed Alone*). Meant as a set of guidelines for life, the short tract consisted of twenty-one injunctions for his students, which he bestowed on his most trusted disciple, Terao Nobumasa.[9]

The last stone of his life's five-storied stupa had been put in place. Now all he needed to do was to ensure that his writings would be preserved for posterity. The *Bukōden* describes how, that same day:

> Musashi handed the *Gorin no sho* to Terao Magonojō Nobumasa, who afterward took the tonsure under the name of Muse. The *Heihō sanjū-kyū kajō* he handed to Terao Motomenosuke Nobuyuki.

Musashi passed away peacefully on June 13, 1645. The *Heihō senshi denki* describes in reverent detail the manner of the swordsman's end:

> At the moment of his death, Musashi had himself raised up, had his belt tightened, and his *wakizashi* inserted into his belt.
>
> Then he sat there kneeling on the floor with one knee raised, leaning on his *katana* with his left hand, until his spirit departed from earth.

Musashi was laid in his coffin wearing his armor and helmet. Except for the sword by Ōhara Sanemori, he was accompanied by all his weapons, as he had requested.

The next day, the long road from the Taishō temple leading down to the Shira river was thronged with people wanting to get a last glimpse of the famous swordsman. The rainy season had started and it was pouring down thick and fast as Kumamoto's dignitaries gathered at the Taishō temple to attend a sober ceremony led by the temple's chief abbot, Ōshō Genkō Wanao, in which they commemorated the life of a man who had become an integral part of life in Kumamoto.[10]

The ceremony was attended by all who had known and practiced with Musashi. Foremost among them were his his old friends Shiota Hamanosuke and Sawamura Daigaku, closely followed by his star deshi, the two Terao brothers Nobumasa and Nobuyuki, and his many many other deshi.

Special guests of honor were Nagaoka Okinaga and his son, Yoriyuki. Lord Mitsunao could not attend the service, as he was visiting Edo at the time. Yet three days later, at Musashi's third-day memorial service, he would go down to the Tōkai temple in Edo's Shinagawa district to offer incense for Musashi's departed spirit.[11]

Shortly after the procession left the Taishō temple, Musashi's coffin was placed on a large rock in the Maesugi horse grounds, just east of the temple. There, amid the pouring rain, Musashi's Buddhist mentor, Akiyama Wanao, performed Musashi's last rites. No sooner had he said a requiem for his friend than a bright bolt of lightning split the grey curtain of rain, followed by a deep peel of thunder that seemed to roll on forever.

From there, the solemn procession moved along the main road leading down to the river. Having reached the riverbank, Musashi's coffin was carried aboard one of Lord Mitsunao's ships and ferried upstream to the village of Oe, on the other side of the river. There Musashi was buried in a special tomb that Nagaoka Okinaga had built for the master swordsman.[12]

## Iori's Peace of Mind

Musashi's funeral befitted the great swordsman: short, sober; down to earth. All who had known him felt the man had been honored with a worthy burial, none more so than his surviving son, Iori. Since Musashi's move to Kumamoto, Iori had seen little of his adoptive father, yet the news of his death filled the thirty-three-year-old with deep sadness, for what he had achieved had been made possible by Musashi.

Unable to leave his post in Kokura, he had been forced to leave the care of his aging father in the hands of his counterpart in Kumamoto, Nagaoka Kenmotsu. As one of Mitsunao's chief retainers Kenmotsu had taken it upon himself to make sure the needs of the old swordsman were met during his final days.[13]

More than six months before Musashi's death, on December 14, 1644, Iori had written to Kenmotsu to say that:

> Though we have not yet had the occasion to meet, I want to express my gratitude for the care you have shown for Musashi. I would like to visit you at once to show my respect, but I am tied down by urgent matters and thus cannot act according to my wishes. I hear you are on intimate terms with Musashi and therefore take the liberty of commending him into your care.

Three days later, on December 17, Kenmotsu had replied with a long letter in which he sought to put Iori at ease, while at the same time relating how Musashi was faring:

> As you say, we have not yet had the pleasure of meeting, but I read your letter with gratitude. Master Musashi fell ill at a time he had withdrawn to a place not far from Kumamoto, upon which he was brought to a physician and given medicine to drink.
>
> However, as he did not show any signs of improving, and since it was difficult to nurse him sufficiently at the place where he was staying, mas-

> ter Nagaoka Okinaga and I implored him to come to Kumamoto so that we could nurse him there, yet he would not comply. Lord Mitsunao, too, kindly urged him to do so and frequently dispatched a physician, nursing him in various ways, but since it was difficult to conduct such care where he was staying, he was urged to regularly come to Kumamoto, so that, the day before yesterday, he finally came down to Kumamoto.
>
> There, we increased his care, never letting up our guard in our directions to his servants, including Lord Mitsunao, who appointed a physician to be at his side constantly, so please put your mind at rest. At present there are no changes and his condition is stable. I fully understand you would like to visit your father, but that you are unfortunately barred from doing so. Please rest assured that we are fully committed to his care.

Aware that Iori might already be upset by the notion that his father had spent much of his last days outside the comfort of his home in Kumamoto, Kenmotsu carefully stayed clear of mentioning Musashi had spent two full winter seasons in the damp and cold Reigan Cave to write his life's work.

Kenmotsu's letter had the desired effect, for Iori had nothing but praise for the way his father was being cared for by those in Kumamoto, even after he had passed away. On June 21, 1645, one week after he had received tiding of his father's death, Iori wrote to Kenmotsu to let him know that:

> Upon my recent return, I immediately read your letter and I want to express my deepest gratitude

> that, from the moment my father fell ill, Lord Mitsunao appointed Terao Motomenosuke to remain at his side and see to his care.
>
> Fate sadly ordained it should be to no avail, yet you painstakingly organized his funeral service, his third day memorial service, as well as the building of his tomb, for which great blessing I sincerely express my deepest gratitude.
>
> I am also deeply grateful that Lord Mitsunao visited Musashi's sickbed, that he sent a representative to his funeral service, and that he went to the length of offering incense at the [Tōkai] temple at the time of his memorial service.
>
> I offer this letter to pay my initial respect but hope to hear your what your specific wishes are.

The two men exchanged several more letters over the next few weeks, Iori reiterating his deep indebtedness toward all in Kumamoto for the kind care with which they had treated his father, and Kenmotsu expressing his gratitude for the various gifts that had accompanied Iori's letters.[14]

## In Death's Wake

All who had known Musashi cherished his memory and exerted themselves to preserve his legacy for posterity. He was sorely missed by his deshi, who found it hard to master his style of fencing without his inspired guidance, however cantankerous he might have been at times. It now fell to the two Terao brothers to teach Musashi's many deshi and pass on his heritage to the next generation of swordsmen. Their most prominent deshi was

Nagaoka Naoyuki, the young son of master Yoriyuki, who would go on to serve the Hosokawa until the end of his life.

Most inheritors of Musashi's legacy were warriors of lower rank, including Dōke Heizō, Uragami Jūsaemon, and Murakami Masahide. Many of them prospered, but not all of them were able to turn Musashi's art to their advantage. Not long after his teacher's death, Masahide tried to leave the service of the Hosokawa to pursue a life of *musha shugyō*. His request was turned down. Three years later his properties were confiscated and Masahide was forced to take up life as a farmer in Sakuchi, some ten miles north of Kumamoto.

The presence of the stubborn old warrior was also missed by those who occupied a higher station in life, especially master Yoriyuki. During his five years in Kumamoto, Musashi had spent many a happy evening with Yoriyuki at his *yashiki* and had grown very fond of the fun-loving nobleman. Those sentiments were reciprocated by Yoriyuki, who in turn had come to appreciate the old swordsman's worldly-wise humor. The *Bukōden* describes how:

> Afterwards, when master Yoriyuki went out falcon hunting, he visited Musashi's grave. Summoning the village elder, he told him not to tarry in keeping the grave clean and tidy and gave him fifty bags of rice by way of payment.

Musashi's old Buddhist friend, Akiyama Wanao, also found it hard to fill his days without the old warrior around. He missed the sharpness of his thought and the depth he had brought to their discussions on matters of religion and philosophy by drawing parallels with the art of *heihō*. Like the great friendship between Yagyū Munenori and the famous monk Takuan Sōhō,

Wanao and Musashi had come to appreciate their mutual professions and found they could learn much from each other. With age and approaching death Musashi had come to realize that religion and martial ethics touched on each other in more profound ways than he had ever imagined.

Their talks had not just dwelt on the art of *heihō* and its bearing on religion, for Musashi was not only a consummate swordsman. He had been at home with arithmetic, architecture, botany, archery, horsemanship, etiquette, music, calligraphy, painting, and poetry. The monk knew that the void such accomplished and rounded men leave behind is hard to fill. In essence, however, he simply missed his friend as a human being. To the monk Musashi had been "the model of a fine human being," a man with a "magnanimity of heart that did not care about trifles."

The *Bushū denraiki* describes how, almost a hundred years after his demise, Japan's greatest swordsman was still remembered by his fellow countrymen whenever they entered Kumamoto along the Ōzu Kaidō:

> A stone memorial was erected at a place now known as Mound Musashi. It is said that even today, warriors and commoners alike dismount from their horse when they pass in front of Mound Musashi.[15]

# THE KOKURA HIBUN

## Introduction

The *Kokura hibun* is a lengthy epitaph celebrating the life, exploits, and character of Miyamoto Musashi. It is inscribed on a fifteen-foot obelisk-like stone monument, which overlooks the Straits of Shimonoseki.

The Kokura Monument was erected in 1654, on the initiative of Musashi's adopted son, Miyamoto Iori, nine years after Musashi passed away. It stands on the crest of Temukeyama, a hill some two hundred feet in height on the outskirts of Akazaka, in the northern district of the port of Kokura. In the distance, protruding from behind the island of Hikoshima to the northwest, one can just make out the island of Funashima, the scene of Musashi's most famous duel.

Though the provenance of its text is uncertain, the *Kokura hibun* is believed to have been written by Akiyama Wanao (1618–73), abbot of the Taishō temple in Kumamoto.

## Looking up at the Heavens the True and Perfect Art of Heihō is Eternal even in Death

Heihōsha Without Equal under the Heavens

Epitaph of Shinmen Musashi Genshin,
last descendant of the Akamatsu of Harima.
Died at Kumamoto in the province of Higo on
May 19, the second year of Shōhō [June 13, 1645].
Erected on April 19, in the third year of Shōō
[June 4, 1654] by his pious son.

"Look for the chances and respond to the changes." This is the way of accomplished general. The practice of the martial arts and the study of soldiery are the preoccupation of an army. Who was it that let his heart play at the gate of *bun* and *bu*, that let his hands work on the practice grounds of the martial arts, and gained fame for his courage in doing so? It was the nobly-born Musashi Shingen, scion of the Shinmen, last descendant of the Akamatsu of Harima, the man whose Buddhist name is Niten. By nature he had a magnanimity of heart that did not care about trifles. Truly, was this not the man called Musashi Shingen?

He became the progenitor of the Niten art of *heihō*. The Buddhist name of his father, Shinmen, who came from a house known for its mastery of the *jitte*, was Muni. This tradition was passed on to Musashi, who, as a result of training from dusk till dawn, came to understand that the *jitte* was many times more efficient than the single sword. However, the *jitte* was not a conventional weapon, whereas it was normal for samurai to wear two swords. And since there was no harm in applying the principles of the jitte to the art of fighting with two swords, he chose to abandon the tradition of fighting with the *jitte* and founded an art in which one fought with two swords.

Musashi truly was a rare swordsman. Whether he wielded a *shinken* or a *bokutō*, none could escape him, either by ducking or by running away. The force of his thrust was such that it resembled a projectile from a crossbow, and even the great Yōyū would not have been able to surpass him.

All things considered, Musashi was a man who totally mastered the art of *heihō* and embodied valor. Thus, at the age of thirteen, he challenged to a duel a man by the name of Arima Kihei, a Shintō-ryū swordsman from Harima, and defeated him instantly. Then, in the summer of his sixteenth year, he went to the province of Tajima. There he again challenged a swordsman and struck him dead in the blink of an eye so that before long his name was known throughout town.

Afterwards, Musashi went up to Kyoto, where lived the Yoshioka, known as the Foremost Heihōsha in Japan. Musashi challenged them, and fought for his honor with a Yoshioka descendant by the name of Seijūrō on the grounds of the Rendai temple outside the [former] capital. It was supposed to be a real contest but Musashi floored Seijūrō with a single blow of his *bokutō*, causing the latter to pass out. And because it was agreed beforehand that they would only exchange a single blow Musashi did not take Seijūrō's life. The latter's deshi came to his aid, lifted him on a stretcher, and took him home. There he was given various medical treatments and eventually recovered. In the end, he abandoned the martial life and took the tonsure.

However, Yoshioka Denshichirō, too, left Kyoto to fight it out with Musashi. He attacked Musashi with a five-foot *bokutō*. Seizing the opportunity, Musashi wrested the *bokutō* from him and struck him with his own weapon, so that Denshichirō fell to the ground and expired.

The followers of the Yoshioka school were filled with bitterness, conspiring among themselves saying, "We cannot stand up to him with technical skill alone. Let us therefore resort to tactics." And thus, feigning that they had come to practice, Yoshioka Matashichirō gathered his deshi and awaited Musashi in ambush outside Kyoto at Sagarimatsu. There were several hundreds of deshi, intending to kill Musashi in a single attack with swords, as well as bows and arrows. Musashi, however, had a talent for anticipating such events and, seeing through their dishonest scheme, he secretly said to his deshi, "This is no affair of yours, quickly leave this place. Even if my sworn enemies had assembled an army, to me it would be no more than a drifting cloud, so why should I fear them?" And when Musashi proceeded to scatter his enemies apart it seemed as if a wild dog was chasing away wild beasts. When Musashi returned to the capital having displayed his power all its citizens were in awe. His gallant vigor, his superior calculation, defeating a vast force singlehandedly, these were the marvelous exploits of a man of war.

Now prior to this, successive generations of the Yoshioka clan had served as fencing instructors to the shogun. They were called the Foremost Heihōsha in Japan. In the time of Shogun Yoshiaki, Musashi's father, Shinmen Munisai, was summoned to the capital and ordered to duel with the Yoshioka. Of the three bouts the Yoshioka swordsman won once, while Munisai won twice. In reward for this he received the title of Heihōsha Without Equal in Japan. Given this precedent, when Musashi came to Kyoto and defeated the Yoshioka swordsmen several times, the Yoshioka school of swordsmanship ceased to exist.

Now near here there lived a master swordsman whose name was Ganryū. When Musashi made it known that he wanted to duel with Ganryū the latter proposed that they fight with real swords. But Musashi responded saying, "Feel free to use a real sword and display your skills with it, but I will fight with the *bokutō* and reveal its secrets." And thus both men solemnly pledged in writing that they would meet in a duel on Funashima, an island in the sea between the provinces of Buzen and Nagato. And it was there that both men met at the same time. Ganryū came charging toward Musashi wielding his three-foot *tachi*, throwing at him all the techniques he had at his disposal. But Musashi struck him dead with one single blow of his *bokutō*, and with such speed that it seemed faster than lightning. Since Ganryū died on this island the people henceforth referred to it as Ganryū Island.[1]

From his thirteenth year until his prime of life Musashi fought more than sixty duels without ever being defeated. He would invariably say that, "In order to seize victory, one has to strike one's opponent the very moment they raise their eyebrows in surprise." And each time he met with someone in a duel he lived up to this dictum. From of old thousands, nay tens of thousands have met in a duel. However, except for Musashi, I have never heard of anyone to squarely face a great swordsmen and strike him dead, be it in the present or the past, in the capital or in the countryside. By now Musashi's reputation has spread throughout the country and such is the extent of his undiminished fame that it is impressed on the minds of present-day people though the oral traditions of their elders. Truly, is it not a marvel, is it not a mystery? Indeed, the excellence of his precocious talent is unparalleled.

Musashi would often say that the art of *heihō* should mature in one's hands and govern one's heart, and that as long as one remains utterly unselfish and impartial one can command armies in the field and even the management of the affairs of state need not be difficult. Musashi's valor at the time of the rebellion started by Lord Ishida Mitsunari, the favorite of Taikō Toyotomi Hideyoshi, or at the time of the disturbance caused by Lord

Toyotomi Hideyori, cannot be expressed in words, even if oceans had mouths and valleys tongues, and thus I will remain silent on this matter.

Not only was Musashi a consummate swordsman, he was also at home with etiquette, music, archery, horsemanship, calligraphy, arithmetic, and poetry. Moreover, be it in his dabbling in the arts or his skillful pursuit of his profession, he was never idle. He was the model of a fine human being.

Musashi died in the province of Higo. On his deathbed he wrote the words "Looking up at the heavens the true and perfect art of *heihō* is eternal, even in death," and it is these words that have inspired me to commemorate his legacy. Hence, I, his pious son, have founded this monument, so that they may be passed on and seen by successive generations into eternity.[2]

# OLD PROVINCES

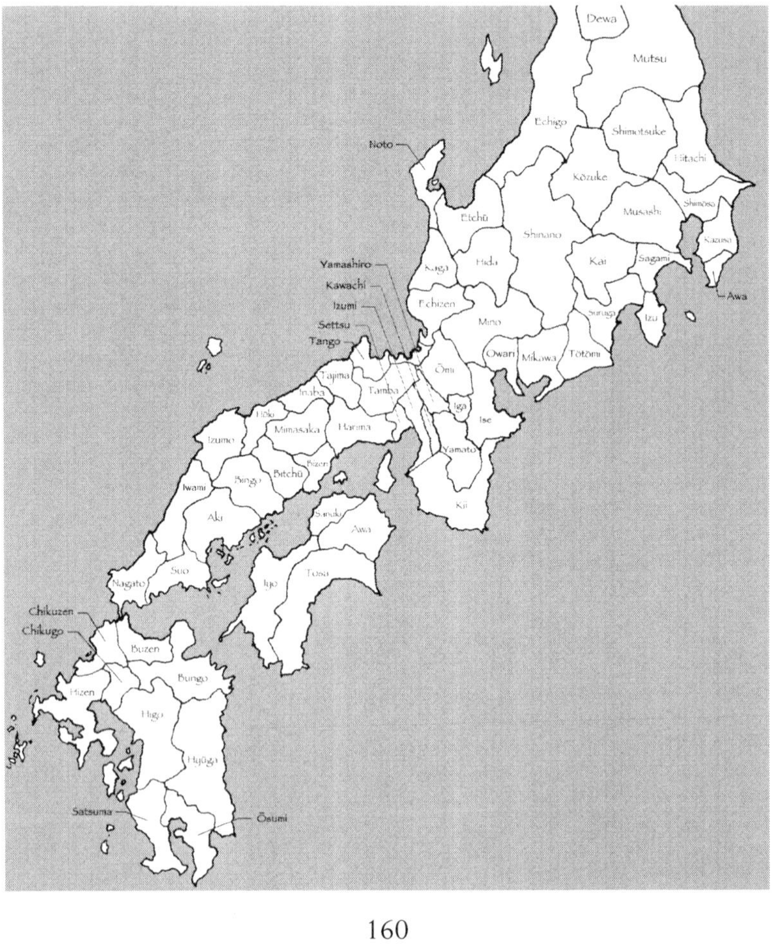

# Old Provinces and Their Modern Equivalents

| | |
|---|---|
| Aki: | Hiroshima |
| Awa: | Tokushima |
| Bingo: | Hiroshima |
| Bitchū: | Okayama |
| Bizen: | Okayama |
| Bungo: | Ōita |
| Buzen: | Fukuoka |
| Chikugo: | Fukuoka |
| Chikuzen: | Fukuoka |
| Dewa: | Yamagata, Akita |
| Echigo: | Niigata |
| Echizen: | Fukui |
| Etchū: | Fukuyama |
| Harima: | Hyōgo |
| Hida: | Gifu |
| Higo: | Kumamoto |
| Hitachi: | Ibaraki |
| Hizen: | Nagasaki |
| Hōki: | Tottori |
| Hyūga: | Miyazaki |
| Iga: | Mie |
| Inaba: | Tottori |
| Ise: | Mie |
| Iwami: | Shimane |
| Iyo: | Ehime |
| Izu: | Shizuoka |
| Izumi: | Osaka |
| Izumo: | Shimane |
| Kaga: | Ishikawa |
| Kai: | Yamanashi |
| Kawachi: | Osaka |
| Kazusa: | Chiba |
| Kii: | Wakayama |
| Kōzuke: | Gunma |
| Mikawa: | Aichi |
| Mimasaka: | Okayama |
| Mino: | Gifu |
| Musashi: | Saitama, Tokyo |
| Mutsu: | Aomori |
| Nagato: | Yamaguchi |
| Noto: | Ishikawa |
| Ōmi: | Shiga |
| Ōsumi: | Kagoshima |
| Owari: | Aichi |
| Sagami: | Kanagawa |
| Sanuki: | Kagawa |
| Satsuma: | Kagoshima |
| Settsu: | Osaka |
| Shimōsa: | Chiba |
| Shinano: | Nagano |
| Suō: | Yamaguchi |
| Suruga: | Shizuoka |
| Tajima: | Hyōgo |
| Tamba: | Kyoto |
| Tango: | Kyoto |
| Tosa: | Kōchi |
| Tōtōmi: | Shizuoka |
| Wakasa: | Fukui |
| Yamashiro: | Kyoto |
| Yamato: | Nara |

# CASTLES, TEMPLES, AND SHRINES

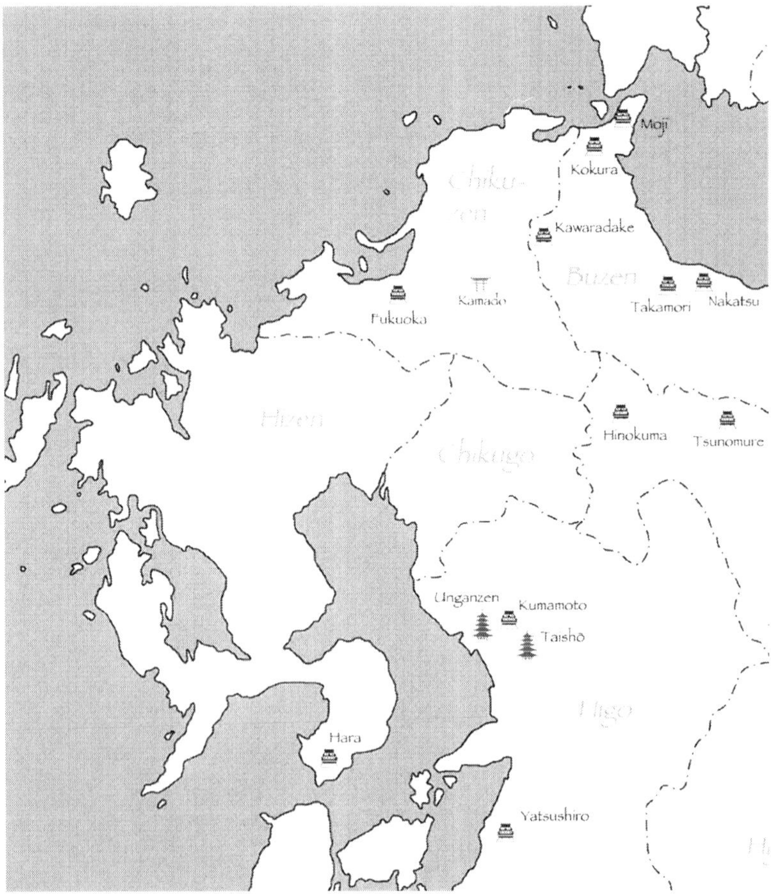

Iwami
Nagato
Suo
Moji
Kokura
Chiku-
zen
Kawaradake
Buzen
Takamori
Nakatsu
Tomiku
Aki
Kitsuki
Kamado
Fukuoka
Chikugo
Hinokuma
Tsunomure
Hiji
Usuki
Bungo
Saiki
Unganzen
Kumamoto
Taishō
Higo
Nobeoka
Yatsushiro
Hyūga

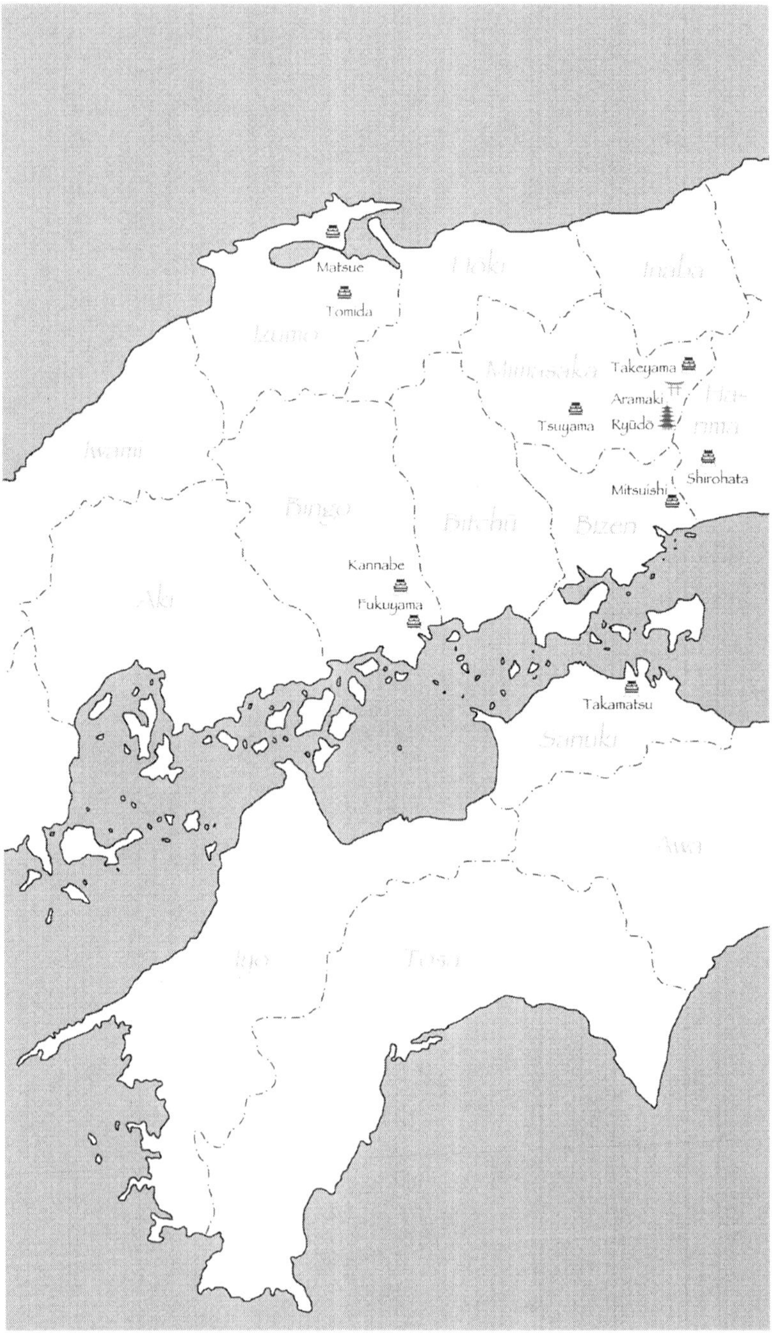
Matsue
Tomida
Takeyama
Aramaki
Tsuyama
Ryūdō
Shirohata
Mitsuishi
Kannabe
Fukuyama
Takamatsu

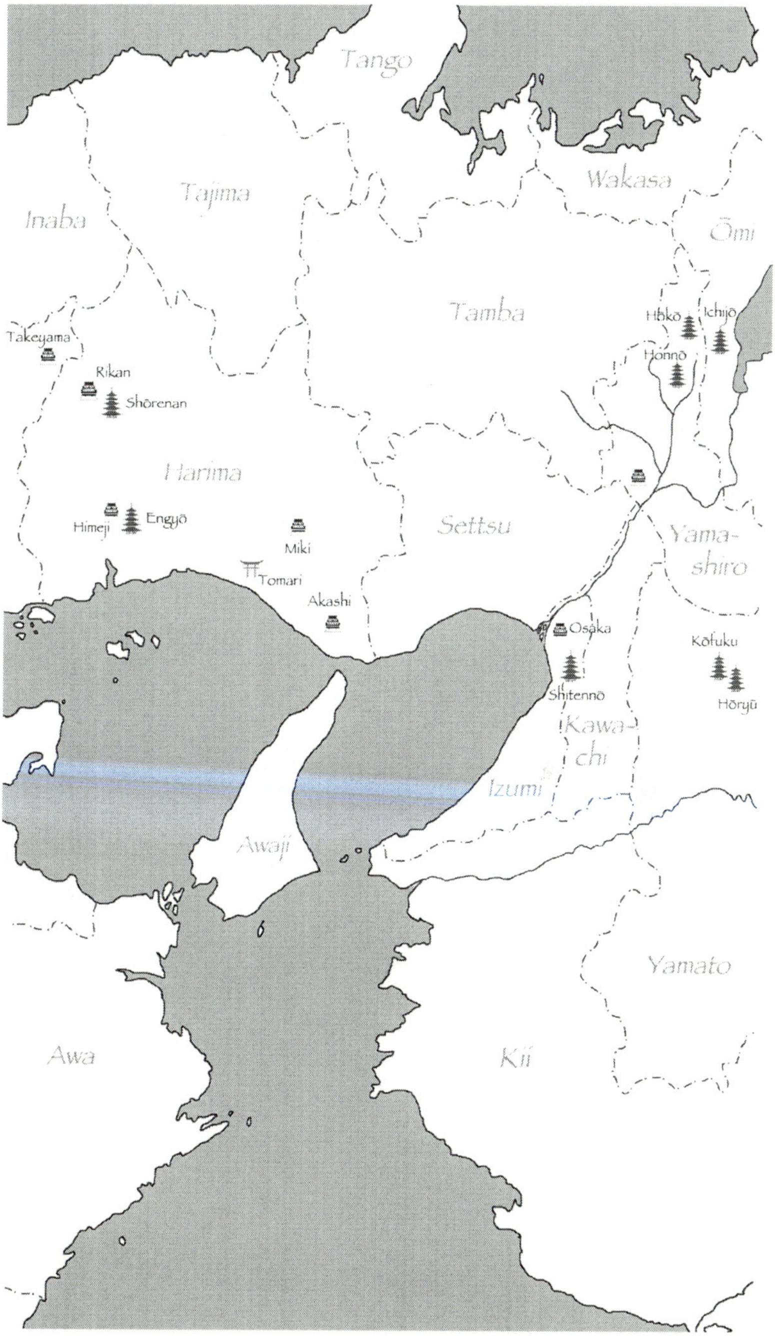
Tango
Tajima
Inaba
Wakasa
Ōmi
Tamba
Takeyama
Rikan
Shōrenan
Harima
Himeji
Engyō
Miki
Tomari
Akashi
Settsu
Honkō
Ichijō
Honnō
Yama-
shiro
Osaka
Shitennō
Kōfuku
Hōryū
Kawa-
chi
Izumi
Awaji
Yamato
Awa
Kii

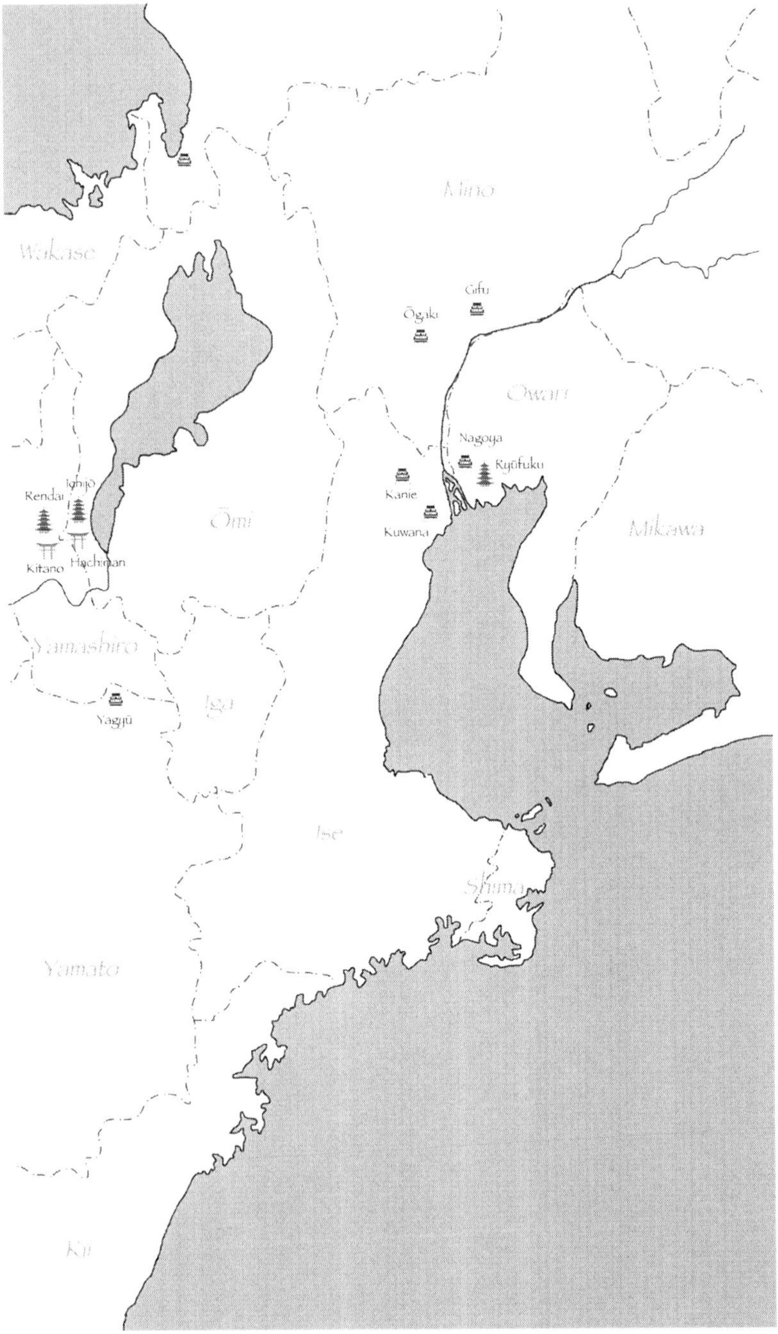
Mino
Wakase
Gifu
Ōgaki
Owari
Nagoya
Ryūfuku
Ichijō
Rendai
Kanie
Kuwana
Ōmi
Mikawa
Kitano
Hachiman
Yamashiro
Iga
Yagyū
Ise
Shima
Yamato
Kii

Nōtō
Ettchū
Shinano
Kaga
Hida
Ichijōdani
Echizen
Mino
Kai
Gifu
Owari
Nagoya
Koromo
Ōmi
Mikawa
Suruga
Ise
Tōtōmi
Iga

Shimotsuke
Kōzuke
Shinano
Musashi
Kai
Sagami
Yugyō
Kanonji
Suruga
Izu

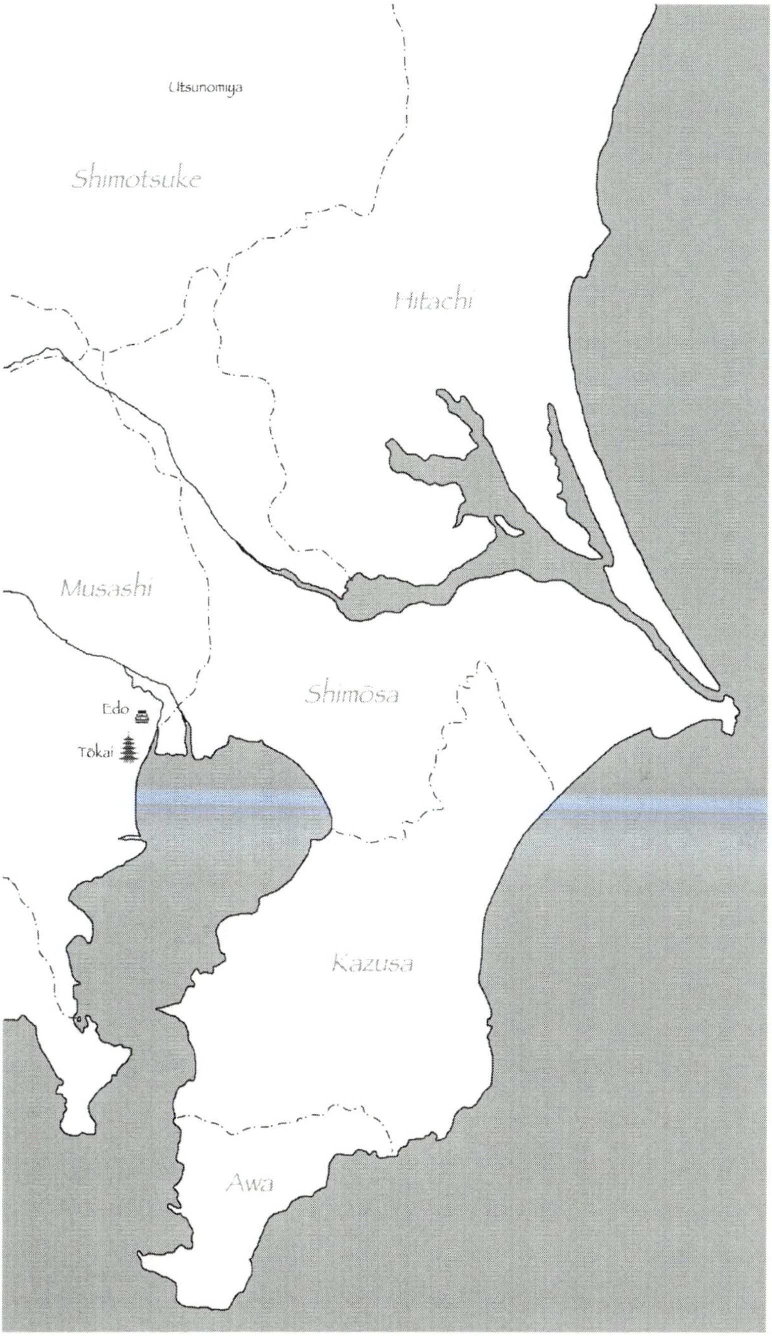
Utsunomiya
Shimotsuke
Hitachi
Musashi
Shimōsa
Edo
Tōkai
Kazusa
Awa

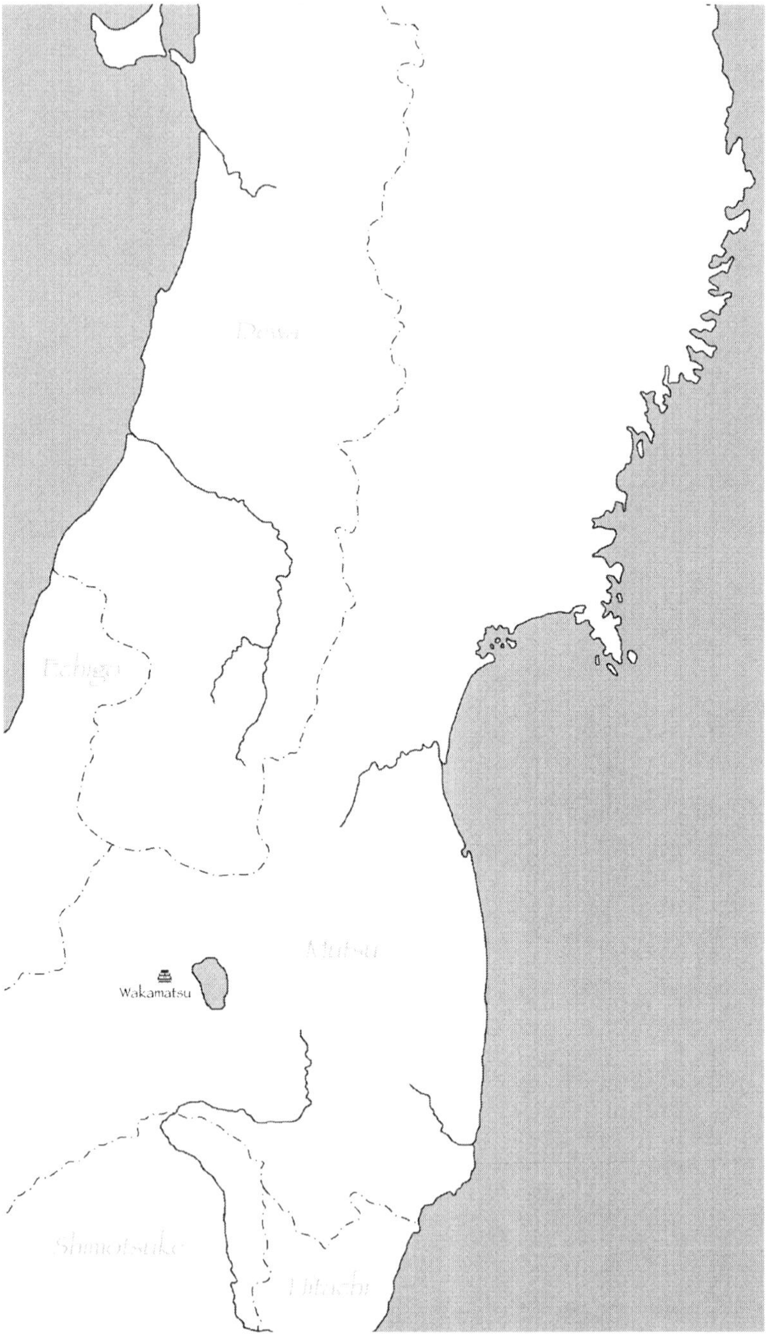
Wakamatsu

# HISTORICAL PERIODS

## Japan

Nara 710–94
Heian 794–1185
Kamakura 1185–1333
Muromachi 1333–1568
Momoyama 1568–1600
Edo 1600–1868

## China

Han 202 BC–AD 220
Three Kingdoms 221–65
Six Dynasties 265–581
Sui 581–618
Tang 618–906
Five Dynasties 907–60
Northern Song 960–1127
Southern Song 1127–1279

Yuan 1271–1368
Ming 1368–1644
Qing 1644–1911

## Periods of Military Rule

Kamakura Bakufu 1185–1333
Muromachi Bakufu (Ashikaga Bakufu) 1333–1568
Edo Bakufu (Tokugawa Bakufu) 1603–1867

# BATTLES, SIEGES, AND REBELLIONS

## Battles

Battle of Shizugatake 1583
Battle of Komakiyama 1584
Battle of Nagakute 1584
Battle of Sekigahara 1600
Battle of Shigakihara 1600
Battle of Dōmyōji 1615

## Sieges

Siege of Odawara castle 1590
Siege of Gifu castle 1600
Siege of Ōgaki castle 1600
Siege of Kitsuki castle 1600
Siege of Tomiku castle 1600
Siege of Usuki castle 1600
Siege of Saiki castle 1600
Siege of Tsunomure castle 1600

Siege of Hinokuma castle 1600
Siege of Kawaradake castle 1600
Siege of Kokura castle 1600
Siege of Osaka castle 1614–15
Siege of Hara castle 1638

## Rebellions

Honnō Rebellion 1582
Shimabara Rebellion 1637

# DOMAINS AND DAIMYOS

## Akashi

Ogasawara Tadazane 1616–17

## Fukuoka

Kuroda Nagamasa 1600–23

## Fukuyama

Mizuno Katsunari 1619–39

## Himeji

Ikeda Mitsumasa 1616–17
Honda Tadamasa 1617–31

## Kokura

Hosokawa Tadaoki 1600–20
Hosokawa Tadatoshi 1620–32
Ogasawara Tadazane 1632–67

## Kumamoto

Hosokawa Tadatoshi 1632–41
Hosokawa Mitsunao 1641–50
Hosokawa Tsunatoshi 1650–1712

## Nakatsu

Kuroda Yoshitaka 1587–89
Kuroda Nagamasa 1589–1600

## Okayama

Tokugawa Yoshinao 1607–50

## Owari

Tokugawa Yoshinao 1607–50

# SCHOOLS OF SWORDSMANSHIP

## Asayama Ichiden-ryū

Founder: Asayama Ichiden Shigetatsu
Region: Tango, Tanba
Period: Muromachi

## Chūjō-ryū

Founder: Chūjō Nagahide
Region: Mikawa
Period: Muromachi

## Gan-ryū

Founder: Sasaki Kojirō
Region: Echizen
Period: Edo

## Hōzōin-ryū

Founder: Hōzōin Kakuzenbō In'ei
Region: Nara
Period: Momoyama

## Kyōhachi-ryū

Founder: Saichi Hōgen
Region: Yamashiro
Period: Kamakura

## Nen-ryū

Founder: Nenami Okuyama Jion
Region: Mutsu
Period: Muromachi

## Nitō Tetsujin-ryū

Founder: Aoki Jōemon
Region: Musashi
Period: Edo

## Shintō-ryū

Founder: Iizasa Chōisai Ienao
Region: Shimosa
Period: Muromachi

## Takeda-ryū

Founder: Minamoto no Yoshiari
Region: Kai
Period: Heian

## Takenouchi-ryū

Founder: Takenouchi Hisamoro
Region: Mimasaka
Period: Muromachi

## Toda-ryū

Founder: Toda Nagaie
Region: Echizen
Period: Muromachi

## Tōgun-ryū

Founder: Kawasaki Kaginosuke
Region: Echizen
Period: Muromachi

## Tōri-ryū

Founder: Shinmen Muni
Region: Mimasaka
Period: Momoyama

## Yagyū Shinkage-ryū

Founder: Yagyū Muneyoshi
Region: Nara
Period: Muromachi

## Yoshioka-ryū

Founder: Yoshioka Naomoto
Region: Yamashiro
Period: Muromachi

## Shinkage-ryū

Founder: Kamiizumi Ise no Kami Nobutsuna
Region: Kōzuke
Period: Muromachi

# LINEAGES

As with so many of Japan's martial schools, or *ryūha*, those spawned by Musashi have thrived and diversified, as well as disintegrated, over the centuries. One of the reasons for this diversification is that Musashi took on deshi well before his style had evolved into a fixed form. Having received a license from Musashi to practice his current style, these men went on to propagate their particular schools, even though Musashi himself continued to hone and develop his art. This resulted in schools that differed distinctly from each other. Today, there are many *ryūha* that trace their origins back to the style of swordsmanship practiced by the master himself. The main division is that between the practitioners of the Enmei-ryū line (the style practiced by Musashi during the early part of his career), and the practitioners of the Niten Ichi-ryū line (the style practiced by Musashi during the latter part of his career).

Today, the most widely practiced schools descended from those two major styles are the Heihō Niten Ichi-ryū, the Noda-ha Niten Ichi-ryū; and the Owari Enmei-ryū, the Musashi Enmei-ryū Hangan-ha, and the Musashi Enmei-ryū Kenjutsu.

# The Niten-Ichi-ryū Lineage

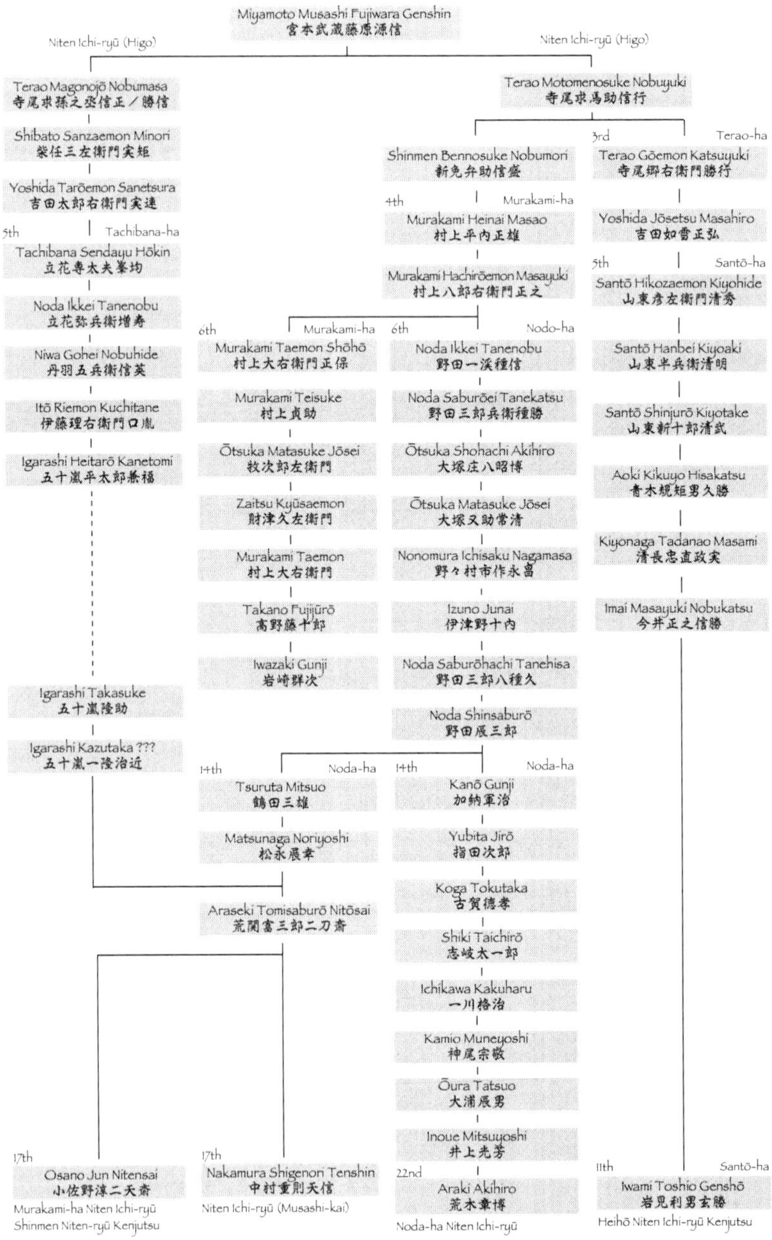

# The Enmei-ryū Lineage

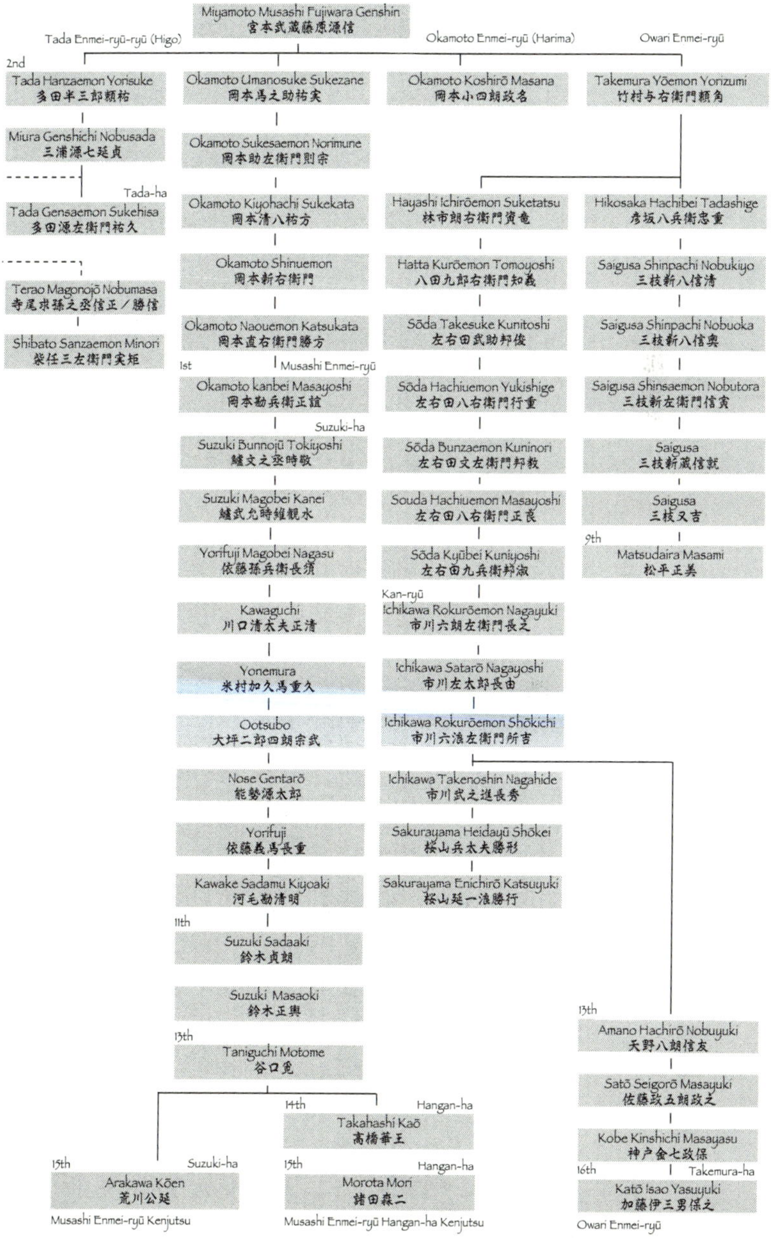

# WEBSITES

## Japanese

**Shinmen/Murakami-ha Niten-ryū Kenjutsu**
Kokusai Suigetsujuku Bujitsu Kyōkai
www.japanbujut.exblog.jp

**Heihō Niten Ichi-ryū Kenjutsu**
Heihō Niten Ichi-ryū
www.hyohonitenichiryunihon.wordpress.com
www.nihonkobudokyoukai.org/martialarts/034/

**Noda-ha Niten Ichi-ryū Kenjutsu**
Noda-ha Niten Ichi-ryū
www.nihonkobudokyoukai.org/martialarts/035

**Niten Ichi-ryū Musashi-kai**
Niten Ichi-ryū Musashi Kai
www.musashikai.jp

**Musashi Enmei-ryū Kenjutsu**
Musashi Enmei-ryū Kai
www.ne.jp/asahi/system/color

**Musashi Enmei-ryū Hangan-ha Kenjutsu**
Musashi Enmei-ryū Hangan-ha
www32.ocn.ne.jp/~seitai/emmei-hangan.htm

## English

**Shinmen Niten-ryū Kenjutsu**
International Suigetsujuku Bujitsu Association
www.isba-world.com

**Murakami-ha Niten Ichi-ryū**
International Suigetsujuku Bujitsu Association
www.isba-world.com

**Heihō Niten Ichi-ryū Kenjutsu**
Hyoho Niten Ichi Ryu
www.hyohonitenichiryu.wordpress.com

**Niten Ichi-ryū Musashi-kai**
Niten Ichi-ryu Musashi Kai
www.musashikai.jp/english-page

## French

**Heihō Niten Ichi-ryū Kenjutsu**
Hyoho Niten Ichi Ryu
www.nitenichiryu.wordpress.com

## German

**Heihō Niten Ichi-ryū Kenjutsu**
Hyoho Niten Ichi Ryu
www.nitenichiryu.de

## Dutch

**Heihō Niten Ichi-ryū Kenjutsu**
Hyoho Niten Ichi Ryu
www.hyohonitenichiryunederlands.wordpress.com

## About Miyamoto Musashi

**English**
www.musashi-miyamoto.com
www.miyamotomusashi.com

**French**
www.musashi-miyamoto.net

## General Information

**English**
www.koryu.com
www.samurai-archives.com
www.ejmas.com

**French**
www.koryuweb.wordpress.com

# GLOSSARY

| | |
|---|---|
| *ageya*: | Luxurious restaurant with geisha entertainment. |
| *ashigaru*: | Foot soldier. |
| *biwa*: | Japanese lute. |
| *bokutō*: | Wooden sword used for practice. |
| *bu*: | The martial arts. |
| *bun*: | The literary arts. |
| *burei-uchi*: | Killing someone for reasons of insolence. |
| *bushi*: | Warrior. |
| *chūdan*: | Middle guard, one of Musashi's five *kamae*, or stances in which one awaits an attack in a defensive position, ready to parry and strike at any given moment. |
| *daimyō*: | Fuedal lord. |
| *denki*: | Biography. |
| *deshi*: | Pupil or disciple of a master of an art or craft who has committed him- or herself to study the art or craft in question for a number of years. |
| *dōjō*: | Hall with a smooth wooden floor or covered with mats for the practice of martial arts. |
| *eboshi*: | Headgear traditionally worn by nobles in court dress, but also used in Shintō ceremonies. |

| | |
|---|---|
| *fūdai daimyō*: | Vassal *daimyō*. |
| *gedan*: | Lower guard, one of Musashi's five *kamae*, or stances in which one awaits an attack in a defensive position, ready to parry and strike at any given moment. |
| *genpuku*: | Coming of age ceremony. |
| *go*: | Japanese chess. |
| *gorintō*: | Five-storied stupa. |
| *haori*: | Lightweight silk jacket worn by men as a component of the *hakama*. |
| *hatamoto*: | Direct retainer, or "bannerman," of the shogun. |
| *hatasashi*: | The poles of banners carrying a clan's *kamon*. |
| *heihō*: | Art or method of warfare, here generally employed to mean the martial arts, and in particular Musashi's Niten Ichi-ryū. |
| *heihōsha:* | Practitioner of the art of *heihō*. |
| *hidari no waki*: | Middle guard, one of Musashi's five *kamae*, or stances in which one awaits an attack in a defensive position, ready to parry and strike at any given moment. |
| *hikiwatashi*: | Transfer of a fiefdom from one *daimyō* to another. |
| *hōshin*: | To empty one's mind and allow it to respond to new challenges. |
| *hoshu jutsu*: | Compendium of seizing, holding, and binding techniques employed to arrest culprits or deal with those captured alive during siege warfare. |
| *isshin ittō*: | Technique in which one moves in on one's opponent, stoops down, and achieves victory by lifting him up from his legs as he is about to strike from above. |
| *jitte*: | A traditional weapon consisting of an iron rod that may vary in length between ten inches and a yard with a fork-like extension situated just above the hilt. |

| | |
|---|---|
| *jō*: | Wooden staff. |
| *jōdan*: | Upper guard, one of Musashi's five *kamae*, or stances in which one awaits an attack in a defensive position, ready to parry and strike at any given moment. |
| *junshi:* | Medieval tradition in which a retainer immolated himself on the death of his lord. |
| *jūjutsu*: | Bare-handed form of combat art based on a variety of grappling techniques. |
| *kabuki*: | Classical Japanese dance-drama known for its stylized drama and the elaborate make-up of its performers. |
| *kaki*: | Family records. |
| *kakimono bugyō*: | Magistrate in charge of a fiefdom's archive. |
| *kakun*: | Moral guidelines handed down by the head of a clan to younger males. |
| *kamae:* | Defensive stance in which one awaits an attack in a defensive position, ready to parry and strike at any given moment. |
| *kamon*: | Family crest. |
| *kan*: | 3.75 kilograms. |
| *kana*: | The phonetic Japanese syllabary. |
| *kanazōshi*: | Traditional type of book printed in *kana*, the phonetic Japanese syllabary. |
| *kanji*: | Chinese ideograph. |
| *kanjō bugyō*: | Magistrate of Payments. |
| *karō*: | Chief retainer of a *daimyō*. |
| *katana*: | Sword. |
| *katsu-totsu*: | Onomatopea used to describe the quick, cadence-like succession in which two strokes with the sword are executed, *katsu* as one raises one's sword to stab, *totsu* as one strikes down. |
| *karusan hakama*: | *Hakama* with trouser legs that are tapered toward the lower end so that they fit tight round the shins. |

*kazoedoshi*: Traditional East Asian method of keeping age.

*kodachi*: Literally, "small *tachi*," it is the shortest of the pair of swords traditionally worn by samurai.

*koku*: Medieval unit of measurement, approximately 278 liters. Here it is used to express the annual rice yield of a plot of land, one *koku* being sufficient to feed a person for a year.

*kū*: Air, emptiness.

*kumihoka*: Outside the regular class of warriors.

*makura bokutō*: "Pillow" *bokutō*, a short version of the traditional wooden practice sword.

*metsuke*: Inspector.

*migi no waki*: Right-hand guard, one of Musashi's five *kamae*, or stances in which one awaits an attack in a defensive position, ready to parry and strike at any given moment.

*miso*: Seasoning paste made of fermented soy beans.

*mizukuruma*: "Water mill" technique, in which the sword is swept close along the floor and then brought up in a wide, circular motion.

*mokuroku*: Written inventory of the techniques and tenets of a school of swordsmanship.

*musha bugyō*: Magistrate of Warriors.

*musha shugyō*: Literally, "warrior training," but in the context of *budō*, the old practice of ascetic self-discipline that goes back to the ancient traditions of the so-called *yamabushi*, or mountain monks.

*musha shugyōsha*: Practitioner of *musha shugyō*.

*naginata*: Pole sword.

*narezushi*: Traditional form of fermented *sushi*.

*nebari o kakuru*: Literally, "applying glue," a technical term to emphasize the importance of keeping one's sword firmly against that of one's opponent, as if they had been glued together.

*nengō*: The name of an era.

*obi*: A belt worn under a samurai's *hakama* into which the sheaths of his two swords are inserted.

*omoimono*: Classical Japanese term that can mean either a loved one or a prostitute.

*renga*: Series of short verses that are linked into one single poem through a collaborative effort.

*rōnin*: Masterless samurai.

*ryūha*: A particular branch of a school of swordsmanship.

*ryūsui no uchi*: Technical term meaning to make oneself big, both physically and mentally, by drawing one's sword way back behind one's body and striking a large and strong blow, but slowly, almost as if in slow motion.

*sankin kōtai*: A bakufu policy during the Edo period in which daimyo were required to spend alternate years in their domain and the capital of Edo in order to prevent rebellions.

*sekka no atari*: Technique in which one strikes the opponent's sword the moment one's own sword and that of one's opponent are about to touch without even slightly raising one's sword.

*seppuku*: Ritual suicide.

*shaku*: Measure of length, about one foot.

*shiai*: Duel between two practitioners of a school of combat.

*shidachi*: One of the two roles in *budō*, in which the student responds to an attack and can thereby acquire correct tempo, stance, and perception of opportunity.

*shihan*: Chief instructor.

*shinai*: Weapon made of joined segments of bamboo and used in competitive practice.

| | |
|---|---|
| *shinken*: | Real sword, as opposed to the wooden *bokutō*, or practice sword. |
| *shikomitsue*: | A sword the hilt and scabbard of which are crafted from the same wood so that, when sheathed, the sword is indistinguishable from a walking stick. |
| *shimono*: | Component of the *hoshu jutsu*. |
| *shinzan*: | Newcomer. |
| *shōgun*: | Hereditary military governor during Japan's fuedal era. |
| *shuriken*: | Small, sharpened, hand-held blade thrown from a short distance. |
| *sōhei*: | Warrior monks of the great Buddhist temples. |
| *sōjutsu*: | Art of fighting with the *yari*. |
| *sumi-e*: | Ink drawing. |
| *sumō*: | Traditional full-contact competitive wrestling. |
| *sutra*: | Rule or aphorism in Sanskrit literature. |
| *tachi*: | Longest of the pair of swords traditionally worn by samurai. |
| *taishō*: | Chief warrior or commander. |
| *tantō*: | Traditional Japanese dagger with a blade between 5.9 to 11.8 inches in length. |
| *taryū shiai*: | Literally, "contest of different schools," used to refer to a duel between practitioners of different schools of combat. |
| *tatami*: | Traditional Japanese floor mat made of woven soft rush straw and filled with rice straw. |
| *teki-uchi*: | Killing someone for reasons of revenge. |
| *teppō ashigaru*: | *Ashigaru* (foot soldiers) armed with rifles (*teppō*). |
| *torikago*: | Component of the *hoshu jutsu*. |
| *uchidachi*: | One of the two roles in *budō* in which the instructor initiates an action, controlling the tempo, but allowing the *shidachi* to strike the winning blow. |
| *umamawarigumi*: | A daimyo's elite household mounted guard. |

*uruzuki*: Additional month added every few years to make up for discrepancies between calendar months and seasons in the lunisolar calendar.

*wakizashi*: Literally, "side inserted sword," is an auxiliary sword with a blade between 12 and 24 inches in length used for fighting at close quarters.

*wakō*: Japanese pirates during Japan's middle ages.

*yamabushi*: Reclusive mountain monks of the Japanese Alps, who practiced austerities in the harsh environment of the mountains in order to attain superhuman powers.

*yari*: Spear or lance.

*yashiki*: Samurai mansion.

*yazama*: Arrow loophole.

*yukata*: A casual summer *kimono* with straight seams and wide sleeves made of cotton and usually unlined.

*zanshin*: To remain alert and leave one's mind on the fallen opponent.

*zōei bugyō*: Magistrate of Construction.

# NOTES

## Introduction

1 All passages quoted here from Musashi's *Gorin no sho*, popularly translated as the *Book of Five Rings*, have been translated by the author from an edition edited and annotated by Kamiko Tadashi. This text is based on a copy of the *Gorin no sho* that was passed down in 1667 by Terao Magonojō Nobumasa (Katsunobu) to his student Yamamoto Gensuke (Genzaemon Katsuhide), and which is currently in the possession of the Hosokawa family. See Kamiko Tadashi, *Gorin no sho*, 13.

2 The Kokura monument can be seen today and though somewhat faded by the wear and tear of a few centuries, its text is still decipherable. The earliest record to carry the *Kokura hibun* in full is the *Bukōden*. A full Japanese transcript of the inscription is reproduced in Matsunobu Ichiji, *Miyamoto Musashi zensho*, 292.

3 Literally meaning "books written mainly in *kana*," the phonetic Japanese syllabary and not the difficult *kanji*, or Chinese ideographs, the *kanazōshi* ranged from essays, military chronicles, to travel guides and were printed during the first eight decades

(1600–80) of the Edo period. See Kimura Akira, *Kaijō monogatari*, Nagano, 1985.

4 See Fukuda Masahide, *Miyamoto Musashi kenkyūron bunshū*, 51–52.

5 See Fukuda Masahide, *Miyamoto Musashi kenkyū dainishū, Bushūdenraiki*, 171–172.

6 See Kondō Heijō, *Shiseki shūran*, volume 24. Tokyo, 1967.

7 See Hinatsu Shigetaka, *Honchō bugei shōden*. Tokyo, 2003.

8 For a full translation of the *Bushū denraiki* and the *Bukōden*, and an exhaustive account of the gestation of all four works, see De Lange, William, *The Real Musashi, The Bushūdenraiki*; and De Lange, William, *The Real Musashi: The Bukōden*. The Japanese originals of the two texts are reproduced in Fukuda Masahide, *Miyamoto Musashi kenkyū dainishū, Bushūdenraiki*, 344–67; and Matsunobu Ichiji, *Miyamoto Musashi zensho*, 300–314.

9 See Nagao Susumu, *18 seiki ni okeru kenjutsu no henshitsukatei ni kansuru kenkyū; Gekken sōdan no bunseki o chūshin ni*, Meiji Daigaku Ninbun Kagaku Kenkūsho Kiyō, volume 45, 1999, 126. Also see Kaku Kōzō. *Kyokui Ichiryū tamashii no waza ni nihonjin no minamoto o saguru*, 115–16.

10 See Hirano Yōsai, *Harima kagami*; and Fukuda Masahide, *Miyamoto Musashi kenkyūron bunshū*, 85–86.

11 See Kosuge Ren, *Bisan hōkan*.

12 See Akabane Tatsuo, *Musashi "Enmeiryū" wo Manabu*, 100–124.

13 In his *Tōsakushi* (1851), Masaki Teruo explicitly states that the *Honchō bugei shōden* (1714) is wrong in claiming that Musashi hailed from Harima. In doing so Teruo seems to go against a number of other records on Miyamoto Musashi, many of which were written decades, if not centuries, before the *Tōsakushi*. The *Harima kagami* (1762), for instance, states that "Miyamoto Musashi hailed from the village of Miyamoto in the vicinity of Ikaruga in the district of Ittō." More importantly, in his *Gorin no sho*, Musashi himself claims that he was a native of Harima.

There may, however, be specific reasons why Musashi preferred to consider himself a native of Harima, rather than Mimasaka. First of all his father, with whom he had a troubled relationship, came from Mimasaka, whereas his beloved stepmother, Yoshiko, came from Harima. It was at her place, the village of Hirafuku in Harima, too, where he spent the happiest years of his childhood. Not surprisingly, Harima was also where he settled down during the middle years of his life. See Fujimaki Masayuki, *Tōsakushi*, 12–32.

Another reason for Musashi's willful misrepresentation of his roots may be the fact that, like many of the other western provinces, the province of Mimasaka had been the breeding ground of Tokugawa dissent in the run-up to the Battle of Sekigahara (1600). Indeed, Ukita Hideie, at that time the daimyo in control of both provinces of Bizen and Mimasaka, was one of the ringleaders of the Mitsunari alliance and the first to mobilize his troops when he held a ceremony for those who would go into battle at the Hōkoku shrine in Fukuoka. This was on September 8, eleven days before Ishida Mitsunari and his co-conspirators decided to move against Ieyasu at a secret conference at Mitsunari's stronghold of Sawayama castle.

14 The *Mimasaka ryakushi* also is the only record to mention the specific reason why Shinmen Munetsura entered the service of the Kuroda, i.e., the annihilation of the Ukita clan. In the Battle of Sekigahara Ukita Hideie chose the side of the western alliance under Ishida Mitsunari. Defeated in battle he fled to the Ibuki Mountains, from where, with the help of Shimazu Yoshihiro of Satsuma, he made his way in disguise to the province of Ōsumi (today's Kagoshima prefecture). Also deprived of his former possessions (but not necessarily because he fought under Ukita during the same battle), Shinmen Munetsura entered the service of Kuroda Yoshitaka sometime after 1600, the year in which the latter was promoted to his new estate

in Chikuzen in reward for his role in the Battle of Sekigahara. See Yabuki Masanori, *Mimasaka ryakushi*, 143–45.

This much is borne out by the *Keichō shichi-nen shoyakunin chigyōwari*, a record of the distribution of land among the various retainers for the seventh year of Keichō (1602), in which Munetsura is listed as having a fief of two thousand *koku*. He next makes his appearance in the *Keichō nenchū samurai-chū jija chigyō*, a record of the distribution of land among the retainers and the various temples and shrines of the Kuroda clan in Chikuzen from the ninth year of Keichō (1604). Significantly, unlike Muni, Munetsura is listed as a newcomer (*shinzan*). In the code of the records this means that Munetsura entered the service of the Koroda sometime after 1600. See See Fukuda Masahide, *Miyamoto Musashi kenkyūron bunshū*, 112–18.

15 See Fukuda Masahide, *Miyamoto Musashi kenkyūron bunshū*, 25–26.

16 The record carrying Musashi's name, the *Ōsaka o-jin no otomo*, was discovered among the possessions of the descendants of Nakayama Shōgen, who had served as one of the elders of the Mizuno fiefdom.

The *Ōsaka o-jin no otomo*, moreover, is not the only roll call to mention Musashi's name in connection to the siege. A similar roll call, kept among the archives of Fukuyama castle confirms that Musashi was one among the 230 mounted warriors (in addition to some 4300 warriors on foot) mobilized under Katsunari's command. The roll call, titled *Ōsaka o-jin o-ninzu tsukeoboe*, was originally among the papers of the Oba, a clan of Mizuno retainers from Fukuyama. Today, two copies, one drafted in 1752, the other in 1818, are still kept in the Kagami Yagura, the castle's eastern turret, and both carry the name of a certain Oba Heiba.

Moreover, not only does the *Ōsaka o-jin o-ninzu tsukeoboe* mention that Musashi was among Katsunari's mounted warriors, it explicitly states that he was the fourth among a group of ten mounted warriors attached to none other than Sakushū-sama, the honorary name of Katsunari's son, Katsushige (later Katsutoshi). Two men among the remaining nine are marked as "taking part as *rōnin*," whereas no such label is put on Musashi. See Fukuda Masahide, *Miyamoto Musashi kenkyū dainishū*, 189–198; and *Miyamoto Musashi kenkyūron bunshū*, 19–24.

Musashi's participation in the siege of Osaka castle under Mizuno Katsunari is also supported by the *Sōkyū sama o-degatari*. Though, unlike the two roll calls, it does not touch on Musashi's role during the siege of Osaka castle, it does mention that during the suppression of the Shimabara Rebellion (in which Katsunari played a prominent role), "a man by the name of Miyamoto Musashi said that he had ridden into battle under Lord Katsunari." See Fukuyama-shi Kyōiku Iinkai, *Oba-ka Bunsho*, part 1, Fukuyama, 1974, 178.

Had Musashi fought among the western forces, why, furthermore, should he have adopted Mikinosuke, the third son of another Ieyasu ally, Nakagawa Shimanosuke, who served Katsunari as *musha bugyō*, his Magistrate of Warriors, and died during the siege of Osaka castle? Mikinosuke's background, by the way, is not provided by the *Kōkō zatsuroku*, but by an ancestral record drawn up in 1696 and submitted to the administrators of the Okuyama fiefdom in the province of Bizen by a certain Miyamoto Kohei, head of a contingent of *ashigaru* of the Ikeda clan and a nephew of Miyamoto Mikinosuke. See Fukuda Masahide, *Miyamoto Musashi kenkyū dainishū*, 189–198; and *Miyamoto Musashi kenkyūron bunshū*, 19–24.

17 Though Hōkin's claim in his *Bushū denraiki* that Musashi joined his father in Nakatsu and entered the service of Kuroda Yoshitaka is contested by some, there is little doubt that Musashi's father, Munisai, did indeed live in Nakatsu at this time, as his name is mentioned in the local records of the Kuroda clan for 1604.

Going by what Hōkin is saying, it seems that Munisai had left the castle town of Takamori and joined his lord, Yoshitaka, in Nakatsu, the seat of the Kuroda headquarters. See Fukuda Masahide, *Miyamoto Musashi kenkyūron bunshū*, 112–127.

Unless Musashi had completely fallen out with his father (which is contradicted by the *Bushū denraiki*, as well as the *Numata kaki*) it is unlikely that, at the tender age of sixteen, Musashi would have ended up fighting among the western forces in the Battle of Sekigahara, in other words, that he fought opposite the forces of Kuroda Nagamasa, the son of Muni's lord, Kuroda Yoshitaka. Nor is there any clue to suggest under whom he might have done so. And if he indeed had been fighting among the ranks of one of Mitsunari's allies, why should he later have relied with such consistency and apparent faith on the hospitality of Ogasawara Tadazane (Akashi), Nagaoka Okinaga (Kokura), and Hosokawa Tadatoshi (Kumamoto), all chieftains who had fought and earned their promotions by joining Ieyasu's side.

Here, too, Musashi's eastern loyalties are again supported by the *Kōkō zatsuroku*, the *Ōsaka o-jin no otomo*, and the *Ōsaka o-jin o-ninzu tsukeoboe,* which all clearly state that during the siege of Osaka castle Musashi served among the troops of Mizuno Katsunari, yet another chieftain who fought on Ieyasu's side throughout his military career. See Fukuda Masahide, *Miyamoto Musashi kenkyū dainishū*, 160–162; and *Miyamoto Musashi kenkyūron bunshū*, 26–41.

18 See Murakami Genzō, *Zuihitsu Sasaki Kojirō*; and Kawaguchi Sunao, *Sasaki Kōjirō*.

19 A case in point is Tachibana Minehira, alias Tanji Hōkin, who practiced Musashi's Niten Ichi-ryū from his early childhood, refused to move closer to his master's castle in order to be close to his teacher, traveled up to Akashi from Kyushu twice to practice with the third progenitor of the Niten Ichi-ryū (Minehira would go on to become the fifth), refused to marry in order

to deepen his understanding of Musashi's heritage, and who finally spent ten years of his life in a small hermitage on the estate of his brother writing the *Bushū denraiki*. Though not included in my translation, Hōkin added his own biography, as well as that of his Niten Ichi-ryū predecessors. See Fukuda Masahide, *Miyamoto Musashi kenkyū dainishū*, 360–67.

## Chapter 1

1 Musashi's birthplace is contested by different Japanese historians, as well as the various records. The *Harima kagami* claims it was the village Miyamoto in the vicinity of Ikaruga, a reference to the Ikaruga *shōen*, or Ikaruga manor in Harima province. Today that village no longer exists. It disappeared from the map toward the end of the nineteenth century, when the district of Itō was merged with that of Issai to create today's district of Ibo. The name of Miyamoto lives on as a small area in the Taishi municipality (of the Ibo district, in today's province of Hyōgo).

This is contested by the *Mimasaka ryakushi*. While it confirms that Musashi was a man from the village of Miyamoto, it adds in brackets that it is referring to a village by that name in the district of Yoshino, which was situated in the most eastern part of Mimasaka, the province situated along Harima's northwestern border. This claim is supported by the *Tōsakushi*, which also originates from Mimasaka. Ignoring the fact that even Iori's monument to his father clearly states that Musashi came from Harima, the *Tōsakushi* insists that the *Kokura hibun*, as well as the *Honchō bugei shōden*, are wrong in their claims that Musashi was born in Harima. See Fujimaki Masayuki, *Tōsakushi*.

2 Shinmen Munetsura was the son of Shinmen Munesada. Following the fall of Takeyama castle, the Shinmen were dispossessed. Over the next few decades they made several attempts

to recover what they had lost, but all of their efforts proved abortive. Dispossessed and disillusioned, Munesada passed away in 1558. The care of Munetsura, who was still in his infancy, was taken over by his uncle.

By the time Munetsura came of age, the fortunes of the Shinmen were again waxing. Their first break came with the death, in 1562, of Amago Haruhisa and then, in 1566, with the fall of their Amago stronghold of Tomida castle. During the eighties and nineties, Munetsura served under Ukita Hideie (who had succeeded his father in 1582) in Toyotomi Hideyoshi's campaign to unify the country, as well as the two Korean campaigns during the nineties. See Nagatanigawa Hiroshi, *Sengokudaimyō Amago no Kenkyū*.

3 The *jitte* is a traditional weapon introduced to Japan from China during the early Muromachi Period (1333–1568). It consists of an iron rod varying from thirty centimeters to a meter in length. The *jitte* is a defensive weapon in that it is used to deflect an attack with a sword by stopping its downward thrust by means of a fork-like extension situated just above the hilt.

4 Buni's grave (long believed to have been that of Muni) lies on the grounds of the (later erected) Musashi shrine, situated among the Jigami hills, above the old family *yashiki* in Miyamoto. The date on the withered stone reads "eighteenth day of the fourth month of the eighth year of the Tenshō era [May 31, 1580]."

5 Yoshiko's family, the Bessho, had been an important clan in Hirafuku. They were a junior line of the Akamatsu and Yoshiko's father, Bessho Shigeharu, had been the master of Rikan castle. But when in 1578 he had sought to resist Oda Nobunaga's advance westward, he was defeated and dispossessed. Marrying into the Shinmen, therefore, had been Yoshiko's rescue from a life of hard work and constant need. See Nakanishi Seizō, *Miyamoto Musashi no shōgai*, 34–36; and Kaku Kōzō, *Miyamoto Musashi to iu kenkyaku*, 16-17.

6 Women in Yoshiko's time did not have the same marital rights as men. Divorce laws were different for samurai and commoners (non-samurai could simply hand their wives a short letter), but in essence a samurai had to give his consent. And while men were allowed to keep concubines, if a woman took up living with another man without being divorced, she could even be executed by her own husband. The one way for a woman to obtain a divorce against her husband's wishes was to seek refuge in a Buddhist temple. This recourse proved so popular that these temples came to be known as *kakekomidera*, or "shelter temples." See William E. Deal, *Life in Medieval and Early Modern Japan*, 345–346.

7 The *shuriken*, or "hand hidden blades," were small, sharpened blades that were thrown from a short distance. *Shuriken* came in a variety of shapes, such as steel spikes (*bōshuriken*), or flat pieces of steel with a varying number of pointed blades (*hira shuriken*). Though the throwing of these weapons, or *shuriken-jutsu*, became an art in its own right, the *shuriken* was essentially a supplementary weapon in a warrior's arsenal, intended to wound and unsettle an opponent before one came to blows.

8 Used for itinerant warriors, the concept of *musha shugyō*, or "warrior ascetic practice," derived from monks who disciplined themselves physically in order to "train the mind" (*seishin tanren*), and who were therefore also known as *shugyōsō*.

9 The outcome of these *shiai* were often deadly. The weaker parties who survived such contests often chose to submit themselves to their superiors and follow them on their travels in the hope of ultimately emulating and perhaps surpassing their teachers. It was not uncommon to encounter on the road between one village and another, master swordsmen followed by a group of acolytes. Kihei, too, seems to have been traveling in company, for the messenger sent round to notify Bennosuke speaks of him as his master. See Ozawa Masao, *Miyamoto Musashi*, 6–7.

10 A *karusan hakama* was a Japanese garment modeled after the *calção*, the balloon trousers worn by the Portuguese sailors who reached Kyushu during the middle of the sixteenth century. Unlike traditional *hakama*, the *karusan* had trouser legs that tapered toward the lower end so that they sat tight round the lower shins. They were worn by all classes, but they were particularly liked by those who spent much time on the road, especially itinerant warriors, who appreciated their wide and comfortable legs, while the narrow ends prevented one from tripping over one's own garment. See Bushiseikatsu kenkyūkai, *Bushiseikatsushi*, 44–49.

11 In 1592, in one of his increasingly frequent yet always unpredictable fits of anger, Hideyoshi sent an invading force of some 158,000 troops to the Korean Peninsula. Intended to conquer the Korean Joseon dynasty, the invasion was aborted in 1596 when China came to Korea's aid. The second invasion, which followed a brief interlude of unsuccessful negotiations, was launched in 1597, and involved some 141,000 Japanese troops. It ended with Hideyoshi's death in 1598. Some 100,000 Japanese, more than 185,000 Koreans, and 30,000 Chinese troops, as well as close to a million civilians died in the course of the conflict.

12 There was another reason why Muni would have left Munetsura's service. The succession from Ukita Naoie to his son Hideie had not gone smoothly. A number of Naoie's most senior retainers resented the rigor with which his son had established his authority. All came to a head in 1599, when a riot broke out in the Ukita fiefdom, and many of Naoie's close retainers left his son's service. A number of them entered the service of Tokugawa Ieyasu, who played an active role in resolving the issue. It is almost certain that Munetsura, too, left Hideie's service. It is therefore possible that Munetsura went on to fight under an eastern commander in the Battle of Sekigahara. That would explain why he was able to enter the service of the Kuroda shortly

after the battle. Given that his possessions were part and parcel of the Ukita fiefdom, he would have lost them anyway, regardless of which side he fought for. His fief when he entered the service of the Kuroda, by the way, was only one thousand *koku*, a fifth of what he had owned under Hideie. See Inoue Tomoshige, *O-togishū Miyamoto Musashi*, 43–37.

13 Hayashi Tarōemon was a master lancer from Shinano, who had moved to Harima and, like Muni, entered the service of the Kuroda during the early eighties. Within a few years he had climbed to the position of *ashigaru taishō*, or commander of a battalion of foot soldiers, a capacity in which he was to serve Kuroda Nagamasa in numerous battles, including the Battle of Sekigahara. In reward for his valiant services in that battle he was given a helmet by none other than Nagamasa himself. See Fukuda Masahide, *Miyamoto Musashi kenkyūron bunshū*, 112–127. For a detailed exposition of the various sources related to Musashi's whereabouts during the Battle of Sekigahara, see note 16 to the Introduction.

14 Records of the distribution of land (*bungenchō*) for the Kuroda fiefdom in Nakatsu, drawn up in the seventh year of Keichō [1602], show that Shinmen Muni served the Kuroda on a stipend of one hundred *koku*, and was placed under the command of the *ashigaru taishō* Hayashi Tarōemon, but classed as *kumihoka*. In a similar record for the ninth year of Keichō [1604] Muni is further classified as a *furugo fudai*, a long-standing hereditary vassal, which reinforces the now widely held view among Japanese scholars that Muni had been in the service of the Kuroda clan before he came to live in Nakatsu. See Fukuda Masahide, *Miyamoto Musashi kenkyūron bunshū*, 112–127.

15 This part of Musashi's given name is perhaps least understood, as it is often misread as Genshin. Cause for this confusion is the fact that Musashi's posthumous name (*okurina*) is written with the same characters as Harunobu, but pronounced accord-

ing to the *on-yomi*, or the Chinese-style reading of a character, i.e., Genshin. In Japanese tradition, however, given names (*imina*) were pronounced according to their *kun-yomi*, or the Japanese way of reading Chinese characters, i.e., Harunobu. In other words, when Musashi received his adult name from his father, it would have been pronounced as Harunobu; however, from the moment he took it on his *dharma* name (which was the same as his *okurina*), it should be read as Genshin. Interestingly, Musashi's given name was the same as that of Takeda Shingen, though the first character of the latter's given name was written with a different Chinese character. Musashi's *dharma* name, by contrast, was written with the same characters as the great warlord's *dharma* name, though this time in reverse order.

16 The Plains of Musashi were one of the scenic beauty spots of old Japan. Already in 1290 the court lady Gofukakusa Nijō (1258–1306) recorded in her diary how struck she was by the beauty of the plains, through which she passed as she returned from a pilgrimage to the Zenkō temple in Nagano in the autumn. Its vast, undulating fields of pampas grasses, she recorded, "grow so tall that even a man on horseback disappears from view," and after three days of traveling she had lost all sense of where she was. See Fukuda Hideichi, *Towazugatari*, 325–26; and Brazell, Karen, *The Confessions of Lady Nijō*, 195–96.

17 The Battle of Sekigahara (21 October, 1600) was a decisive moment in Japan's feudal history. For more than two and a half centuries Japan had been in the throws of civil strife. The period of conflict had begun way back in 1333, when Emperor Godaigo (1288–1339) sought to restore to the throne the powers it had enjoyed during Japan's early beginnings. In that conflict two parties rose to the fore, each backing its own imperial contender, who resided in different courts, one in the Muromachi district of Kyoto, and one south of the capital, among the Yoshino mountains. The conflict between the Northern and Southern

courts lasted until 1392, when both parties came to a settlement and the Ashikaga clan, the backer of the Northern court, assumed total control of the country.

For the next half century the Muromachi Bakufu (1333–1568) reigned supreme, until it fell victim to internal corruption and factionalism. As the conflict spiraled out of control the capital, once the flower of the nation, became the stage of trench warfare of unprecedented cruelty that lasted for a decade. In the wake of the so-called Ōnin War (1467–77), the wave of anarchy that had been set in motion swept the countryside until the whole of Japan was ablaze with warfare. Battles were no longer fought by government factions in the cause of national interests but by local warlords, fighting to achieve petty and shortsighted interests that only served to bolster their position amid surrounding and invariably hostile states.

The first drive to bring to an end this Warring States period (1469–1573) was set in motion by the Owari warlord Oda Nobunaga (1534–82), the first of the three great unifiers. Nobunaga was the first to crush the resistance of the powerful monasteries and the Ikko sectarians and bring back into the fold the Home Provinces, which, situated around the capital, were of such strategic importance. His successor, Toyotomi Hideyoshi (1537–98), built on those foundations by subduing the islands of Shikoku and Kyushu. It was Tokugawa Ieyasu (1543–1616), however, who reaped the fruits of their labors, when, in the Battle of Sekigahara, he crushed the predominantly western warlords, led by Ishida Mitsunari, who refused to bow to (his) central authority. See Futaki Kenichi, *Sekigahara gassen*; Kasaya Kazuhiko, *Sekigahara gassen*; and Bryant, Anthony, *Sekigahara 1600: The Final Struggle for Power*.

18 One of the chieftains to invite Shinmen Munisai for practice was the daimyo Kinoshita Nobutoshi, the master of Hiji castle, situated a few miles southward along the coast from the port

of Kitsuki. Fortunately, Nobutoshi kept a day-to-day diary during most of 1613, and from that diary, the *Keichō nikki*, it is revealed that in the spring of that year, Munisai frequently visited Hiji castle. Thus the entry for May 2 [June 19] records how, "though it had been raining since morning, Munisai came round at four o'clock." The next day, the weather improved and that evening both warriors "went out and had dinner together." The meal must have been a lavish affair, for two days later Nobutoshi is again visited by the swordsman "and was given two hats as a present." See Shudō Yoshiki, *Keichō nikki*, 231.

## Chapter 2

1 The Yoshioka-ryū had been founded by Yoshioka Naomoto, a merchant of dyed goods who had been trained in the Kyōhachi school of fencing. Naomoto, better known by his spiritual name of Kenpō, developed his own style of fencing and became the private fencing instructor to the twelfth Ashikaga shogun, Ashikaga Yoshiharu (1511–50).

The success of the Yoshioka clan reached its zenith under Kenpō's younger brother, Naomitsu, who established the Heihōsho, a martial arts school in Kyoto's Imadegawa district. Naomitsu's descendants (three of whom confusingly inherited Naomoto's spiritual name of Kenpō) continued to serve the Ashikaga house as fencing instructors, down to the fifteenth Ashikaga shogun, Ashikaga Yoshiaki (1537–97).

In 1573, the fortunes of the Yoshioka clan took a turn for the worse when Oda Nobunaga, vexed by the shogun's collusion with his arch-enemy Takeda Shingen (1521–73), sent Yoshiaki into exile. The Yoshioka clan continued to practice their school of fencing, but its close association with the Ashikaga house meant that it would never again enjoy the degree of esteem it had known under Naomitsu. See Ozawa Masao, *Miyamoto Musashi: nitō ichiryū no kaisetsu*, 21–22.

2 There is a lot of uncertainty surrounding the exact names of the Yoshioka swordsmen with whom Musashi dueled. According to the *Bukōden* and the *Bushū denraiki* Musashi dueled with three members of the Yoshioka clan who went by the names Seijurō, Denshichirō, and Matashichirō. The *Yoshioka-den*, however, mentions two men by the names of Genzaemon Naotsuna and Mataichi Naoshige. The *Koro usawa* only mentions a certain Yoshioka Kanefusa. The *Gekken sōdan* on the other hand speaks of a certain Yoshioka Kenpō, a name usually associated with the founder of the Yoshioka-ryū, Naomoto, but also used by many of his descendants. It is probably because of this uncertainty that the *Honchō bugei shōden* stays clear of calling the men by name and simply refers to them by their family name. Most historians now tentatively agree that the men's full names probably were Yoshioka Seijūrō Naotsuna and Yoshioka Denshichirō Naoshige, and that their father was Yoshioka Naokata, who in turn was the son of the school's co-founder, Yoshioka Naomitsu. See Watatani Kiyoshi, *Nihon kengō no hyakusen*, 142.

3 A *makura bokutō*, or pillow *bokutō*, is a short version of the traditional wooden practice sword that can easily be taken along in the small confinement of a palanquin. The term probably refers to keeping a short sword next to one's pillow (*makura*) during the night in case of emergency. It certainly does not imply that it used to be hidden under a pillow, as Japanese pillows at this time consisted of no more than a narrow block of wood with a thin strip of padding along the top.

4 Though most sources make mention of Sagarimatsu as the place of ambush, it remains a vexingly elusive designation as there are many places in and around Kyoto that are historically associated with the name. Today, the showdown is widely believed to have taken place near the Ichijō temple, which is situated east

of Kyoto and the spot where Musashi faced down his enemies is marked by a bronze statue. This is very likely, since the area around the temple is known as Sagarimatsu. See Ozawa Masao, *Miyamoto Musashi: nitō ichiryū no kaisetsu*, 22–23.

5 Paradoxical though it may seem today, many of the monasteries during Japan's middle ages were far more than religious centers; they were also centers of political, even military power. Indeed, many of the thousands of monasteries that adorned the Japanese landscape were more fortified strongholds than places of pious meditation. They had complex defenses manned by garrisons of battle-hardened *sōhei* or "warrior monks," usually consisting of groups of several hundred, although their ranks could easily be multiplied by the ring of an alarm bell. Within the temple grounds young monks would practice the art of combat from early dawn till late at night.

Such practice was no mere pastime but a tradition born out of necessity and pursued with a spiritual devotion that had its equal only in the warrior's pride in ancestry. The preferred weapon of the warrior monks was the *yari* (the Japanese lance) or the *naginata* (the pole sword), weapons of up to several yards in length, by which one could keep even a mounted opponent at bay. So wealthy and so well organized were the main Buddhist sects that temple complexes such as the Ishiyama near Osaka and mount Hiei near Kyoto were considered virtually impregnable, even against the most powerful of warlords.

If not already constrained by religious inhibitions, most of Japan's medieval warlords prudently chose to form alliances with, rather than antagonize the Buddhist sects. It was not until the end of the sixteenth century, when Oda Nobunaga, the first of Japan's three great unifiers, set out to destroy these bulwarks of religious resistance, before the power of the sects was finally and irrevocably broken. See Hioki Shōichi, *Nihon sōhei kenkyū*; and Adolphson, Mikael S, *The Teeth and Claws of the Buddha*.

6 Edo at the turn of the sixteenth century was the most exciting town in Japan for a swordsman. Only the previous year, Tokugawa Ieyasu founded the Edo Bakufu. A decade earlier, while governing the Kantō area on behalf of Hideyoshi, he had made Edo castle his new headquarters. Built in the middle of the fifteenth century, the castle was now too small and its facilities outdated. To accommodate the increase in personnel and official functions he launched a large-scale reconstruction. An immense force of more than a hundred thousand men was put to work to dig wide moats, flatten hills, and heave into place the huge blocks of granite from which the walls and foundations were constructed. He added a new western and a new northern wing, increasing the circumference of the main castle to a staggering ten miles. No one who entered any one of its thirty-eight gates could fail to be impressed with the wealth and power of what was also known as the Tokugawa Bakufu. See Fukai Masaumi, *Edojō*; and Hara Fumihiko, *Ushinawareta Edojō*.

7 Today only copies of the *Heidō kagami* exist, though their provenance is disputed by some Japanese historians. The copy addressed to Mizuno Katsunari consists of thirty-eight articles. Other extant copies, by contrast, only contain twenty-eight or even twenty-one articles. The one addressed to Katsunari is dated "an auspicious day" in the twelfth month of the thirteenth year of Keichō [January, 1609]. This means that Musashi had met and befriended Katsunari by the time he was twenty-five. This, in turn, provides us with a clue as to how Musashi came to serve Katsunari during the siege of Osaka castle. If indeed Katsunari had come to know Musashi in Edo and had been impressed with his skills it is easy to understand that he would have chosen him to serve as one of his son's guard during such a dangerous campaign.

Another confusing factor is the signature at the end of the document, which runs "Miyamoto Musashi no Kami Fujiwara no Yoshitsugu." Although it confirms that the swordsman had by this time already used the name Musashi, it is one of the few documents to feature the name Yoshitsugu. If correct, it is not clear from where Musashi took this name as it is not a name carried by any of his direct ancestors. See Akabane Tatsuo, *Musashi "Enmeiryū" wo Manabu*, 18–49, 202–218.

8 Over the following years Katsunari continued to serve Ieyasu, most conspicuously so in the run-up to the Battle of Sekigahara, when he distinguished himself in the sieges of the castles of Gifu and Ōgaki. His valor gained him the rank of fifth-level retainer. See Hirai Takao, *Fukuyama kaiso Mizuno Katsunari*.

9 Musashi's reluctance to be placed under Yagyū Munenori is understandable given the status of the Yagyū clan. Yagyū Tajima no Kami Munenori (1571–1646) was one of the most highly respected swordsmen in Musashi's day.

Though Munenori belonged to an ancient house of warriors, for many years the future of the Yagyū clan had been uncertain. In 1580, they lost their castle as a result of Oda Nobunaga's efforts to pacify the Home Provinces. Five years later they lost their lands during Toyotomi Hideyoshi's nationwide land survey. By then the internecine warfare in the region had forced the Yagyū to go into hiding. Only under Tokugawa Ieyasu did their fortunes recover.

That recovery began in 1594, when, impressed by a demonstration of the Yagyū Shinkage-ryū, Ieyasu hired Munenori's father, Muneyoshi (also pronounced Munetoshi), as his personal *shihan*. Carried along by Ieyasu's successes the Yagyū had rapidly recovered from their misfortunes. Munenori succeeded his father and was admitted to the league of *hatamoto*, the small group of direct retainers to the shogun, the very elite of the country. By the time Musashi was approached by the Bakufu the Yagyū fiefdom had a total revenue of ten thousand *koku*, making Munenori the first and only man in Japanese history to have risen to the rank of daimyo chiefly through his (and his father's) skill with the sword.

Munenori, then, was in many ways Musashi's opposite. Where Musashi had no ambitions for high office, Munenori personified it; and where Musashi paid little heed to his personal appearance to the point of neglect, Munenori did not shy away from the circumstance and pomp that came with high office. See Tokunaga Shinichirō, *Yagyū Munenori*.

## Chapter 3

1 Kojirō was not just any wandering swordsman. At a young age he entered the service of the powerful Asakura clan, which had its headquarters in Ichijōdani castle. The Asakura were known to be great patrons of the martial arts, especially of the Toda school of fencing, which traced its ancestry way back to the legendary fifteenth-century warrior-monk Nenami Jion and his Nen school of fencing.

Chief propagator of the Toda-ryū in Kojiro's day was the famous Toda Seigen, who had under his wing a large number of aspiring swordsmen, including his star deshi Yamazaki Rokusaemon (who was later adopted by the Toda and given the name Toda Shigemasa), and Kanemaki Jisai. It was probably under Jisai that Kojirō acquired many of the Toda techniques.

Following the destruction of the Asakura by Oda Nobunaga's forces in 1573 Kojiro embarked on a *musha shugyō* until, in 1610, in his early fifties, he became a fencing instructor to Hosokawa Tadaoki. The *Nitenki* claims that he was only eighteen when he dueled with Musashi, even though its origin, the *Bukōden*, clearly states this was the age at which he founded his Ganryū. See Kojima Hidehiro, *Sugao no kengōtachi*, 162–67.

2 The famous *mizukuruma*, or "water mill," technique employed by Kojirō evokes an image in which the swordsman boldly brandishes his sword in a large, rotating fashion, but this is not

necessarily so. Traditional Japanese water mills do not merely consist of a single wheel that scoops up the water, but of a conveyor-belt-like chain of buckets mounted at one side on an axis, and on the other side on a large wheel that is driven by one or more footmen. The action of the water mill consists of a sweeping motion in which the water is first driven along in front of the buckets through a wooden gutter after which it is scooped up as the buckets rise one by one on the large axis. In the *mizukuruma* technique, then, the sword is similarly swept close along the ground and then brought up in a large, circular motion akin to that of the rising water bucket. This is borne out by the fact that most accounts claim that Musashi's *hakama* was cut in the duel. The image that arises, then, is one in which Kojirō strikes at Musashi with his sword in two large upward motions, first toward the left and then toward the right. See Ozawa Masao, *Miyamoto Musashi*, 34–38; and Fukuda Masahide, *Miyamoto Musashi kenkyū dainishū*, 167.

3 The *migiwaki no kamae* is the last of Musashi's five *kamae*, or stances, of *chūdan*, *jōdan*, *gedan*, *hidari no waki*, and *migi no waki*, in all of which one awaits an attack in a defensive position, ready to parry and strike at any given moment. They are set out in detail in the Scroll of Water (*Mizu no maki*), the second chapter of Musashi's *Gorin no sho*. When resorting to the *migiwaki no kamae*, Musashi explains, one parries the opponent's attack at the height of the right armpit and then swiftly raises one's blade to a *jōdan* position (above the head) to bring it down in a straight curve through the center of the body. Mastering this method of parrying, Musashi notes, is essential in order to be able to understand the way of the longsword: "When you have become accustomed to the wielding of a blade in this stance, you will be able to handle even heavy blades freely." Ozawa Masao, *Miyamoto Musashi*, 34–38; and Fukuda Masahide, *Miyamoto Musashi kenkyū dainishū*, 167.

In 1603 Ieyasu had seized control and founded the Edo Bakufu (1603–1867) by having himself appointed Sei-I Tai Shogun, or Barbarian Subduing Generalissimo, and abolishing the *go-tairō*, the Council of Five Regents. The council had been called into life in 1598 by Toyotomi Hideyoshi when, from his deathbed, he sought to ensure that he would be succeeded by his son, Hideyori, who was then only five years old. Ieyasu stopped short, however, of dealing with Hideyori, as many warlords still looked up to the latter heir as their true overlord. Instead, Ieyasu sought to contain Hideyori and his allies by building and reinforcing a large number of castles throughout the Home Provinces. The largest castle in the region, however, remained Osaka castle, and it was there that Hideyori was allowed to reside and receive visiting vassals. Several attempts were made to reconcile the Toyotomi and Tokugawa clans, but with the successive deaths of their most staunch vassals the house of Toyotomi became increasingly isolated. In their isolation the Toyotomi became ever more intransigent, giving Ieyasu all the more reason to remove this obstacle to absolute power.

The friction between the two parties came to a head in 1614, when the house of Toyotomi celebrated their reconstruction of the Hōkō temple with an inscription on the temple bell that read: "May the state be peaceful and prosperous; in the east it greets the pale moon, and in the west bids farewell to the setting sun." Likening the house of Ieyasu (which had its power base in the eastern provinces) to the moon—and a pale one, at that—and the house of Toyotomi (whose supporters resided chiefly in the western provinces) to the sun, went a step too far for Ieyasu. Having furthermore been informed by his spies that Hideyori was steadily amassing troops at Osaka castle, in the winter of 1614 Ieyasu raised a force of more than one hundred and sixty thousand men and laid siege to the castle. See Kasaya Kazuhiko, *Sekigahara no gassen to Ōsaka no jin*.

2 Though neither the *Bukōden* nor the *Bushū denraiki* are clear on which side and under whom Musashi served in the summer campaign, it is now widely accepted among Japanese historians that he did so under the command of Mizuno Katsunari (1564–1651). For a detailed exposition of the various sources related to Musashi's connection to Mizuno Katsunari and his role during the siege, see note 16 to the introduction. Also see Fukuda Masahide, *Miyamoto Musashi kenkyūron bunshū*, 14–30.

3 A *mokuroku* is a written inventory of the techniques and tenets of a particular school of fencing. It is in many ways the medieval equivalent of a contemporary teaching license.

4 See Fukuyama-jō Hakubutsukan Tomo no Kai, *Mizuno Katsunari oboegaki*, 68.

5 In reward for his contribution to Ieyasu's Osaka campaigns Katsunari was initially promoted to the Kōriyama fiefdom, a fief of sixty thousand *koku* in Yamato province. Given Katsunari's huge contribution, the promotion was frowned upon by many, not least by Katsunari himself, as he had expected a fief of at least two-hundred thousand *koku*. Yet it had been precisely his reckless valor that vexed Ieyasu (who could ill afford to lose such a valuable ally), and so cost Katsunari a more lofty promotion.

Katsunari's pride was somewhat restored in 1619, when Ieyasu's son, Hidetada, promoted him to the Fukuyama fiefdom in the province of Bingo. At the time, the fief was still only worth a hundred thousand *koku* (another one thousand were added in 1626), but it did control the western part of the Inland Sea, making it—as well as Katsunari's appointment—

of strategic importance to the Bakufu. In 1622, to better police the sea, he therefore abandoned his more inland headquarters of Kannabe castle for the newly built Fukuyama castle at the mouth of the Ashida River. See Hirai Takao, *Fukuyama kaiso* [illegible]

[illegible] studied the art of swordsmanship under none other than Toda Seigen, chief propagator of the Toda-ryū, the official school of swordsmanship of the Asakura clan. Following the demise of the Asakura Kaginosuke had led the life of a *rōnin*, until he was taken in by Tōgun Sōjō, abbot of the Hiezan monastery near Kyoto. Kaginosuke continued his study of the art of swordsmanship under Sōjō, naming his school after the Hiezan monk.

7 Interestingly, the *Nihon kendō-shi*, published in 1925, also features Musashi's meeting with Miyake, followed by a duel in the garden of Musashi's dwelling, although it is not clear on where exactly Musashi was staying. The *Nihon kendō-shi* also claims that Miyake's given name is Gunbei, and not Gundayū. More importantly, Miyake is not a retainer of Honda Tadamasa, but of his son, Honda Masatomo (1599–1638), at that time the [illegible]

[illegible] was compiled some three decades after the *Bisan hōkan*, there are several reasons why it seems unlikely that Musashi should have dueled with one of Masamoto's retainers. For one, it is hard to imagine that Masamoto's retainers would have an interest—or, indeed, the liberty—to challenge Musashi if he were staying in Himeji. Himeji, after all, fell under the jurisdiction of his father, Tadamasa. They would have had even less authority to do so in Hirafuku had Musashi been staying with his stepmother. The fiefdom of Hirafuku at the time belonged to Ikeda Teruoki, one of the few members of the Ikeda clan who had been allowed to hang on to their possessions in Harima with the redistribution of lands in the wake of Ikeda Mitsumasa's demotion to the fiefdom of Tottori. See Harimagaku Kenkyūsho, *Harima*.

8 Like Honda Tadamasa, Ogasawara Tadazane was a *fūdai*, or vassal daimyo, whose role it was to guard the Bakufu against conspiracies by any of the *tozama*, or outside daimyo, those who had failed to choose the side of the house of Tokugawa in the previous conflicts. Given that much of the initial resistance against the Tokugawa had emanated from western Honshū, it was not surprising that many of the domains to the west of Akashi and Himeji were ruled by *tozama* daimyo. It was to form a buffer against these potentially hostile daimyo (and a first line of defense around Osaka and Edo castles, the centers of Bakufu power) that, before he passed away in 1616, Tokugawa Ieyasu had devised the delicate distribution of fiefdoms by which the loyal Honda and Ogasawara clans had acquired their new domains. And it was to bolster that first line of defense that, on the specific order of Ieyasu's son and successor, Hidetada, Tadamasa was ordered to take in hand the construction of Akashi castle and its environs. See Kurobe Tooru, *Akashijō wo meguru rekishi no tabi*.

9 Miyamoto Mikinosuke's grave can still be visited on the temple grounds of the Engyō temple. His grave is situated behind that of Honda Tadatoki. Immediately behind Mikinosuke's grave is that of Miyata Kakubei. As Mikinosuke's retainer, it was Kanbei's role—and honor— to serve as his *kaishaku*, the person whose role it was to behead the one committing *seppuku* and thus relieve them from the terrible pain that accompanied this ritual. Left to Mikinosuke's grave is that of Tadatoki's only other page, Iwahara Gyūnosuke. See Kawaguchi Sunao, *Miyamoto Musashi 101 nazo*, 118.

10 From the family records of the Miyamoto clan in Kokura, as well as a *munafuda* (a sign staked to a traditional building stating the building's donor, builder, and date of construction) recently uncovered from the Tomari shrine of Yoneda village, it is now clear that Iori was indeed a native of Harima, where he was born as the second son of a certain Tawara Hisamitsu, a samurai in the service of Bessho Nagaharu (1558–80), the lord of Miki castle. Hisamitsu's lord had initially supported Nobunaga's drive westward, but due to his wife's clan relations, he stubbornly refused to submit to the rule of Toyotomi Hideyoshi, at that time Nobunaga's chief general in the region. Banding up with the other Besshō chieftains he began to attack Hideyoshi's forces, even calling in the help of the powerful Mōri. His resistance proved so fierce that at one stage, Hideyoshi's army was forced to retreat, which so enraged the great general that he laid siege of Miki castle. Finally, in January 1580, having held out for a year and ten months, the members of the Bessho clan agreed to commit *seppuku* on the condition that those who had served them would be spared. Reduced to the life of a *rōnin*, Tawara Hisamitsu took up farming near Yoneda, where he had two sons, the second of whom was Iori. See Utsunomiya Yasunaga, *Miyamoto Shingen denshiryō shūsei*, 121–40; and Fukuda Masahide, *Miyamoto Musashi kenkyūron bunshū*, 205–13.

This version of events is largely confirmed by the *Harima kagami*, which claims that Iori "was born in the village of Yoneda. His father, who was called Jinbei, was formerly a samurai at Miki castle of the Bessho clan, but following the fall of the castle, he moved to the village of Yoneda, where he sired Iori." See Hirano Yōsai, *Harima kagami*, 154.

11 Aoki Jōemon originally hailed from the home province of Kawachi. The *Heihō senshi denki* describes how "when Musashi was twenty-eight or nine there was among the many followers who were granted permission to practice and teach his art

of fencing a man by the name of Aoki Jōemon. It seems that Tsuchiya Minasaemon, a retainer of Lord Naitō of the Murakami fiefdom in Echigo, has made a name for himself in teaching the art of fencing with two swords. That is to say, it is the style of fencing for which Aoki Jōemon received a license when Musashi was still young, and I have heard that its methods are different, as well as its meanings." See Fukuda Masahide, *Bushū denraiki*, 153, 278–80.

12 Though Shigemori's *yashiki* has long since been destroyed, a stone which had become Musashi's favorite place to sit while sojourning in his host's garden has survived. The stone has been moved to the precincts of the Bingo Go-kuni shrine, situated on the castle ground's northern perimeter, where it graces the temple grounds under the name of Musashi Meisō Ishi (Musashi's Meditative Stone).

13 *Uchidachi*, or "striking longsword," is used to describe the offensive role in practicing a fencing technique. The *uchidachi*, which is usually performed by the teacher, takes the initiative by making the first move, thus allowing the *shidachi*, or "receiving longsword," to respond and practice a specific technique by striking the winning blow. What Musashi is saying, then, is that in his art of fencing the opponent is never able to strike a blow, let alone a winning one.

14 Following his defeat at Musashi's hands Gonnosuke is said to have retreated to the Kamado shrine in Dazaifu, where he spent his days in meditation and the perfection of his *jō* techniques, or *jōjutsu*. Out of these evolved what is today known as the Shintō Musō school of *jōdō*. See Okada Kazuo, *Miyamoto Musashi no subete*, 174; and Ozawa Masao, *Miyamoto Musashi*, 49–50.

Oddly, the *Nitenki* claims that the duel between Musashi and Gonnosuke did not take place in Akashi but in Edo. The account, however, is much shorter and far less specific. See Fukuhara Josen, *Miyamoto Musashi no tankyū*, 172.

## Chapter 5

1 As the third son of Hosokawa Tadaoki, Tadatoshi had been bound to remain lord of Moji castle, a minor figure in the larger feudal scheme of things. But when, in the wake of the Battle of Sekigahara, his eldest brother was disinherited, it was Tadatoshi, and not his second eldest brother (who would later join Toyotomi Hideyori at Osaka castle out of resentment and die during the siege), who was chosen to succeed his father and become master of Kokura castle and the clan's fiefdom in Buzen. See Haruna Akira, *Hosokawa sandai*, 303–400.

2 Kumamoto had once been the fief of Katō Kiyomasa, whose invaluable role in Japan's unification had earned him the vast estate. When Kiyomasa died in 1611 his estate passed to his third son, Tadahiro. At an age of only ten, however, Tadahiro was utterly incapable of running such a huge domain, and it was not long before he became the object of a fierce contest between two factions of counselors, each vying for control over the young and impressionable daimyo.

For several years the dispute simmered until, in 1618, faced with appeals from both factions, the Bakufu became fully aware of the internal troubles. It relieved a number of Tadahiro's counselors from their duties, hoping that with age Tadahiro would come to grips with the remainder. But the measure failed to bring stability to the fiefdom, as Tadahiro failed to develop the kind of administrative qualities his father had possessed. Finally, on July 9, 1632, while on a visit to Edo, Tadahiro was stripped of his title and banned to the northern province of Dewa. See Fukuda Masahide, *Katō Kiyomasa 'saishi' no kenkyū*, 87–89.

3 Better known as the Kasadera Kannon, this temple is believed to have been founded in 733 by a monk named Zenkō when he carved an image of the Jūichimen Kannon, the bodhisattva with

eleven faces, from a piece of driftwood from the nearby river. A memorial stone in the temple's cemetery still commemorates Musashi's death. It was erected in 1744 by Sōda Hōsei, the fifth-generation practitioner of Musashi's Enmei-ryū in Owari. See Akabane Tatsuo, *Musashi "Enmeiryū" wo Manabu*, 128–29.

4 Sugawara no Michizane (845–903) was one of the great scholars and administrators of the Heian period (794–1189), the golden age of the Japanese imperial court. He had risen to high rank by the end of the century, but in 901 his brilliant career had come to an ignominious end when he was accused of plotting against the throne and exiled to Kyushu. Forced to leave his wife behind in the capital, the fifty-six-year-old Michizane made the long journey south well aware that his days in the sun were numbered. His only consolation was the company of his son and daughter, but not long after he had taken up his new and insignificant post as local administrator his son died. The sensitive courtier never recovered from the blow. His health failed, and in 903 he died a broken man.

Soon the diviners of his time found reasons to believe that the great scholar had not found peace in death, for in the years that followed, the capital was struck by an inexplicable chain of calamities. The first omens of Michizane's wrath manifested themselves when, one by one, the men who had conspired in his downfall died under mysterious circumstances. To appease Michizane's spirit, in 923 the then emperor, Daigo, posthumously reinstated the former minister, but the series of calamities failed to cease. In 930, the Great Audience Hall of the palace was hit by lightning. It caught fire and a number of courtiers perished in the flames, including the man who claimed to have overheard Michizane's admission of guilt. For weeks on end ferocious rainstorms continued to torment the capital until, at long last, racked by the strain of fear and guilt, the emperor himself died at the age of forty-five. After that the calamities ceased, but the reverence paid to Michizane continued.

In 905 an altar was established near his grave site, the same place that in 919 the foundations were laid for the Anraku temple. The temple was to become a place of worship for the spirit of the great and gifted scholar, who, in time, became deified as the Tenman Daijizai Tenjin, the Heaven-filling Supreme Lord and Heavenly deity, the god of learning and calligraphy. The vertical scroll carrying Musashi's calligraphy and a *bokutō* allegedly also crafted by Musashi are still kept in the Tōkōin. See Akabane Tatsuo, *Musashi "Enmeiryū" wo Manabu*, 130.

5 Another man to become a fervent practitioner of Musashi's Enmei-ryū in Owari was Hikosaka Hachibei Tadashige. Born in 1624, Tadashige was still a boy when Musashi visited Nagoya. Yet Tadashige might well have seen him in action, for when he reached his twenties, he began studying Musashi's style of fencing under Yamada Moritsugi, a student of Aoki Jōemon, who had studied directly under Musashi and his father and had gone up to Edo to open a dojo where he taught his Nitō Tetsujin school of fencing. When Tadashige's brother took a position in another fiefdom, the swordsman moved back to Owari, where, through Terao Naomasa's offices, he entered Tokugawa Yoshinao's service and continued his study under Takemura Yōemon Yorizumi, the man later sent to Nagoya by Musashi to teach his Niten Ichi school of swordsmanship. See Akabane Tatsuo, *Musashi "Enmeiryū" wo Manabu*, 106.

6 The only original source to mention this encounter is the *Bushū denraiki*. To be true to the text, the *Bushū denraiki* only speaks of Matsudaira Izumo no Kami. This has led a number of historians to believe that Musashi was the guest of Matsudaira Naomasa (1601–1666), the grandson of Tokugawa Ieyasu and the lord of Matsue castle. Matsue castle, after all, is located in what once was the province of Izumo, leading them to assume

that the honorific title of "Izumo no Kami" must have referred to its master, Matsudaira Naomasa. This, however, is to ignore the fact that it was Matsudaira Katsutaka (1589–1666) who bore the title of Izumo no Kami, and not Naomasa (whose honorific title was Dewa no Kami). Katsutaka's clan, moreover, was related to the Ogasawara (Tadazane's fourth son was adopted by Katsutaka's eldest brother), and it is very plausible that he and Musashi met at Akashi or Kokura castle.

Another strong indication that the event was not staged at Matsue but at Matsuyama is the fact that the same record states that Musashi "stayed at the house of Lord Matsudaira Izumo no Kami," (*Matsudaira Izumo no Kami no ie ni ari*), rather than at his castle, which would logically have been the case had he been the guest of Lord Naomasa, the master of Matsue castle. If, therefore, Musashi's host was Katsutaka and not Naomasa, the duel would have been held somewhere in the vicinity of Matsuyama castle, where Katsutaka would have stayed in an official accommodation, rather than the castle itself. See Fukuda Masahide, *Bushū denraiki*, 198–99.

7 Only when we closely read Musashi's own explanation of the two techniques by which he parried and defeated Katsutaka can we truly understand what went on in that library room of Matsuyama castle. The two techniques of *nebari o kakuru* (applying glue) are both described in the Scroll of Water (*Mizu no maki*) of the *Gorin no sho*. "When the opponent parries your attack with a *tachi*," Musashi writes, "keep your sword firmly against his, as if they had been glued together." The term "gluing," is meant "to convey the intent of keeping the swords together and that you should not go in with too much force. When one parries an opponent's sword in this way it does not matter how gently it is done." Musashi goes on to point out that "gluing" should not be confused with getting entangled with one's opponent. "Gluing is strong, but getting entangled is weak. It is

necessary to distinguish between the two." *Sekka no atari*, by contrast, is a technique in which one "strikes the opponent's sword the moment when one's own sword and that of one's opponent are about to touch without even slightly raising one's sword." In this technique, "it is important to strike quickly, while observing three points: a firm stance, a firm posture, and a firm grip." See. Kamiko Tadashi, *Gorin no sho*, 104, 112–113.

8 Takagi Umanosuke Shigesada was a retainer of Mōri Nagatsugu (1610–98). Umanosuke had studied the Takenouchi-ryū, one of the oldest schools of *jūjutsu* found in Japan. Building on what he had learned and combining it with his own experience in Nagatsugu's service, Umanosuke founded his own school called the Takagi-ryū. See Fukuda Masahide, *Bushū denraiki*, 228–30.

9 Takada Matabei Yoshitsugu (1590–1671) hailed from the province of Iga. At a very young age he had become adept with the *yari*, studying the art of fighting under none other than Hōzōin Kakuzenbō In'ei (1521–1607), the famous abbot of the Kōfuku temple and founder of the Hōzōin school of spear fighting. Yoshitsugu had entered the service of Ogasawara Tadazane while the latter was still lord of Akashi castle in Harima. Like Musashi he had moved down with his lord to Kyushu and participated in the siege of Hara castle during the Shimabara Rebellion. See Fukuda Masahide, *Bushū denraiki*, 282–84.

10 The *chūdan*, or middle position is the first of Musashi's five *kamae*, defensive stances set out in detail in the Scroll of Water (*Mizu no maki*), the second chapter of Musashi's *Gorin no sho*. "In the *chūdan no kamae*", Musashi explains, "one points the tip of one's *tachi* to his face. When the enemy strikes, deflect his longsword to the right and press on." It seems that this is exactly what Musashi did with Yoshitsugu's *yari*, causing it to hit his right leg. Kamiko Tadashi, *Gorin no sho*, 90–91.

11 The *Bushū denraiki* is one of the few records to make any mention of Musashi's relation with women and the only one to men-

tion the birth of a child. There are, however, good reasons why so few should mention this tragic episode. One reason, admittedly, is suggested by Hōkin himself, when he asserts that Musashi never again mentioned this deeply painful event to anyone. See Fukuda Masahide, *Bushū denraiki*, 255–57.

Another reason for the reticence of the chroniclers might be found in the kind of liaison that produced the child. Hōkin describes the woman as an *omoimono*, a word that can mean either a loved one or a prostitute, but there are strong reasons to suspect that the woman who was the object of Musashi's affections belonged to the latter group. Indeed, she may have been an inhabitant of the Yoshiwara pleasure quarters in Edo, a place Musashi might have visited when he accompanied Lord Tadazane on a visit to the capital.

While it was quite normal in Musashi's day for men to frequent the pleasure quarters of Edo and the like, any child that was the product of such relationships was an embarrassment. It is only to Musashi's credit that he deeply loved the child. Yet it is also understandable that if Musashi's other early biographers were even aware of the liaison and its product they balked at committing it to paper. All of them, after all, were his disciples by descent and their chief aim was to extol the virtues of the master, rather that expose his weaknesses, however human.

It is not surprising, then, that the only other source to make mention of such a liaison is Shoji Kasutomi's *Dōbō goen*. Writing his work in 1720, seven years before Hōkin was to complete his own, Katsutomi cannot have had any knowledge of the *Bushū denraiki*, nor is it, given the geographical divide, likely that Hōkin had read the *Dōbō goen*. We cannot even be sure whether Kumoi was the mother of the unfortunate child or just one of Musashi's mistresses. See Kaku Kōzō, *Miyamoto Musashi to iu kenkyaku*, 181–183.

12 Ogasawara Nagatsugu (1615–66) was the eldest son of Tadazane's brother, Ogasawara Tadanaga (1594–1615). Tadanaga, in turn, was the eldest son of Ogasawara Hidemasa (1569–1615). Both Hidemasa and Tadanaga had fallen during the fierce fighting at Tennōji during the summer campaign against Osaka castle. Given that Tadanaga was Hidemasa's eldest son, Nagatsugu would normally have succeeded his (dead) father as clan leader. However, as Nagatsunu was born weeks after his father's death, the leadership had gone to Nagatsugu's uncle, Tadazane, who was Hidemasa's second son.

13 The Shimabara rebellion, so called after the peninsula on which it took place, was the last serious military conflict to upset the centrally imposed order of the Edo Bakufu. Chief source of the rebellion was the harsh regime of the local daimyo, Matsukura Katsuie (1598–1638), who imposed such heavy taxes on the already severely impoverished populace that many simply starved. See Shimura Kunihiro, *Shimabara gassenki*.

14 Musashi's letter to Arima Naozumi is reproduced in Matsunobu Ichiji, *Miyamoto Musashi zensho*, 286.

15 It is not clear what affliction Musashi suffered from. Yet given the symptoms it was most likely dyspagia, which affects the foodpipe and can be caused by cancer. This would explain why Musashi was unable to verbally respond to Iwama Rokubei Masanari (see chapter 6). It is also supported by the *Bushū denraiki*, which states that Musashi was taken ill with esophageal cancer (*ekkaku*), or cancer of the foodpipe, before he found the time to write out a fair copy of his *Gorin no sho*.

16 *Shimono* and *torikago* are both components of the so called *hoshu jutsu*, a compendium of seizing, holding, and binding techniques employed to arrest culprits or deal with those who were captured alive during siege warfare. As such they helped to form the foundation of the modern day martial art of *jūjutsu*. See Hottashi Giken, *Karate jutsu, jūjutsu, hoshu jutsu*.

17 The *jōdan no kamae* is the second of Musashi's five *kamae* defensive stances set out in detail in the Scroll of Water (*Mizu no maki*), the second chapter of Musashi's *Gorin no sho*. "In the *jōdan no kamae*," Musashi explains, "one holds the *tachi* over one's head and strikes the opponent the moment he is about to strike." Kamiko Tadashi, *Gorin no sho*, 91–02.

The *ryūsui no uchi*, or the "flowing water blow," is also featured in the Scroll of Water. "When the opponent retreats quickly, dodges quickly, and quickly parries your *tachi*, make yourself big, both physically and mentally, draw your sword way back behind your body and strike a large and strong blow, but slowly, almost as if there were a stagnation in its motion, like one might observe in the rush of a river, which tends to flow slower—but with much more force—as it reaches deeper parts." Kamiko Tadashi, *Gorin no sho*, 102.

18 Yagyū Munenori was the son of Yagyū Muneyoshi, once the lord of Yagyū castle, in the northeastern part of Yamato province. Muneyoshi was one of the greatest swordsmen of the sixteenth century and became Tokugawa Ieyasu's fencing instructor in 1594 after he had lost his castle and territories in Toyotomi Hideyoshi's land reforms. Both father and son were renowned practitioners of the Yagyū Shinkage school of fencing, a blend of their own Yagyū traditions and the Shinkage school developed by the great Kamiizumi Nobutsuna, who stayed at Yagyū castle during the late 1560s. See Tokunaga Shinichirō, *Yagyū Munenori*.

## Chapter 6

1 Sakazaki Naizen was a descendant of the Okada, a clan distantly related to the *Bukōden*'s author. The Okada hailed from the province of Owari where they had served Oda Nobunaga's father, Oda Nobuhide (1510–51). They had served a string of

masters until, probably sometime after the turn of the seventeenth century, they entered the service of the Hosokawa. It was not long after that Naizen was adopted by Sakazaki Kiyosaemon, who by then had risen to the position of Junior Head of Pages on a stipend of close to two thousand *koku*. By the time Musashi wrote his letter, Naizen had succeeded his adoptive father as Junior Head of Pages on a stipend of one thousand *koku*.

2 Rokubei Masanari was the eldest son of Takeda Yoshinobu, a descendant of the great Takeda Shingen (1521–73), famous through his epic battles at Kawanakajima with his arch-rival Uesugi Kenshin. At the turn of the sixteenth century Masanari entered the service of Ogasawara Hidemasa (1569–1615), the father of Musashi's current host, Tadazane. In 1609, however, he had entered the service of Tadatoshi's father, when he accompanied Hidemasa's second daughter, Hosokawa Chiyohime (1597–1649), upon her marriage into the Hosokawa clan—an important and sensitive appointment, only granted to retainers who enjoyed their master's absolute trust.

3 Musashi's letter to Sakazaki Naizen is quoted in full in Toyoda Masanaga's *Bukōden*. See De Lange, William, *The Real Musashi: The Bukōden*, 32–33. The letter is also reproduced in Tominaga Kengo, *Shijitsu Miyamoto Musashi*, 109; and in Nakanishi Seizō, Miyamoto *Musashi no shōgai*, 209–210.

4 It is not clear why the place was called Chiba castle, as the former castle, too, was know by the name of Kumamoto, albeit written with different characters. Today, the area is still known as the Chiba castle district, or Chibajō *machi*, although it is now situated outside the castle grounds. See Nishigaya Yasuhiro, *Kumamotojō*, 26–29.

5 Given that the edict takes effect retroactively (it is signed August 27, issued on August 28, but takes effect on August 21), it is clear that Hosokawa Tadatoshi was keen that Musashi should receive his stipend from the moment he arrived, and not from

the date the edict was issued. Hence, it is almost certain that Musashi arrived in Kumamoto on August 21, 1640. It is also clear that Tadatoshi already anticipated that Musashi would remain in Kumamoto until his death, as the edict dictates that Musashi should receive his stipend in perpetuity. See Inoue Tomoshige, *O-togishū Miyamoto Musashi*, 154–65.

6 Yoriyuki was in fact Hosokawa Tadaoki's sixth son. His mother was one of Tadaoki's concubines and the eldest daughter of Naoshita Shichinosuke, one of Tadaoki's retainers. Yoriyuki had been adopted by Nagaoka Okinaga.

7 A banner (*hatasashi* or *sashimono*) here is the Japanese equivalent of the European medieval heraldic banner. Medieval Japanese banners were narrow vertical flags that identified the chieftain under whom soldiers were fighting by their family crest (*kamon*) or the clan's battle slogan.

*Sashimono* could be worn by foot soldiers (*ashigaru*), who attached the bamboo pole to which the banners were fastened to their backs. They could also be carried by mounted warriors, in which case the bamboo pole was inserted into a special holder attached to the saddle.

8 The Shinchō district was and still is situated just south of Kumamoto castle, not far from the old site of Chiba castle where Musashi resided.

9 Shocking though it may seem today, this episode is a typical example of the harsh medieval Japanese tradition of *burei-uchi*, the killing of someone for reasons of insolence. Together with the custom of *teki-uchi*, the killing of someone for reasons of revenge, and *megataki-uchi*, the killing of an unfaithful wife and her lover, *burei-uchi* had become part of the standard repertoire by which samurai were expected to uphold their own reputation and that of their lord.

In Musashi's day, these various forms of severe reprisal were accepted by the Bakufu as legitimate ways to retore one's honor, a value prized higher than any other in medieval Japan. Toward the end of the Tokugawa era, however, they came to be considered as overly harsh and could no longer be resorted to at will. See Eiko Ikegami, *The Taming of the Samurai*, 244–245.

10 The unrelenting spite with which Aoki Jōemon is rebuked by Musashi may be partly attributable to the bias of the author of the *Bushū denraiki* himself. Jōemon's Nitō Tetsujin-ryū, after all, represented an altogether different line of Musashi's school of fencing than the one Tanji Hōkin was trying to preserve. See Fukuda Masahide, *Bushū denraiki*, 153, 278–80.

Jōemon had established himself in Edo where he founded a school called Nitō Tetsujin-ryū. It is, in this respect, interesting to see what Niwa Nobuhide, the author of the *Heihō senshi denki* has to say on the matter. In his work Nobuhide describes how "when Musashi was twenty-eight or nine there was among the many followers who were granted permission to practice and teach his art of fencing a man by the name of Aoki Jōemon. It seems that Tsuchiya Minasaemon, a retainer of Lord Murakami Naitō of Echigo, has made a name for himself in teaching the art of fencing with two swords. That is to say, it is the style of fencing for which Aoki Jōemon received a license when Musashi was still young, and I have heard that its methods are different, as well as its meanings."

As the founder of his own particular line of Musashi's heritage, it was natural for Nobuhide to be critical of any contenders, yet his criticism of Aoku Jōemon is more balanced than that of Hōkin, albeit somewhat lacking in detail.

11 *Katsu* and *totsu* are onomatopoeia that derive from Sanskrit and introduced to Japan by practitioners of Zen Buddhism, who used the terms to communicate states of mind that cannot be expressed in speech. In the martial arts the words are used to invoke a cadence, very much like the effect of clash and echo among the mountains.

Describing the *katsu-totsu* technique in the Scroll of Water of the *Gorin no sho*, Musashi explains that "both *katsu* and *totsu* are used when attacking and pinning down an enemy or when an enemy seeks to return a blow, in which case you raise your sword as to stab him from below but strike him from above with a return strike." The term *katsu-totsu* describes the quick, cadence-like, succession in which the two moves are executed, "*katsu* as one raises one's sword to stab, *totsu* as one strikes down."

12 Shimizu Hōki (1573–1649) was not just any swordsman. He was a famous warrior in the island of Kyushu. He had won fame during the second Korean campaign, when he fought under the great Katō Kiyomasa. In 1602 he entered the service of Hosokawa Tadaoki on a stipend of two thousand *koku*. By the time Musashi came to Higo, Hōki had climbed to the lofty position of senior scribe on a stipend of close to five thousand *koku*. It seems that Hōki was a keen practitioner of the Yagyū Shinkage-ryū, which may account for Musashi's snub.

13 Akiyama Gentei Wanao (1618–73), was the second abbot of the Taishō temple, built in 1637 to serve as the Hosokawa family temple in Kumamoto.

14 Musashi's poem on love is quoted in Kaku Kōzō, *Miyamoto Musashi to iu kenkyaku*, 181. Also see note 11 to chapter 5.

## Chapter 7

1 Today, the most widely known version of this treatise consists of thirty-five articles, consequently by the title *Heihō sanjū-go kajō*). To make matters more confusing, there is also a version comprising forty-two articles (*the Heihō shijū-ni kajō*). It is not clear whether clauses were deleted or added by Musashi's followers. The fact remains that the *Bukōden* clearly states that Musashi wrote a treatise consisting of thirty-nine articles.

The *Nitenki*, by contrast, refers to thirty-five articles, but this might simply be due to the fact that its author was only familiar with a version comprising that number. In the absence of any evidence to the contrary, we have to assume that the *Bukōden* is correct, especially because it mentions that, on June 6, 1645, while on his deathbed, Musashi handed "the thirty-nine articles" over to his deshi Terao Motomenosuke Nobuyuki, and not thirty-five. The full text of the *Heihō sanjū-go kajō* is reproduced in Matsunobu Ichiji, *Miyamoto Musashi zensho*, 278–85. For a full English translation see Kenji Tokitsu, *Miyamoto Musashi*, 199–216.

2 This is the text [translated by the author] of the eighth injunction from the *Heihō sanjū-go kajō*, entitled *Kokoromochi no koto* ("Concerning One's State of Mind"). See Matsunobu Ichiji, *Miyamoto Musashi zensho*, 279–80.

3 Musashi's letter to Lord Hosokawa Mitsunao is not dated or signed, and is therefore ignored by some scholars. The document however, is certainly from the period, is certainly in Musashi's hand, and given its content, can only be related to Musashi. And while it does not carry an addressee, a space is left open in the letter's opening line where one would expect to see the name of the person who had requested that Musashi put his ideas into writing. Called an *ketsuji*, or "missing character," in Japanese, these deliberate omissions were used as a sign of respect for emperors or people of high nobility. This means that, if indeed written by Musashi, the letter can only have been addressed to Hosokawa Mitsunao, the daimyo of the Kumamoto fiefdom. See Inoue Tomoshige, *O-togishū Miyamoto Musashi*, 168–69.

4 The cave on Mount Iwato which Musashi visited to write his magnum opus is now known as the Reigandō, or Reigan Cave. The Reigan Cave was already a place of pilgrimage in Musashi's day, for the cave is situated on the grounds of the

Unganzenji, a temple belonging to the Sōtō sect. The temple is believed to have been built during the Northern and Southern Courts period (1334–1392) by the Chinese monk Dong Ling Yong Yu (Tōryō Eiyo), who visited Japan on the invitation of Ashikaga (1306–1352). The name Reigan, incidentally, is comprised of the two characters of *rei* (spirit) and *gan*, the first character of Ganryūjima, the island on which Musashi fought his most famous duel with Sasaki Kojirō. See Nakanishi Seizō, *Miyamoto Musashi no shōgai*, 258–59.

5 Musashi's letter to Terao Naomasa is reproduced in full in Akabane Tatsuo, *Musashi "Enmeiryū" wo Manabu*, 105–106.

6 The Japanese *gorintō* (*stūpa*) or "five-ringed tower" traces its origins to the Indian *pâli*, a sacred tumulus or burial mount containing a relic of Buddha or a saint. Introduced to Japan during the Heian period (794–1185), the development of the Japanese *stupa* soon fell under the influence of indigenous sects, in particular the "secret teachings" (*mikkyō*) of the Shingon Buddhist school promoted by Kūkai (774–835) and Kakuban (1095–1143).

The *gorintō* is assembled of five differently shaped stone segments, each placed on top of each other and each carrying a deeply symbolic meaning: the square foundation stone at the base represents the four elements; the hemispherical dome represents the attainment of wisdom; the conical spire represents transition to enlightenment; the crescent moon represents one's receptivity to the teachings of heaven; and the circular disc at the pinnacle represents perfection through the fusion of wisdom and principles, and thereby Buddhahood.

On another symbolic level, the five segments represent the different stages in a student's spiritual progress: the will to perfection in the square base; the attainment of equanimity in the hemispherical dome; the pursuit of truth in the conical spire; the development of awareness and intuition in the crescent moon; and finally, perfection in the circular disc.

Significantly, here the five segments also represent the five elements of earth, water, fire, wind, and heaven.

The five-storied architecture can also be found in the *gojūtō*, the five-storied towers of Buddhist temples such as the Hōryūji and Kōfukuji, as well as the stone lanterns found in Japanese and Chinese gardens, and is still widely used for memorial monuments and tombs.

7 Sawamura Daigakunosuke Yoshishige (1560–1650) was a longstanding Hosokawa retainer, who had joined the clan in 1582. Twenty four years Musashi's senior, he was already eighty five when he visited Musashi at his deathbed. A native of Wakasa, Yoshishige had a military record at least as impressive as that of his friend. At the time of Musashi's birth he had already fought several battles, claiming the head of an enemy general, a feat for which he received a reward from Toyotomi Hideyoshi in person. He was also the adoptive father of Sawamura Usaemon Tomoyoshi (1605–65), Musashi's senior deshi who had been present at the banquet under the cherry trees.

8 Musashi's letter to Nagaoka Yoriyuki is quoted in Tominaga Kengo, *Shijitsu Miyamoto Musashi*, 131.

9 Musashi's *Dokkōdō* should be seen in the light of the custom in his day for clan leaders to leave a list of injunctions for posterity, the so-called *kakun*, to be handed down from generation to generation. Some of the most famous lines in this vein are from the hand of Hōjō Shigetoki (1198–1261), who left a long list of instructions to his son, Nagatoki (who had just been appointed to the important office of the shogun's deputy at Kyoto), exhorting him to "use the same kind of language and give the same kind of treatment to all, so you may get the best out of the worst." A somewhat different approach was taken by the pragmatic Asakura Takakage (1493–1548), who advised his successors not to "appoint people without ability to lands or posts simply because they have

served the Asakura for generations." Most famous among all these writings are Tokugawa Ieyasu's *Teachings on the Conduct of Life*, in which he reminds his subjects that "a man's life is like a long journey with a heavy burden," so that one "need not hurry," for "patience is the foundation of eternal peace."

Two versions of Musashi's last work are still in existence, one consisting of nineteen, the other twenty-one injunctions. Both carry the title of *Dokkōdō*, or *The Way to be Followed Alone*. Though both versions carry Musashi's signature it is almost certain that at least one was drafted by one of his followers. Though there is no conclusive evidence as to which of the two might be genuine, it is widely assumed Musashi wrote twenty-one injunctions and therefore the longer version is probably genuine. See Matsunobu Ichiji, *Miyamoto Musashi zensho*, 290; and Fukuda Masahide, *Miyamoto Musashi kenkyūron bunshū*, 196.

10 Contrary to widespread belief, Musashi's funeral service was not conducted by Akiyama Gentei Wanao, but by Ōshō Genkō Wanao (1588–1653). This much is borne out by the correspondence between Musashi's son, Iori, and his counterpart in Higo, Nagaoka Kenmotsu, in the wake of Musashi's death (see below). The reason for this misconception is that the *Bukōden* states that Musashi's coffin "was brought to the Maesugi horse grounds, where Akiyama Wanao performed the last rites." Given that Ōshō Genkō was the chief abbot of the Taishō temple at the time, the main service would have been conducted by him. See Inoue Tomoshige, *O-togishū Miyamoto Musashi*, 1184–85.

11 Nagaoka Okinaga remained in the service of the Hosokawa for the rest of his life. On Hosokawa Tadaoki's death in 1646, Okinaga inherited Yatsushiro castle. He remained master of Yatsushiro castle, and ended up serving four successive Hosokawa leaders. Upon his death on July 24, 1661, his son, Yoriyuki, inherited Yatsushiro castle and served the Hosokawa like his father until his death in 1666. Both Okinaga and Yoriyuki outlived their

lord, Mitsunao, who died in 1650, only thirty-one years old. They continued to serve Mitsunao's son, Tsunatoshi, who remained daimyo of the Kumamoto fiefdom until 1712. See Inoue Tomoshige, *O-togishū Miyamoto Musashi*, 256.

12 Today the village of Oe and the district of Akita have been swallowed up by Kumamoto's suburbs, while the district of Akita was abolished as a result of land reforms during the Meiji era. In Musashi's day, however, the village of Oe was situated on the eastern banks of the Shira River, roughly a mile or so northeast of Kumamoto castle. Spelled with a different initial character, this part of Kumamoto is now called Ōe.

13 Born as Komeda Yoshichirō, Kenmotsu (1586–1658) was the eldest son of Komeda Koremasa, a retainer in the service of Hosokawa Tadaoki. In 1607, following a dispute with a senior retainer, Kenmotsu left the service of the Hosokawa and subsequently joined the ranks of Toyotomi Hideyori's troops during the siege of Osaka castle. In 1623 he returned to Kumamoto and reentered Tadatoshi's service on a stipend of two thousand *koku*, upon which he received the name Nagaoka Kenmotsu. Over the following years Kenmotsu steadily climbed in rank until, in 1634, he reached the position of senior retainer with a total fief of ten thousand *koku*.

14 Four days after Iori's letter of June 21, Kenmotsu acknowledged he had received Iori's letter, writing: "As you say, during Musashi's recent illness, Lord Mitsunao appointed Terao Motomenosuke to take care of Musashi, yet in the end he regrettably passed away. You said various kind things about our care for Musashi during his illness and the funeral service after he passed away, and I would like to thank you for your generous letter. I will certainly write to you again in the near future."

Iori's next and last extant letter to Kenmotsu is dated July 22, 1645. In it he acknowledges receipt of Kenmotsu's reply and reiterates "my sincere gratitude for Lord Mitusnao appointing Terao Motomenosuke to attend on Miyamoto Musashi during his illness, as well as the blessing of having the funeral and memorial service conducted at the Taishō temple by Ōshō [Genkō] Wanao in the wake of his death, down to your directions regarding his grave. For this reason I have, through the office of Iwama Rokubei [Masanari] in Edo, expressed my gratitude in a letter to Lord Mitsunao. I hope you will excuse me for saying so, but please feel free to do whatever is required in this respect. Again, so as not to limit myself to written tokens of appreciation, I hereby send you a box of walnuts, as well as a box with two hundred bonito."

Kenmotsu's reply, dated July, 27, 1645, reads: "I read the letter you entrusted into the messenger's care. I passed on to Lord Mitsunao the kind words you wrote concerning his appointment of Terao Motomenosuke during master Musashi's illness, as well as the various arrangements he made in the wake of Musashi's death. I would also like to thank you for the box of walnuts and the box with bonito you cared to send us over such a long distance." See Inoue Tomoshige, *O-togishū Miyamoto Musashi*, 171–80.

15 Still called Musashizuka, or the Musashi burial mound, it is today located in Yuge, in the Ryūta township in Kumamoto's Kita (northern) ward. Situated on the beautiful grounds of Musashizuka Park, it is widely recognized to be Musashi's grave site. According to the *Heihō senshi denki*, however, Musashi's remains were (at some stage) recovered from his grave in Higo and transferred to Kokura "on the request of Ogasawara Tadazane, who thought it more fitting that Musashi be buried in Kokura, near the rest of his descendants."

If Musashi's remains were indeed transferred to Kokura, it is most likely that this was done by his son, Iori, when, in 1654, on the ninth anniversary of his father's death, he erected a monument on the crest of Temukeyama, a small hill on the outskirts of Akazaka. It might have been at that juncture that Iori had Musashi's tombstone in Kumamoto transferred to what was then still the separate village of Yuge, on the opposite bank of the Shira river from Oe, some five miles upstream. Yuge was situated along the Ōzu Kaidō, the old highroad that connected Kumamoto to the rest of Japan.

## The *Kokura Hibun*

1 Oddly, by stating that both swordsmen "met at the same time," Wanao seems to suggest that both swordsmen arrived at Funashima Island at the same moment. Both the *Bukōden* and the *Bushū denraiki* claim that the men arrived at different times, although they fail to agree on who arrived first.

2 It is remarkable, too, that Wanao has nothing to say about his hero's activities at the time of the Battle of Sekigahara and the siege of Osaka castle, fourteen years later. It is perhaps due to his limited knowledge of Musashi's early life that the abbot chooses to remain silent on the issue.

# BIBLIOGRAPHY

## Works in English

Adolphson, Mikael S. *The Gates of Power*. Honolulu, 2000.

—. *The Teeth and Claws of the Buddha*. Honolulu, 2007.

Bryant, Anthony. *Sekigahara 1600: The Final Struggle for Power*. Oxford, 1995.

Carroll, John. *Lightning in the Void*. New York, 2006.

Cleary, Thomas. *Code of the Samurai*. Tokyo, 1999.

Deal, William E. *Life in Medieval and Early Modern Japan*. Oxford, 2006

De Lange, William. *Famous Japanese Swordsmen*, Vols. 1–3. Warren, CT, 2008.

—. *The Real Musashi: Origins of a Legend, The Bukōden*. Warren, CT, 2011.

—. *The Real Musashi: Origins of a Legend, The Bushudenraiki*. Warren, CT, 2010.

Dening, Walter. *Japan in Days of Yore*. London, 1976.

Dunn, Charles J. *Every Day Life in Traditional Japan*. Boston, 1969.

Friday, Karl F. *Hired Swords*. Stanford, 1992.

—. *Legacies of the Sword*. Honolulu, 1997.

Hiroaki Satō. *Legends of the Samurai*. New York, 1995.

Ikagami Eiko. *The Taming of the Samurai: Honorific Individualism and the Making of Modern Japan*. Harvard, 1997.
Nitobe, Inazo. *Bushidō, the Soul of Japan*. Boston, 2012.
Jansen, Marius. *Warrior Rule in Japan*. Cambridge, 2008.
Kaufman, Stephen F. *Musashi's Book of Five Rings*. New York, 2004.
Miyamoto Musashi. *The Book of Five Rings*. Translated by Bradford J. Brown. Toronto, 1982.
Miyamoto Musashi. *The Book of Five Rings*. Translated by William Scott Wilson. Tokyo. 2002.
Miyamoto Musashi. *The Book of Five Rings*. Translated by D.E. Tarver. Lincoln, NE, 2002.
Miyamoto Musashi. *The Book of Five Rings*. Translated by Thomas Cleary. Boston, 2000.
Turnbull, S.R. *The Samurai*. New York, 1977.
Sansom, George. *A History of Japan*. Vols 1–3. Tokyo, 1963.
Sato Hiroaki. *Legends of the Samurai*. New York, 1995.
—. *The Sword and the Mind*. New York, 1985.
Sōhō Takuan. *The Unfettered Mind*. Translated by William Scott Wilson. Tokyo, 1986.
Stone, Justin F. *Bushido*. New York, 2001.
Sugawara Makoto. *Lives of Master Swordsmen*. Tokyo, 1982.
Tokitsu Kenji. *Miyamoto Musashi: His Life and Writings*. Boston, 2005.
Turnbull. S.R. *The Samurai*. New York, 1977.
—. *War in Japan 1467–1615*. Oxford, 2002.
—. *Warriors of Medieval Japan*. New York, 2005.
—. *Warriors of Japan*. Honolulu, 1994.
Vaporis, Constantine Nomikos. *Tour of Duty: Military Service in Edo, and the Culture of Early Modern Japan*. Honolulu, 2008.
Varley, Paul. *Warriors of Japan*. Honolulu, 1994.
Wilson, William Scott. *Ideals of the Samurai*. Burbank, CA, 1982.
—. *The Lone Samurai*. Tokyo, 2004.
Yamamoto Tsunetomo. *Hagakure*. Translated by William Scott Wilson. Tokyo, 1979.
Yoshikawa Eiji. *Musashi*. Tokyo, 1995.

## Works in Japanese

Abe Takeshi. *Sengoku jinmei jiten*. Tokyo, 1990.
Akabane Tatsuo. *Musashi "Enmei-ryū" wo Manabu*. Tokyo, 2010.
—. *Musashi to Yagyū Shinkage-ryū*. Tokyo, 2012.
Aramaki Nitōsai. *Nitō-ryū no naraikata*. Tokyo, 1994.
Dōmon Fuyuji. *Miyamoto Musashi no jinseikun*. Tokyo, 1993.
—. *Miyamoto Musashi*. Tokyo, 2002.
—. *Musashi heihō kakumei no ikikata*. Tokyo, 2002.
—. *Musashi no michi*. Tokyo, 2003.
Domoto Akihiko. *Kendō kojutsu-shi*. Tokyo, 1988.
Ezaki Junpei. *Nihon kengō retsuden*. Tokyo, 1970.
—. *Yagyū Munenori*. Tokyo, 1971.
Fujimaki Masayuki and Masaki Teruō. *Tōsakushi*. Tokyo, 1973.
Fukuda Akira. *Chūsei katarimono bungei*. Tokyo, 1981.
Fukuda Hideichi. *Towazugatari*. Tokyo, 1978.
Fukuda Masahide. *Miyamoto Musashi kenkyū dainishū*. Tokyo, 2005.
—. *Miyamoto Musashi kenkyūron bunshū*. Tokyo, 2003.
—. *Katō Kiyomasa 'saishi' no kenkyū*. Tokyo, 2012.
Fukuhara Josen. *Miyamoto Iori no gisho*. Okayama, 1984.
—. *Miyamoto Musashi seitanchi no kakushō*. Tokyo, 1969.
—. *Miyamoto Musashi shashinshū*. Tokyo, 1970.
—. *Miyamoto Musashi no kenkyū*. Tokyo, 1973.
—. *Miyamoto Musashi no tankyū*. Okayama, 1978.
—. *Miyamoto Musashi tanjōchi no kakushō*. Tokyo, 1969.
—. *Ōhara no shiseki to densetsu, Miyamoto*. Tokyo, 1970.
Funabashi Takeshi. *Nagoya no Miyamoto Musashi*. Tokyo, 2004.
Futaki Kenichi. *Gassen no butaiura*. Tokyo, 1976.
—. *Sekigahara gassen*. Tokyo, 1982.
Hagiwara Hiroo. *Miyamoto Musashi kensei no himitsu*. Tokyo, 1084.
Harada Mukashi. *Shinsetsu Miyamoto Musashi*. Tokyo, 1984.
Harimagaku Kenkyūsho. *Harima*. Tokyo, 2013.
Haruna Akirai. *Hosokawa sandai*. Tokyo, 2010.
Hasegawa Shin. *Nihon adauchi isō*. Tokyo, 1974.

Hayashiya Tatsusaburō. *Chūsei geinoshi no kenkyū*. Tokyo, 1960.
Hinatsu Shigetaka. *Honchō bugei shōden*. Tokyo, 2003.
Hioki Shōichi. *Nihon sōhei kenkyū*. Tokyo, 1972.
Hirai Takao. *Fukuyama kaiso Mizuno Katsunari*. Tokyo, 1992.
Hirotani Yūtarō. *Nihon kendō shiryō*. Tokyo, 1943.
Hottashi Giken. *Karate jutsu, jūjutsu, hoshu jutsu*. Tokyo, 1957.
Ichikawa Kakuji. *Miyamoto Musashi: Niten Ichi-ryū no ken to Gorin no Sho*. Tokyo, 1985.
—. *Miyamoto Musashi: Niten Ichi-ryū no sekai*. Tokyo, 1984.
Imai Masayuki. *Niten Ichi-ryū seihō*. Tokyo, 1987.
Imamura Yoshio. *Shiryō Yagyū Shinkage-ryū*. Vols. 1–2. Tokyo, 1995.
—. *Yamato Yagyū ichizoku*. Tokyo, 1974.
Imano Nobuo. *Edo no tabi*. Tokyo, 1986.
Inoue Tomoshige. *O-togishū Miyamoto Musashi*. Tokyo, 2003.
Ishioka Hisao. *Hyōhōsha no seikatsu*. Tokyo, 1988.
Kaionji Chōgorō. *Bushō retsuden*. Vols. 1–6. Tokyo, 1964.
Kaku Kōzō. *Miyamoto Musashi jiten*. Tokyo, 2001.
—. *Miyamoto Musashi daijiten*. Tokyo, 2003.
—. *Nazo no kensei Miyamoto Musashi*. Tokyo, 1995.
Kamiko Tadashi. *Gorin no sho*. Tokyo, 1997.
Kasaya Kazuhiko. *Sekigahara gassen*. Tokyo, 2008.
—. *Sekigahara gassen to Ōsaka no jin*. Tokyo, 2007.
Katsube Mitake. *Bushidō*. Tokyo, 1971.
Kawaguchi Sunao. *Miyamoto Musashi 101 nazo*. Tokyo, 2002.
—. *Sasaki Kōjirō*. Tokyo, 2002.
Kawamura Akira. *Miyamoto Musashi*. Tokyo, 1998.
Kaku Kōzō. *Kyokui Ichi-ryū*. Tokyo, 2009.
Kitagawa Hiroshi. *Gunkimono no keifu*. Kyoto, 1985.
Kitajima Matsumoto. *Edo jidai*. Tokyo, 1958.
Kogure Masao. *Nitō-ryū no kensei Miyamoto Musashi*. Tokyo, 1983
Kojima Hidehiro. *Kengō densetsu*. Tokyo, 1997.
—. *Miyamoto Musashi no shinjitsu*. Tokyo, 2002.
—. *Sugao no kengōtachi*. Tokyo, 1998.
Kondō Heijō. *Shiseki shūran*. Volume 24. Tokyo, 1967.

Kosuge Ren. *Bisan hōkan*. Tokyo, 1897.
Kubo Michio. *Miyamoto Musashi*. Tokyo, 1998.
Kumei Sao. *Fuhai no kyokui Gorin no sho wo yomu*. Tokyo, 1998.
Kurobe Tooru. *Akashijō wo meguru rekishi no tabi*. Tokyo, 2000.
Kuroda Yoshitaka. *Akashi han ryakushi*. Tokyo, 1981.
—. *Shiwa Akashi-jō*. Tokyo, 1975.
Kuwata Tadachika. *Chosaku-shū*. Vols. 1–10. Tokyo, 1980.
—. *Miyamoto Musashi nyūmon*. Tokyo, 1974.
—. *Nihon no kengō*. Vols. 1–5. Tokyo, 1984.
Maeda Hideki. *Gorin no Sho no tetsugaku*. Tokyo, 2003.
—. *Ken to shisō*. Tokyo, 2009.
Maki Hidehiko. *Kengō zenshi*. Tokyo, 2003.
Matsumura Hiroshi. *Rekishi monogatari*. Tokyo, 1979.
Matsunaga Yoshihiro. *Ningen Miyamoto Musashi*. Tokyo, 1984.
Maruoka Muneo. *Miyamoto Musashi meihin shūsei*. Tokyo, 1984.
Matsunobu Ichiji. *Miyamoto Musashi zensho*. Tokyo, 2003.
Miki Seiichirō. *Teppo to sono jisai*. Tokyo, 1981.
Miyamoto Kenji, *Geijutsuka Musashi*. Tokyo, 2003.
Mishima Yukio. *Hagakure nyūmon*. Tokyo, 1967.
Mitsuse Ryū. *Shin Miyamoto Musashi*. Tokyo, 1981.
Mizuno Yasuo. *Sengoku daimyō Asakurashi to Ichijōdani*. Tokyo, 2002.
Morimoto Shigeru. *Miyamoto Musashi wo aruku*. Tokyo, 2002.
Muneta Hiroshi. *Miyamoto Musashi: sono jitsuzō to kyozō*. Tokyo, 1976.
Murakami Genzō. *Zuihitsu Sasaki Kojirō*. Tokyo, 1952.
Nagatanigawa Hiroshi. *Sengokudaimyō Amago no Kenkyū*. Tokyo, 2005.
Nagazumi Yasuaki. *Gunki monogatari no sekai*. Tokyo, 1978.
Nakajima Michiko. *Yagyū Sekishūsai Muneyoshi*. Tokyo, 2003.
Nakamura Akira. *Shinkage-ryū Kamiizumi Nobutsuna*. Tokyo, 2004.
Nakamura Kichiji. *Buke no rekishi*. Tokyo, 1967.
Nakanishi Seizō. *Miyamoto Musashi no saigo*. Tokyo, 1987.
—. *Miyamoto Musashi no shōgai*. Tokyo, 1975.
Nakayama Hakudō. *Kendō kōwa*. Tokyo, 1937.
Nakazato Kaizan. *Nihon bujutsu shinmyō ki*. Tokyo, 1985.
Nanjō Norio. *Nihon no meijō, kojō jiten*. Tokyo, 1999.

Naoki Sukeyama. *Nihon kengō retsuden*. Tokyo, 1983.
Naramoto Tatsuya. *Bushidō no keifu*. Tokyo, 1973.
—. *Gorin no sho nyūmon*. Tokyo, 1984.
—. *Musashi to Gorin no sho*. Tokyo, 1981.
Nawata Kazuo. *Musashi*. Tokyo, 2002.
Nishigaya Yasuhiro. *Kumamotojō*. Tokyo, 2009.
—. *Sengoku daimyō jōkaku jiten*. Tokyo, 1999.
Nitobe Inazo. *Bushidō*. Tokyo, 1938.
Okada Kazuo. *Miyamoto Musashi no subete*. Tokyo, 1983.
Okubō Hikozaemon. *Mikawa Monogatari*. Tokyo, 1980.
Ōmori Nobumasa. *Bujutsu densho no kenkyū*. Tokyo, 1991.
Omori Sōgen. *Sho to Zen*. Tokyo, 1973.
—. *Zen no kōsō*. Tokyo, 1979.
Ōtsubo Sashikata. *Shin Miyamoto Musashi-kō*. Tokyo 1982.
Owada Tetsuo. *Sengoku bushō*. Tokyo, 1981.
—. *Toyotomi Hideyoshi*. Tokyo, 1985.
Ozaki Hatsuki. *Miyamoto Musashi*. Tokyo, 1984
Ozawa Chikamitsu. *Ken shin itchi*. Tokyo, 1978.
Saitō Shigeyoshi. *Ganryūshima*. Tokyo, 1930.
Sakai Tadakutsu. *Sekigahara kassen shimatsu ki*. Tokyo, 1991.
Sakuchi Kan. *Kensei Musashi-den*. Tokyo, 1946.
Sasamori Junzo. *Ittō-ryū goku-i*. Tokyo, 1986.
Satome Mitsugu. *Jitsuroku Miyamoto Musashi*. Tokyo, 1989.
Shiba Ryōtarō. *Miyamoto Musashi*, Tokyo, 1999.
—. *Nihon kenkyaku den*. Tokyo, 1982.
—. *Sekigahara*. Tokyo, 1992.
—. *Shinsetsu Miyamoto Musashi*. Tokyo, 1983.
Shimura Kunihiro. *Shimabara gassenki*. Tokyo, 1989.
Shinbo Satoru. *Miyamoto Musashi: heihō to geijutsu*. Tokyo, 2002.
Shirotsuka Tomokazu. *Miyamoto Musashi no tabi*. Tokyo, 1984.
Shudō Yoshiki. *Keichō nikki*. Tokyo, 1980.
So Dōshin. *Shorinji kenpō*. Tokyo, 1963.
Sugai Yasuo. *Issatsu de yomu kengō Miyamoto Musashi*. Tokyo, 2002.
Sugimoto Keizaburō. *Gunki monogatari no sekai*. Tokyo, 1985.

Sukeyama Naoki. *Nihon kengō retsuden.* Tokyo, 1983.
Takahashi tomio. *Bushidō no rekishi.* Vols. 1–3. Tokyo, 1986.
Takano Samirō. *Kendō.* Tokyo, 1915.
Takata Yasushi. *Miyamoto Musashi no jitsuzō.* Tokyo, 1993.
Takayanagi Kaneyoshi. *Edo no kakyū bushi.* Tokyo, 1980.
Takeda Shigeju. *Gorin no Sho no jutsuri tankyū.* Tokyo, 2011.
Tanabe Seiko. *Miyamoto Musashi wo kudoku hō.* Tokyō, 1985.
Tanaka Fumon. *Miyamoto Musashi to kengōtachi no kenpō.* Tokyo, 2011.
Tanizawa Eiichi. *Gorin no sho no yomikata.* Tokyo, 1982.
Terada Toru. *Dō no shisō.* Tokyo, 1978.
Terayama Tanchū. *Miyamoto Musashi no ken to bi.* Tokyo, 2002.
Tobe Shinichirō. *Kōsho Miyamoto Musashi.* Tokyo, 1984.
Tokunaga Shiichirō. *Yagyū Munenori.* Tokyo, 1978.
Tokutomi Sōho. *Kinsei Nihon kokumin-shi.* Tokyo, 1982.
Tominaga Kengō. *Shijitsu Miyamoto Musashi.* Tokyo, 1969.
—. *Nihon kassen zenshū.* Vols. 1–6. Tokyo, 1990.
Tsuge Hisayoshi. *Jissen Gorin no sho.* Tokyo, 1994.
—. *Miyamoto Musashi nijūban shōbu.* Tokyo, 2002.
—. *Miyamoto Musashi no tatakai: saisho no kettō no maki.* Tokyo, 1997.
Tsumoto Yō. *Musashi to Gorin no sho.* Tokyo, 2002.
Uozumi Takashi. *Miyamoto Musashi: heihō no michi o ikiru.* Tokyo, 2008.
—. *Miyamoto Musashi: Nihonjin no michi.* Tokyo, 2002.
—. *Sengoku bushi no kokoroe.* Tokyo, 2001.
Utsunomiya Yasunaga. *Miyamoto Genshin deshiryō shūsei.* Tokyo, 2005.
—. *Miyamoto Musashi: hyakumon hyakutō.* Tokyo, 2007.
—. *Miyamoto Musashi: rengoku no chikai.* Tokyo, 2003.
—. *Miyamoto Musashi to shinshiryō.* Tokyo, 2002.
Watatani Kiyoshi. *Nihon kengō no hyakusen.* Tokyo, 1971.
—. *Bugei ryuha daijiten.* Tokyo, 2003.
Watanabe Ichirō. *Budō no meichō.* Tokyo, 1979.
—. *Gorin no sho.* Tokyo, 1991.
Watanabe Makoto. *Miyamoto Musashi: ken to hito.* Tokyo, 2002.
Yabuki Masanori. *Mimasaka ryakushi.* Tokyo, 1881.
—. *Shintei sakuinshi.* Tokyo, 1975.

Yabushita Hideki. *Miyamoto Musashi densetsu*. Tokyo, 2001.
Yamada Jirokichi. *Nihon kendō-shi*. Tokyo, 1960.
Yamamoto Hirobumi. *Akōjiken to yonjūrokushi*. Tokyo, 2013.
Yamane Yukie. *Tottori-han kendōshi*. Tokyo, 1982.
Yamato Tarō. *Fukuyama monogatari*. Tokyo, 2006.
Yamazaki Masakazu. *Muromachi ki*. Tokyo, 1974.
Yasuda Motohisa. *Bushi sekai no jōmaku*. Tokyo, 1973.
Yasuda Takashi. *Kata no Nihon bunka*. Tokyo, 1984.
Yokoi Kiyoshi. *Chūsei wo ikita hitobito*. Kyoto, 1981.
Yokoyama Masakatsu. *Amagoshi ichimon no ruutsu*. Tokyo,1985.
Yonenaga Kunio. *Miyamoto Musashi: tsugi no itte*. Tokyo, 2002.
Yoshida Seiken. *Nitō-ryū o kataru*. Tokyo, 1941.
—. *Shinden Miyamoto Musashi*. Tokyo, 1942.
Yoshida Yutaka. *Budō hiden sho*. Tokyo, 1973.
—. *Zōhyō monogatari*. Tokyo, 1980.
Yoshikawa Eiji. *Miyamoto Musashi*. Tokyo, 1935.
—. *Zuihitsu Miyamoto Musashi*. Tokyo, 2013.

# INDEX

**M**

N



O

**Musashi, Fact & Fiction: A Guide to the Essential Questions**

In the long and complicated—often hotly contended—narrative of Miyamoto Musashi's life there are a number of important questions that have hitherto remained tantalizingly elusive: Where was he born? Who was his father? Who was his mother? Who were his children? What was his appearance? Who were his benefactors? With whom did he duel? In what battles did he participate? On whose side did he fight? What are his writings? Which paintings are his? Where did he live? And where was he buried?

With time, fact and fiction have merged, while the urge to address these questions has resulted in such a degree of speculation and misinformation that even the Japanese and English Wikipedia entries for Musashi are widely divergent, in part diametrically opposed.

This guide brings order in that chaos by drawing directly from medieval texts and testing them against the latest Japanese research. Through clearly defined themes it highlights the various aspects of Musashi's life. In doing so it finally answers these burning questions, laying to rest many of the misconceptions that blur the true picture of this fascinating medieval Japanese warrior.

## The Real Musashi: The *Bushūdenraiki* (Origins of a Legend I)

Miyamoto Musashi is the most revered and celebrated swordsman in Japanese history. Unfortunately, our modern portrait of this historical hero is derived mainly from popular books, comics, and film, with little heed paid to the early *denki*, chronicles written by men who had known Musashi alive, or who recorded what was passed on to them by those who had.

The *Bushū denraiki* is the earliest *denki* on Musashi in existence. Completed in 1727 by Tachibana Minehide, the fifth generation master of Musashi's Niten Ichi school of swordsmanship, it is one of the most reliable records of Musashi's life and exploits outside those from the hand of the master swordsman himself.

Now, after three centuries, Minehide's insight into this enigmatic and solitary swordsman are available to the English reader. His text throws a new and refreshing light on many aspects of especially Musashi's early life—his troubled relations with his father, his first battle experience during Japan's period of unification, the sad death of his illegitimate child, his many duels, and of course his legendary encounter with Sasaki Kojirō on Ganryū island.

### The Real Musashi: The *Bukōden* (Origins of a Legend II)

Next to the *Bushū denraiki*, the *Bukōden* is one of the earliest chronicles of Musashi still in existence. It was completed in 1755 by Toyoda Masanaga, senior retainer to the Nagaoka, a clan closely involved in the events of Musashi's later life.

Masanaga's work ranks with the *Bushū denraiki* as the most reliable records of Musashi's life and exploits outside those from the hand of the master swordsman himself. Now, for the first time in two and a half centuries, Masanaga's insights into this enigmatic and solitary swordsman are available to the English reader.

Like the *Bushū denraiki*, the *Bukoden* gives its own riveting account of Musashi's encounter with Sasaki Kojirō on Ganryu island, as well as his famed duels with the members of the Yoshioka clan. At the same time it throws a new and refreshing light on many aspects of Musashi's later life—his adoption of Iori, his return to Kyushu in 1634, and of course the gestation of his great work on the philosophy and art of Japanese swordsmanship, the *Gorin no sho*. For those interested in the sword culture of Japan, this true account of its most iconic figure is essential reading.

## The Real Musashi: A Miscellany (Origins of a Legend III)

The *Bushū denraiki* and the *Bukōden* are not the only historical records of Miyamoto Musashi. There are a great number of additional, often long neglected, records that present an original and surprisingly vivid image of the illusive and enigmatic swordsman.

This work contains translations from the *Tomari jinja munefuda*, the *Hayashi razan bunshū*, the *Kaijō monogatari*, the *Numata kaki*, the *Yoshioka-den*, the *Hōkōsho*, the *Bushō kanjōki*, the *Kōkai fuhansho*, the *Watanabe kōan taikiwa*, the *Honchō bugei shōden*, the *Dōbō goen*, the *Korō usawa*, the *Kōkō zatsuroku*, the *Harima kagami*, the *Seiryūwa*, the *Saiyū zakki*, the *Gekken sōdan*, the *Sōkyūsama o-degatari*, the *Mukashibanashi*, the *Tōsakushi*, and the *Mimasa ryakushi*.

Now the insight these works offer into this enigmatic and solitary swordsman are available to the English reader. They throw new and refreshing light on many aspects of Musashi's life—his duels with the members of the Yoshioka clan, the events leading up to his duel with Sasaki Kojirō, his heroic role in the siege of Osaka castle, his contribution to the reconstruction of Akashi castle, his liaisons with women, and his remarkable artistic talents.

## FAMOUS JAPANESE SWORDSMEN

### The Two Courts Period

The story of Nenami Jion, the fugitive warrior monk (*sōhei*) who founded the Nen-ryū, the first school of Japanese fencing; and the story of his friend Chūjō Nagahide, scion of an old family of courtiers who went on to found the Chūjō-ryū, the school that became the formative influence on the great fencing masters of the Toda-ryū.

### The Warring States Period

The story of Iizasa Ienao, raised in the fencing traditions of the ancient Katori and Kashima shrines, and founder of the legendary Shintō-ryū; and the story of Kamiizumi Nobutsuna, master of Japan's old pirate (*wakō*) fencing traditions, founder of the Shinkage-ryū, and patron-teacher to the practitioners of the famous Yagyū clan.

### The Period of Unification

The story of Ono Tadaaki, a *rōnin* from the turbulent Kantō who inherited the old traditions of the Toda and Ittō-ryū and became the shogunal fencing instructor; and the story of Yagyū Munenori, the warrior of the Yagyū Shinkage-ryū who restored his clan's dwindling fortunes through his valiant role in the epic Battle of Sekigahara.

Floating World Editions publishes books that contribute to a deeper understanding of Asian cultures. Editorial supervision: Ray Furse. Book and cover design: Keichō Designs. Printing and binding: Integrated Book Technology. The typeface used is Perpetua.